OVERLOAD!

OVERLOAD!

HOW TOO MUCH INFORMATION IS HAZARDOUS TO YOUR ORGANIZATION

Jonathan B. Spira

WILEY

John Wiley & Sons, Inc.

Published by John Wiley & Sons, Inc., Hoboken, New Jersey.
Published simultaneously in Canada.

For general information on our other products and services or for technical support, please contact our Customer Care Department within the United States at (800) 762-2974, outside the United States at (317) 572-3993 or fax (317) 572-4002.

Wiley also publishes its books in a variety of electronic formats. Some content that appears in print may not be available in electronic books. For more information about Wiley products, visit our web site at www.wiley.com.

Library of Congress Cataloging-in-Publication Data:
Spira, Jonathan B.
    Overload!: How Too Much Information is Hazardous to your Organization / Jonathan B. Spira.
       p. cm
    Includes index.
       ISBN 978-0-470-87960-3 (cloth); ISBN 978-1-118-06415-3 (ebk);
       ISBN 978-1-118-06416-0 (ebk); ISBN 978-1-118-06417-7 (ebk)
    1. Knowledge management. 2. Information resources management.
    3. Information technology—Management. 4. Business communication—Management. I. Title.
    HD30.2.S686   2011
    658.4'038—dc22

                                                                2010053512

Printed in the United States of America
10 9 8 7 6 5 4 3 2 1

To my parents, who taught me about knowledge,
and to the millions of knowledge workers
around the world, who inspired me to combat
Information Overload.

CONTENTS

FIGHTING THE GOOD FIGHT AGAINST INFORMATION BLOAT

In this book, Jonathan Spira addresses the problem of Information Overload and our own responsibilities for it. But this isn't just a question of "don't spam." People usually create content with some purpose in mind. Sometimes it's just self-aggrandizement, in which case this book is not for you.

But if you're sending messages without getting a response, maybe you aren't thinking enough about the recipient. If you do so, you'll get more done with less effort and more control . . . because thinking about the recipients helps you determine what actually gets into their heads.

Take how I came to write this foreword. Jonathan had sent me an e-mail politely asking me to write a few notes for his book. In reply, he got this plaintive away message from me: "staving off e-mail bankruptcy: I am traveling and my deferred message liability is around 4000. I'm hoping to work my way through this, but please don't expect a reply until December 31 or worst case December 32!"

He then wrote again – and didn't get a reply. I was too busy dealing with the very problem he is describing in this book.

We then chatted in Facebook instant messaging, but I responded with little enthusiasm.

What *should* people do to cut through the clutter and elicit a response? In the case of Jonathan's first e-mail, he should have given me much more complete directions. In other cases let's say if an individual had wanted me to recommend him for a job, he should write the forwarding letter for me – which I could edit if I wanted. Otherwise, all I would have to do is add the recipient to the cc line and hit reply.

In the case of someone who wanted help getting an in with a certain company, he could do the research himself – i.e. list the top management and the board of directors – and ask me if I knew anyone there.

If someone has to write to me a second time – I'm looking through my backlog of unanswered e-mails here! – he should not say: "Did you get my last e-mail?" Instead, he should make it easy for me by resending the whole thing – which should not have been that long anyway! I would say that my response rate goes down by 60 percent if there's a file attached.

And so on! Thinking about the person you are engaging with will not just clear up information overload; it's also likely to get you the response you want. This is one of the key points addressed in *Overload!*

(How did Jonathan actually get me to write this? By calling me! Sometimes realtime voice communication beats all this fancy electronic stuff!)

ESTHER DYSON

PREFACE

"Why are you so passionate about the problem of Information Overload?" is perhaps the question I have heard most in the past decade.

The answer is rather simple: Information Overload is killing us. It is death by a thousand paper cuts in the form of e-mail messages, documents, and interruptions.

Information Overload and related issues are now mainstream topics. The phrase itself is being co-opted for multiple purposes (many unrelated to the actual problem), and it's the topic of front-page stories in mainstream newspapers, magazines, and blogs.

No one I know is exempt from the problem as information is all around us. The issue is not only the quantity; it's also the intensity. Information is also appearing in new and unexpected ways.

Just a few days before I sat down to write this preface, the Web site WikiLeaks released 250,000 classified State Department documents including hundreds of diplomatic cables. The question of right or wrong notwithstanding, my first thought was "How will anyone be able to sort through this quantity of material and make any sense of it?"

In 1971, the *New York Times* published the *Pentagon Papers*. At the time, the approximately 7,000 pages supplied by Daniel Ellsberg probably seemed insurmountable, but the knowledge worker journalists at the *Times* managed to present the material in a comprehensible manner.

Today, anyone can go to the Web and see the actual cables released by WikiLeaks as well as tens of thousands of analyses published by various parties.

The Internet has removed the intermediaries, such as newspapers, that even a mere decade ago would have been the place to which someone such as Bradley Manning, the private in the U.S. Army who is suspected of having disseminated the classified documents, would have turned.

Manning didn't even need WikiLeaks. Anyone can publish a Web page and content today, and this, of course, is why we have more and more information coming at us from all directions.

The unfortunate reality is, there is no magic bullet for "fixing" Information Overload at this time, and it is likely that we may never fully resolve the problem. In addition, there is a huge financial cost associated with the problem – according to my research at Basex, the knowledge economy research firm where I serve as chief analyst, Information Overload cost the U.S. economy almost $1 trillion in 2010.

While there is relatively little that we can do about Information Overload, we don't have to grin and bear it. What does help reduce Information Overload and lessen its impact is 1.) raising awareness and 2.) presenting context and history as to why the problem is occurring.

Raising awareness helps because most people are simply unaware of the root causes of Information Overload, such as poor search techniques, unnecessarily copying dozens if not hundreds of colleagues on an e-mail, or calling someone two minutes after sending an e-mail message simply to tell the sender of its presence.

Providing context and history puts things into perspective. The quantity of information has increased in lockstep with advances in technology, beginning with pen and paper and continuing into the Information Age. Not surprisingly, sixteenth-century knowledge workers complained with alacrity about such things as too many books.

In addition, we can also take preemptive steps by teaching knowledge workers more about information and information management and ensuring that they know that their actions (e.g., sending an e-mail to 300 supposedly close colleagues) have a significant impact on their colleagues' efficiency and effectiveness.

In addition, a new class of workers may be required, namely knowledge workers who are capable of efficiently sifting through the torrent of information, separating the wheat from the chaff, and presenting the important nuggets in an accessible manner. That person might be a librarian, researcher, editor, journalist – the titles are almost irrelevant but the information-swamped world will be grateful.

When I was doing a research project in grammar school, I learnt about the Library of Alexandria, built in the third century BCE. The library was charged with collecting all of the world's knowledge, the first effort of its kind, and became a home to scholars from around the world. It also had one of the most original (and possibly apocryphal) acquisition policies ever: It confiscated every book that came across its borders (Alexandria had a man-made port and was an early international trading hub) and copied each one, usually returning the copy, not the original, to its owner.

Today, multiple parties are attempting to build a modern-day Library of Alexandria, albeit an online one. Wikipedia, since its founding in 2001, has amassed over 9.25 million articles in 250 languages that, while not books, represent a good part of the world's knowledge. In a similar vein, Google is assembling the world's known books online. An official Google blog post from August 5, 2010, stated that Google had accounted for 29,864,880 as of that date. Thus far, it has scanned approximately 10 percent of them.

The concept of the Library of Alexandria (and, subsequently, the New York Public Library, which I frequented during another research project) made quite an impression on me. But I also realized how much information was out there. When I started working at my father's company, Spiratone, during school vacations, helping select and deploy office automation systems, I began to see how information flowed throughout an organization, or sometimes how it didn't flow.

The time I spent at Spiratone created an indelible impression of how technology sometimes could work in harmony with business – and sometimes not.

It was in the early 1990s, by which time I had been at Basex for almost a decade, when I began to realize that the spread of then-new technologies within the enterprise, such as e-mail, were probably creating as many problems as they were solving. This contrasted with the prevailing view of such new technologies, which viewed them as a panacea for all the ills of the office.

CNBC interviewed me on productivity issues back in 1993. The reporter, Bob Pisante, opened the segment by saying "It's not just meetings that are taking up a ton of time, there's also a problem with mail. And in this day and age, mail means e-mail. You think you're busy? Jonathan Spira can get 150 e-mails a day."

If only that were the case today.

A NOTE TO THE READER

At the risk of potentially overloading you with information before you even start reading, I wanted to alert you to two important issues relating to this book.

First, while this book is bound and fixed in time and space, its mission is not limited to these pages. The book's companion Web site, Overload Stories (www.OverloadStories.com), has been created in order to allow you to share your own experiences and stories about Information Overload and read what others are going through. You will also be able to review updated research and case studies and participate in a dialogue with me on these issues.

Second, I have written this book with the individual knowledge worker in mind. As a result, throughout the book, my references to the knowledge worker are in the singular tense and this requires a singular pronoun, such as he or she. (It is at this point that I am reminded of Mark Twain's excellent essay, "The Awful German Language," in which he points out that "a tree is male, its buds are female, its leaves are neuter; horses are sexless, dogs are male, cats are female.")

To avoid what would be a rather awkward repetition of "he or she" or "him or her" throughout the book and to maintain a modicum of consistency in pronoun usage, I treat the term "knowledge worker" as a masculine noun that requires a masculine pronoun (i.e., I refer to the individual knowledge worker as "he" or "him"). Of course, Information Overload impacts everyone without regard to gender; it is truly an equal opportunity problem.

ACKNOWLEDGMENTS

Despite suffering from significant overload themselves, many knowledge workers have selflessly contributed their time and thoughts to my research over the past ten years which culminated in this book. Without the thousands of knowledge workers who took my surveys, participated in interviews, attended workshops, and sent me their thoughts, I would never have been able to understand the extent to which Information Overload impacts them and at what cost this occurs.

There are a few people whom I must single out by name, due to their unique contributions.

David M. Goldes, president of Basex and a lifelong friend, who has worked alongside me for 22 years studying knowledge workers and knowledge work and kept me focused on the reason we are doing what we do.

Cody Burke, vice president and senior analyst at Basex, who has served as my partner-in-crime since I started to work on Overload! and contributed a good deal of research and thinking that was incorporated in the book.

Basilio Alferow, vice president and editorial director at Basex, who has tirelessly reviewed my writing and made sense of it, even when it made little sense to me.

Greg Andrew Spira, my brother and a veteran of multiple books himself, who was always happy to review at my text and contribute his knowledge of the book-publishing industry.

Nathan Zeldes, president of the Information Overload Research Group, who, first as Intel's Information Overload czar (a title I created to describe his role) and now from his current position, tirelessly contributed data and his experiences in confronting Information Overload.

Tim Burgard, Stacey Rivera, and Vincent Nordhaus, my editors at Wiley, who provided support, guidance, suggestions, and words of encouragement throughout the process.

Finally, I would like to thank my partner, Daniel Lafler, for his unconditional support and understanding during the preparation of this book.

OVERLOAD!

INTRODUCTION

Information has become the great leveler of society and business. Today, practically everyone is more informed than even the most informed person was a mere 25 years ago yet, paradoxically, knows a smaller percentage of the available knowledge. Governments, too, are far better informed about what other nations are doing (which, we hope, leads to fewer misunderstandings) as well as what the citizenry is up to. Young people in poorer nations – witness India, for example – have been able to capitalize on the flexibility of an information society to create better lives for themselves as knowledge workers, something unimaginable a mere quarter century ago.

Knowledge workers think for a living to varying extents, depending on the job and situation, but there is little time for thought and reflection in the course of a typical day. Instead, information – often in the form of e-mail messages, reports, news, Web sites, RSS feeds, blogs, wikis, instant messages, text messages, Twitter, and video conferencing walls – bombards and dulls our senses.

We try to do our work, but information gets in the way. It's not unlike the game Tetris, where the goal is to keep the blocks from piling up. You barely align one, and another is ready to take its place.

When computers first began to encroach upon our everyday lives, they were in distant, glass-walled rooms run by scientists in white coats. The closest most of us came to them were punch cards that came with utility bills. Indeed the term "Do Not Fold, Spindle, or Mutilate" became a running gag among late-night comedians (as well as the name of a movie in the 1970s about a computer dating service).

Technology was the source of conflict in earlier films as well. Films, such as *Metropolis* (1927) and *Modern Times* (1936), commented on the negative impact of automation in the workplace. *Desk Set* (1957), where Spencer Tracy and Katharine Hepburn clash over the computerization of a TV network's research department, presented an epic man versus machine struggle.

1

Information Overload was first mentioned in 1962 by Bertram Gross in *Operation Basic: The Retrieval of Wasted Knowledge*. It was predicted by Alvin Toffler in *Future Shock* (1970). In 1989, Richard Saul Wurman warned of it in his book *Information Anxiety*.

But Information Overload is no longer a problem of the future; it's something that we have to address and manage right now.

Indeed, the term "Information Overload" has become part of the vernacular. While spending the better part of a week at the remote Blackberry River Inn in Connecticut to focus on writing this book, I found that people I ran into had a lot to say on the topic. They also had an encyclopedic knowledge of the problems that arise from multitasking (something I cover in Chapter 16) and cited several incidents where texting resulted in train crashes and other accidents.

Two 40-ish women dining in a local restaurant and seated next to me asked me about my visit. When I mentioned the topic of the book, they both started rattling off the dangers of multitasking and the problem of finding accurate information online.

Back at the inn, the chief information officer at a large software company quizzed me endlessly on what he could do to make his workforce more efficient and effective, given the severity of the problem.

The Way Work Was

As our work environment changed and evolved, it was accompanied by a significant increase in the amount of information that was being created and that we needed to perform our jobs.

For thousands of years, work was a matter of subsistence. We worked to eat, to survive, to provide our family with food. Life was simpler then. There was a direct correlation between the success of our work and whether there was food on the table, or even if there was a table. The dawn of the Industrial Age changed all that. We went off to factories and offices as fewer and fewer of us lived off the land.

The way we look at work today is inexorably and somewhat romantically linked to 1950s situation comedies where the father, a distant figure, would leave for work in the morning in his suit and fedora, briefcase in hand, returning promptly an hour before dinner, just in time for his wife to ask "Hard day at the office, dear?" A quiet dinner hour usually followed, along with time to discuss homework with the kids and present various life lessons, all of which were to be resolved in under 30 minutes. (The actual work performed by dear old dad during the day was somewhat nebulous in most cases, but it generally involved a desk, a secretary, and occasionally a cranky boss.)

My father, who was not in a situation comedy, was the CEO of Spiratone, a midsize company in the photographic industry. He typically came home from the office at 5:30 in the evening, but his information-laden briefcase was always heavy with work that included memos, ad copy, correspondence, and other paperwork.

After the dinner hour, he retired to his study to do more work. He usually received a few phone calls from colleagues, and they were expected to be working as well. Invariably, a few times a week, the phone would ring and at the other end was a distant-sounding female voice announcing "long distance from Tokyo, Japan, calling": The head of his Tokyo office was on the line.

The reality of that age, however, was that most people did not work in offices but held far more mundane jobs. Indeed, in 1950, more people worked in industrial and factory jobs than anywhere else.

The Age of the Knowledge Worker

Today, 78.6 million people in the United States are knowledge workers, a plurality of the workforce. A "knowledge worker" is defined as a participant in the knowledge economy. The "knowledge economy" connotes an economic environment where information and its manipulation are the commodity and the activity (in contrast to the industrial economy, where workers produce a tangible object with raw production materials and physical goods).

Knowledge workers are found at all economic stations. An accounting clerk is a good example of an entry-level or rudimentary knowledge worker. An architect or engineer is an excellent example of a skilled knowledge worker, as is an airline pilot or physician. And a rocket scientist or Nobel Prize–winning economist is representative of the top echelon of knowledge workers.

Of course, not everyone is or should be a knowledge worker, nor is knowledge work performed simply for its own sake.

Factories will still continue to produce products (although these factories will be increasingly robotized and automated), and, as there are some tasks machines simply can't perform as well as a person, people will continue to be directly involved in the manufacturing process. Knowledge workers may develop product design software that other knowledge workers will then use to design, for example, a refrigerator or automobile, but at the end of the day, a product is still manufactured.

The current economic makeup contrasts sharply with the workforce of 25 years ago where industrial workers represented a majority, and that of the turn of the twentieth century, where manual workers, many agrarian, comprised 90 percent of the workforce.

Mark Rivington's Day

Mark Rivington woke up at 7 A.M. to a news report on his clock radio, a bit surprised to find himself in his own bed since his job requires so much travel.

He continued listening to the news while he showered and ate breakfast. He was still sleepy since he had been up late studying Spanish online for an upcoming trip to Madrid.

After a five-minute walk to catch the 8 A.M. train, he continued on his way to work, reading additional newspapers on his tablet computer. He also listened to music on the built-in music player.

After arriving at work at 9, he logged into his computer at his desk. He pondered the work he was about to do, sitting in front of his computer, staring at the screen, deep in thought. As he began his work, the phone rang, and he answered the call. Ten minutes later, he stared blankly at the computer screen, unable to recall what he was about to write.

At 9:30, he joined an hour-long departmental meeting in a large conference room. Like most meeting attendees his age (Mark is 27), he listened with half an ear and spent most of his time triaging his e-mail inbox on his smartphone.

The meeting was over at 10, and, back in his office, Mark caught up with industry news.

It was time for another meeting, this time on the Web. Participants from a special task force Mark was on were presenting preliminary findings. Mark had to pay attention to what his colleagues were saying and make his own presentation. After the 90-minute meeting, Mark wondered how he would keep track of everything that was discussed and, more important, had to be done.

Mark had grown up with information bombardment. As a child, he had been left by his parents in front of the television for hours at a time. He knew how to use a mouse before he could write the alphabet with a pencil and spent his preteen years on the Web, constantly messaging friends around the world.

Back again at his desk, it was time to catch up on correspondence. One e-mail – marked urgent – caught his attention. A major issue was developing at a supplier's factory in Munich, and Mark would have to travel there to resolve the problem.

Mark researches flights and plans a quick trip to Munich for the next day. Since he doesn't have another meeting until 2:30, he starts researching the problem he hopes to be able to solve. An hour of searches proves fruitless, and he starts to feel overwhelmed by the vast amounts of information on the topic, unable to discern what is accurate and what is not.

His meeting comes just as Mark starts to hit a breaking point. He goes to the meeting and continues his research on his laptop. Everyone is silently tapping away on their laptops or smartphones while two people discuss the meeting topic.

Halfway through the meeting, Mark realizes that one attendee is describing a situation eerily similar to what he will be facing in Munich. He starts taking notes and sends the speaker a meeting request to chat later. The speaker replies a few minutes later (clearly, he was multitasking, too) and a meeting time of 5 P.M. is agreed upon.

After this meeting, Mark needs a break. He relaxes by visiting his favorite hobby discussion forum (high-performance German cars) and participates in several discussions.

As the 5 o'clock meeting time comes closer, Mark realizes he needs to try to assimilate all of the information he has on the factory problem in order to make the best use of his time. He curses the poor search tools but uses the knowledge gained in the meeting to improve his search terms, and he begins to find useful information.

The meeting at 5 proves fruitful, and Mark realizes how difficult it would have been to get the information he needs if not for the chance meeting earlier.

At 6 P.M., Mark remembers he has a customer presentation due tomorrow – before he leaves for Europe. He starts to research new industry figures and 90 minutes later realizes he has enough information for his presentation, but it's far from done. He stops and goes to the gym.

Mark, finished with the gym by 9, catches the late train and starts to review the information for his presentation on his tablet. By the end of his commute, he has his presentation ready.

By 10 P.M., Mark is home, preparing dinner and checking e-mail. Already, there are over two dozen messages from colleagues many time zones away. And he still has to pack for his trip.

A Global Economy

In today's global economy, information has become both a currency and a product. Somewhat contrary to the normal laws of supply and demand that dictate the value of other currencies and products, information has become self-perpetuating, in part because we have built technology that easily allows us to create new information without human intervention.

In fact, we've become so good at generating information that it becomes effortless and, as a result, we end up creating far more than we can manage.

Let me take a step back for a moment. While some may contend that there's no such thing as too much information per se, what does exist without question is an inability to manage the flow of information so that people can easily find what they are looking for and not feel overwhelmed. This is Information Overload.

Information Overload throttles productivity, reduces our capability to absorb and learn, puts our physical and mental health at risk, and interferes with personal and business relationships.

Research that I conducted at Basex, the research firm where I serve as chief analyst, has found that the costs of Information Overload are extremely high, in terms of both dollars and human costs. Indeed, according to research published by Basex in December 2010, Information Overload cost the U.S. economy $997 billion per year.

As the tools we use beep and blurt, day in and day out, one competing with the other for a moment of the knowledge worker's day, they take a toll, not only emotionally and intellectually but on the bottom line as well.

The changes in how we use and view information that will happen over the next half century will not only reshape the globe but turn it inside out. This will in turn change how we view the concept of home, our home and work lives, our business and personal relationships, and perhaps even our national loyalties.

GREAT MOMENTS AND MILESTONES IN INFORMATION OVERLOAD HISTORY

Prior to the 1800s, the tools used by knowledge workers required much effort on the part of the user. Indeed, the earliest knowledge workers used stone, chisels, quills, and parchment to store information. To them, these tools were true innovations and dramatically increased their ability to create, share, and distribute knowledge.

Transmitting information over a distance in earlier days was also tricky. Sending a message might have involved beacon fires, flags, carrier pigeons, drums, mirrors, or even a man on a horse. Clearly, despite the occasional hard drive crash, today's users have it relatively easy by comparison.

Our timeline navigates through many centuries of recording information and details the many innovations that allowed mankind to create, store, and distribute more information to more people. Of course, the easier it became to publish information, the more overloaded we became.

Today, innovation comes quickly and today's state-of-the-art tools become yesterday's news in a nanosecond. What will be available even a few years down the road is hard to fathom, and what we will be using 20 or 30 years hence is the stuff that science fiction is made of. I have no doubt that the individual who updates this timeline in 2084 will look back at today's rather primitive tools and smile knowingly.

Year	Development	Why it was relevant
4000 BCE	Clay tablet	Allowed information to be recorded and stored for the first time
3500–3000 BCE	Papyrus and reed brushes or pens (Egypt)	More portable and easier to use than clay and stone
2697 BCE	Ink (Tien-Lcheu, China)	Further advanced the recording of information
1600 BCE	Alphabet (Sinai)	Made written language possible
First century	Codex (Rome)	Made information truly portable
105	Paper (Ts'ai Lun, China)	Made information lightweight and portable
700	Quill pen (Seville, Spain)	Simplified writing
Ca. 1440	Movable type (Johann Guttenberg)	Made mass reproduction of information possible
1565	Pencil (Borrowdale, England)	Made writing utensils less expensive and easier-to-use
1605	Newspaper (*Relation aller Fürnemmen und gedenckwürdigen Historien,* Strasbourg)	Made possible the distribution of large amounts of news and information
1642	Pascaline Adding Machine (Blaise Pascal)	Automated arithmetic

Courtesy of The Spira Collection

A 1430 proclamation by Jean, count of Foix and of Bigorre. Handwritten documents first appeared after the development of an alphabet and continued to be the predominant means of information distribution until Gutenberg.

Numb. 254.

The London Gazette.

Published by Authority.

From Monday, April 20. to Thursday, April 23. 1668.

Portsmouth, April 19.

ON Thursday last arrived at Spitthead, the Portland and Eagle Fregats from the Downs; the former is intended to put in here to refit, but the other is again put to sea to the Westwards. The Revenge is now in the Dock, and will in few days be in readiness; The Mountague, Monk, Tyger and Bristol expect only a fair wind.

Hull, April 20. The 16th instant was forced into Humber a Fleet of about 100 sail of laden Colliers bound to the Southwards, who still continue there in expectation of a fair wind, and with them arrived there a ship belonging to this Town of 60 Tuns, laden with Wines from Bourdeaux, who in her return was met at sea by a Privateer of 14 Guns, pretending to be French, but supposed Spaniards, who plundered them of their Cloaths, and several other things to a considerable value. The 17th came in in a Swede from Gottenburg laden with Iron, Pitch, Tarr and Deals.

Lisbonne, May 31. After several meetings and consideration about the Mairiage of the King and Queen, on the 24th instant, the sentence passed, annulling and making void the said Marriage to all intents and purposes. On the 28th instant, the Prince Regent and the Queen were by Proxy married in the Capella-Real, the Marqis de Marialva having the Princes power, and the Duke de Cadaval a procuration from the Queen : to morrow the Queen intends to leave the Monastry, to which she has been so long retired, and to take her lodgings in the Alcantara.

The Count de Schomberg, is for the good services done by him to this Crown, Honoured with the Title of Count de Mertola, and for the support of his Honour, has a Pension of sixteen thousand Crowns a year assigned him for his life ; he intends in little time a voyage into France to settle his affairs and concernments here, promising to return again if possible within the space of 6 weeks.

Here has lately appeared a Meteor of a prodigious length and bigness, and is generally believed to proceed from some Comet whose body at present is not visible, by reason of its too neer vicinity to the Sun ; the time of its appearance is immediately after the Sun is past our Horizon.

Several Ambassadors are intended to be in little time employed from hence to the Neighbouring Princes, amongst others 'tis believed, the Marquis de Marialva may be chosen for the person to be sent into Spain, and the Conde de Torre for Rome.

From Tangier we are informed of the good posture of affairs in that Garrison, and the decaying state of Gayland ; and that Tassaletta is marched into South Barbary to settle those parts, and quiet some Commotions amongst the people there.

Hamborough, April 20. The Lunenburg forces which were upon their march towards the United Provinces, upon intelligence that the Bishop of Munster made some difficulty of giving them the liberty of passing through his territories, have made an halt, expecting farther orders.

General Wrangle is now at Wolgast, but as yet there is little discourse of the motion of the Swedish forces.

From Warsaw we are told that the Ambassadors from the Czar of Muscovy are vigorously persuing their Negotiation with His Majesty, for entring into a neerer Alliance with the Crown of Poland, and are endeavouring to insinuate into the Nobility a good opinion of the young Prince of Muscovy, and to prepare a way for his Election to that Crown, upon the resignation or death of the present King.

They also tell us that the Cossacks have lately by stratagem possest themselves of the City of Czernickow, a strong place under the Dominion of the Muscovites, having sent several Carts into the Town, wherein lay concealed a party of stout Soldiers, who upon a signal given, seised one of the gates, and by it let in the rest of their forces, who killed and took prisoners above fifteen thousand Muscovites, plundring the Inhabitants, but the Castle still holds out against them.

The King of Poland intends in few days to depart from Warsaw, and to make a journey into Lythuania, and before his return to visit Dantzig.

From Ratisbonne we are told that the Deputies from the Princes of the Circle of Rhine have thoughts of confirming and strengthning their Alliance ; and that the Cardinal of Saltzburg President of the States of the Empire, was suddenly expected there ; upon whose arrival the business of the Circle of Burgundy would again be taken into consideration.

From Vienna we are informed of the arrival of the Empress Dowager from Neustadt, and that the Spanish Ambassador had lately a return of a considerable sum of moneys from Madrid, with which he intended to raise four new Regiments for the service of that Crown ; but that a late Express bringing news of the great probability of a Peace between the two Crowns of Spain and France, might put a stop to his intended Levies.

They farther inform us that the City of Vienna is much disgusted with the Toleration and Liberty given to the Jews, and are earnest sollicitors for their Banishment ; promising by a liberal Contribution, with which they are willing to charge themselves, to give full satisfaction to the Emperour for the moneys which they annually paid for their permission.

The States of Hungary are now assembled at Presbourg, (preparatorily to the General Diet in little time to be held there) to consider of their Grievances, in Order to the more full discussion of them in their full Assembly.

Vienna, April 15. The Spanish Ambassadour is taking care for the raising four new Regiments of Foot to be sent into the Kingdom of Naples, and has accordingly conferred with several Officers, with whom he is capitulating, and to whom he intends to commit the charge and command of those new Levies.

The Empress Dowager being returned hither from Neustadt, on the 9th instant was present in the Church of the Capucins at the solemn Anniversary observed in memory of the Emperour Ferdinand 3. her Husband, intending after some few days longer stay to return again to Neustadt, and from thence with the Imperial Princesses her Daughters to go to the waters at Baden, where they may continue for some time ; the Emperour intending for Laxenburg to divert himself in hunting.

From Hungary we are told that an Hungarian Captain belonging to the Garrison of Schinta, having for some time held a private correspondency with the Bassa of Newhausel, fearing to be discovered by a letter of his intercepted and brought into Schinta, in much haste left the Garrison with his Family, Wife and Children, and fled for his security to the Turks.

They tell us from Upper Hungary, that a party of 70 Heyduaes being abroad in search after prize, had robbed several Waggons laden with Merchants Goods belonging to the Turks, of a considerable value ; of which, in like ligence being brought by the Countrey people to the Bassa of Waradin who was then abroad with a party of neer 300 men, he immediately

An issue of the London Gazzette from April 23, 1668. The London Gazette is Britain's oldest continuously-published newspaper and was founded in 1665.

Year	Development	Why it was relevant
Ca. 1725	Punch cards (Basile Bouchon and Jean-Baptiste Falcon)	Improved method for controlling machines such as looms and, a century later, served as a means of storing information
1792	Tachygraphe semaphore, renamed Télégraphe in 1798 (Claude Chappe)	Allowed communication of information over distance
1806	Stylographic Writer aka carbon paper (Ralph Wedgwood)	Made it possible to create multiple copies of documents easily
1808	Typewriter (Pellegrino Tumi)	Originally created for the blind, a much faster way to write down information

Courtesy of Western Union

Samuel F.B. Morse (1791–1872) invented the electric telegraph after hearing about the discovery of the electromagnet. He created a dot-dash code for numbers and letters, and in 1844, having perfected the device, he sent the first Morse code message over a long-distance telegraph. The phrase "what hath God wrought" traveled almost instantly from Washington to Baltimore.

Year	Development	Why it was relevant
1830–1835	Electric Telegraph (Joseph Henry) and Morse Code and Electromagnetic Telegraph (Samuel F.B. Morse)	Enabled real-time communication over a distance
1839	Photography (Louis Jacques Mandé Daguerre and William Henry Fox Talbot – separately)	Made the capture of images possible
1844 and 1861	Commercial telegraph line between Washington D.C. and Baltimore (Morse) and Transcontinental Telegraph Line (Western Union)	Expanded the ability to communicate real-time information across the continental United States
1858–1866	Transatlantic cable	Enabled real-time communication across the Atlantic
1868–1871	Commercially successful typewriter and QWERTY keyboard (Christopher Sholes)	Changed the face of correspondence

Courtesy of The Spira Collection

Portrait of a man with a chamfered-box daguerreotype camera, ca. 1856. The daguerreotype, invented in 1839 by Louis Jacques Mandé Daguerre (1787–1851), was the first commercially successful photographic process. Photography quickly became the medium of record for information that could not otherwise be captured.

Year	Development	Why it was relevant
1870	Universal Stock Ticker (Thomas A. Edison and Western Union)	Enabled the transmission of stock price information over telegraph lines, remained in use through 1970
1876	Telephone (Alexander Graham Bell)	Made real-time voice communication possible
1887	Punched card tabulating machine (Herman Hollerith)	Allowed processing of information stored on punch cards
1895	Telediagraph (Ernest A. Hummel)	Enabled images to be sent over great distances using electrically-scanned shellac-on-foil originals
1914	Belinograph (Édouard Belin)	Enabled the scanning and transmission of an image using ordinary telephone lines
1915	Transcontinental telephone line (AT&T)	Enabled voice communication across the U.S.

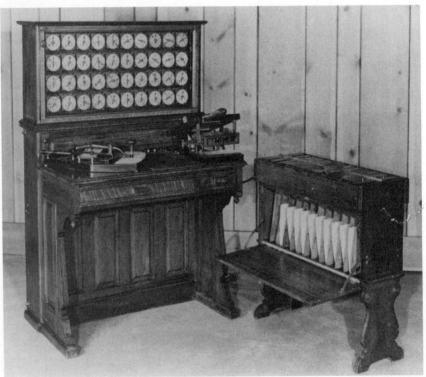

Courtesy of IBM Archives

Herman Hollerith (1860–1929) invented the concept of recording data on machine-readable punched cards and designed a tabulating machine would keep a running total of data. Tabulating Machine Company, which he formed in 1896, later became IBM.

Year	Development	Why it was relevant
1924	Telephotography (fax predecessor)	Enabled the transmission of pictures via telephone or telegraph lines
1930	Television	Made transmission of moving images possible, brought information streams into homes
1936	Gegenseh-Fernsprechanlagen, public videophone service (Deutsche Reichspost)	Made public video calling possible although the service lasted only a few years
1938	Xerography (Chester Carlson)	Led to the plain-paper photocopier
1940	Spread-spectrum communications (Hedy Lamarr and George Antheil)	Enabled secure communications and a signal with a wider bandwidth
1946	ENIAC Electronic Digital Computer (J. Presper Eckert and John Mauchly)	Inaugurated the age of general purpose digital computing
Ca. 1953	Repetitive typewriter (M. Schultz Company)	Enabled mass production of documents
1957	Sputnik satellite (USSR)	Enabled global telecommunications
1959	Xerox 914 plain paper copier	Enabled easier and higher quality copying of information
1960	DEC PDP-1 (Programmed Data Processor) Mini-computer (Digital Equipment Corp.)	Moved computing from the data center into the office

Courtesy of Xerox Corporation

The Xerox 914 was the first automatic office copier to make copies on plain paper.

Year	Development	Why it was relevant
1961	IBM Selectric Typewriter	Marked the beginning of desktop publishing thanks to the ability to switch fonts (via different typing elements)
1962	oNLine System (NLS) (Doug Engelbart and Stanford Research Institute)	Introduced hypertext browsing, online editing, mouse, windowing, information organized by relevance
1962–1968	Packet switching networks (Paul Baran, Donald Davies, Leonard Kleinrock – separately)	Removed the possibility of a single point of outage as data is split into packets that can then take different routes to a destination
1964	Transcontinental microwave communications (AT&T and Western Union, separately)	Enabled the replacement of land lines, leading to lower telecommunications costs
1964	IBM Magnetic Tape Selectric Typewriter	Allowed data to be stored in a typewriter for word processing
1964	IBM System/360 mainframe computer	Expanded scientific and commercial computing applications via a family of mainframe computers
1966	Telecopier 1 fax machine (Xerox)	Made possible the scanning and transmission of documents over telephone lines

Courtesy of IBM Archives

The IBM Magnetic Tape "Selectric" Typewriter, unveiled in 1964, pioneered the application of magnetic recording devices to typewriting, giving rise to the concept known today as word processing.

Year	Development	Why it was relevant
1969	ARPANET (Advanced Research Projects Agency, U.S. Department of Defense)	Led to modern-day Internet
1971	E-mail (Ray Tomlinson at BBN)	Allowed individuals to send and receive messages electronically
1971	Floppy Disk (IBM)	Enabled easy movement of information and data from one computer to another
1973	Westar commercial communications satellite, (Western Union)	Heralded the age of satellite-based communications
1973	Xerox Alto (Xerox Palo Alto Research Center)	Introduced the graphical user interface and the metaphor of a desktop to computing
1973	Graphical User Interface, Xerox Palo Alto Research Center	Replaced text commands, making computers easier to use

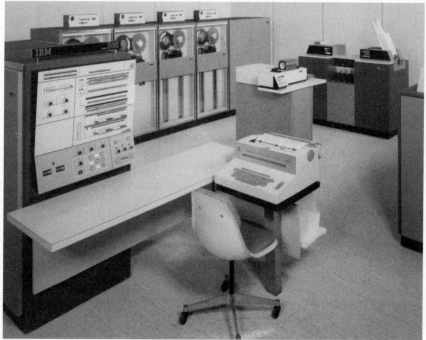

Courtesy of IBM Archives

The IBM System/360 mainframe computer, announced by IBM in 1964. The System/360, with a choice of five processors and 19 combinations of power, speed, and memory, was the first large "family" of computers to support interchangeable peripheral equipment and software. It represented a bold departure from the prevailing one-size-fits-all industry standard for mainframes.

Year	Development	Why it was relevant
1973	Mobile Phone (Martin Cooper and Motorola)	Enabled placing and receiving phone calls from outside the home or office without using wires
1973	EARS laser printer (Xerox)	Increased the speed and quality of office printing
1973	International connection to ARPANET (Univ College of London and Royal Radar Establishment)	Presaged a global Internet
1973	IBM 3340 Direct Access Storage Facility hard drive (code-named Winchester)	Led to inexpensive local storage
1973	Ethernet (Xerox)	Enabled local area networking
1973	FTP	Made possible the copying of files from one host to another
1973	TCP/IP (Robert Kahn and Vint Cerf, Stanford)	Enabled more efficient transmission and routing of traffic
1974	Hypertext (Ted Nelson, in *Computer Lib/Dream Machines)*	Enabled the World Wide Web and an easy-to-use method of sharing information via embedded references (hyperlinks) in text
1974	Altair 8800 Personal Computer	Brought computing into the home
1974	Telenet (BBN)	Made packet-switched networking available to the general public
1976– 1977	Apple I and Apple II personal computers	Popularized home and hobby computing
1978	WordStar (MicroPro International)	First commercially successful word processing software

Courtesy of Dan Bricklin and Bob Frankston

The idea for VisiCalc, the first electronic spreadsheet, occurred to Dan Bricklin while he was a student at the Harvard Business School. He, along with codeveloper Bob Frankston, originally imagined a group of people sitting around a table with a pointing device, where each user could draw graphics and formulae, which would be recalculated as necessary, on a shared screen. A far simpler version was developed on the Apple II based on a grid of rows and numbers and released in 1979.

Year	Development	Why it was relevant
1979	VisiCalc (Dan Bricklin and Bob Frankston)	First spreadsheet, revolutionized how data is organized and presented
1980	Usenet	Allowed users to read and post messages and served as predecessor to today's online Internet forums
1980s	WordPerfect, XyWrite, MultiMate, Microsoft Word, and pfs: Write	Solidified the migration of word processing from dedicated hardware to PCs
1981	IBM Personal Computer	First standards-based PC, moved computing to the desktop
1981	Xerox Star (also known as the Xerox 8100 Information System)	Introduced a graphical user interface, icons, folders, a mouse, Ethernet networking file servers, print servers, and e-mail
1982–1983	GRiD Compass 1101, and Gavilan SC laptop computers	Presaged a new movement in portable computing
1984	Breakup of AT&T/Divestiture of Bell System (Judge Harold Green and the U.S. Department of Justice)	Created a deregulated and competitive environment in the U.S. telecommunications industry that led to the Information Age
1984	MacWrite	Introduced users to WYSIWYG word processing and graphical user interfaces
1985	MacPublisher	Enabled computer-based WYSIWYG desktop publishing

Courtesy of IBM Archives

When IBM introduced the IBM PC in 1981, the company thought it might sell 250,000 personal computers over five years. Instead, the PC changed the entire IT landscape with its explosive growth.

Year	Development	Why it was relevant
1986–1988	NSFNET (National Science Foundation)	Created an open network that served as the backbone of the Internet by allowing academic and regional networks to connect
1989	HTML [Tim Berners-Lee at CERN (Conseil Européenne pour la Recherche Nucléaire – European Laboratory for Nuclear Research)]	Enabled the development of the Web and gave users the ability to describe the appearance of Web pages using tags
1990	Archie Internet search	Allowed users to index and find FTP files
1990	Microsoft Windows 3.0	Inaugurated a widespread change to GUI-based operating systems
1991	Wide Area Information Servers	Enabled indexing and search on remote computers
1991	World Wide Web (Time Burners-Lee at CERN)	Enabled browsing of information using a system of interlinked hypertext documents accessible over the Internet
1992	Apple Newton personal digital assistant	Enabled personal information to be stored in a handheld device
1993	Mosaic browser	Opened up the Web to the general public

Courtesy of PARC, a Xerox company

The 1981 Xerox Star was the commercialized version of the Xerox Alto. It was intended largely for document creation and its keyboard design in particular reflects this. The Star, also known as the Xerox 8100 Information System, introduced much of the functionality we still take for granted today.

Year	Development	Why it was relevant
1994	IBM Simon	Enabled mobile access to information by combining a phone, PDA, pager, and fax
1994	Justin's Links from the Underground (Justin Hall)	Laid a foundation for popularity of blogs and bloggers
1995	Microsoft Internet Explorer	Brought Microsoft into the browser business
1995	Alta Vista (Digital Equipment Corp.)	Enabled better search through a searchable, full-text database of a large portion of the Web
1996	Nokia 9000 Communicator	Spawned the smartphone industry
1997	SixDegrees.com	Set the stage for the rise of Friendster, Myspace, Facebook, and LinkedIn among others
1997	Google	Provided better search results through the incorporation of relevancy
1998	Open Diary (Bruce Ableson)	Allowed readers to post comments on blogs, leading to an increase in popularity
1999	Wi-Fi 802.11b standard	Enabled a revolution in wireless computing devices
2001	3G standard for mobile communications	Enabled faster mobile data communications as well as simultaneous voice and data

Courtesy of Research in Motion Limited

Research in Motion's BlackBerry 5810 and 5820 smartphones were the first commercially successful devices to combine phone, secure e-mail, text messaging, a browser, and organizer applications into a single wireless device.

Year	Development	Why it was relevant
2002–2004	Friendster, MySpace, Bebo, LinkedIn, and Facebook	Allowed users to share and interact with information based around social networks
2002	Handspring (later Palm) Treo 180	Influenced the development of the modern smartphone
2002	BlackBerry	Enabled mobile access to information by combining a phone, PDA, secure e-mail, texting, and Web browsing
2004	Voice-over-IP (VoIP)	Marked the beginning of accessible Internet telephony
2006–2007	Twitter	Enabled a new type of short messaging culture
Ca. 2006	Cloud computing	Allowed knowledge workers to access systems and information from anywhere
2007	Apple iPhone	Created an innovative Web-based model for apps and information sharing on mobile devices
2010	Apple iPad	Rejuvenated the long-nascent tablet computer market and drove acceptance of larger portable computing devices with smartphone-like operating systems

Courtesy of Basex, Inc.

Apple's iPad tablet computer had a dramatic impact on the portable computing market and the Facebook social network became both an important means of sharing information as well as an additional source of Information Overload.

HOW WE GOT HERE

All men, by nature, desire to know.

—Aristotle

An examination of how mankind started to create information in the earliest days of civilization, and how throughout the ages, those who work with information have increasingly found there is too much.

INFORMATION, PLEASE?

Our knowledge is a receding mirage in an expanding desert of ignorance.

—Will Durant

"Let your fingers do the walking" was the ubiquitous slogan for the Yellow Pages, developed back in 1964 by Geers Gross. It presaged a culture that today can find anything and everything online. The premise back in 1964 was that, rather than going from store to store, you could find what you were looking for in the commercial telephone book.

Back then, getting information was practically synonymous with asking the telephone company operator for a number. My, how things have changed: Today it might be a challenge to locate a telephone book or getting a live person on the line when calling directory assistance.

Given the information explosion that followed the introduction of the Web into almost every corner of the earth, now our fingers never stop walking. (With an amazing lack of foresight, the tagline was scrapped in 1998 by the Yellow Pages Publishers Association; at the time, the association's president called it "a little boring." Little did he know.)

Almost every generation has had access to more information than the one preceding it. It was maintained by some historians that Aristotle (384 BCE–322 BCE), in his day, knew everything – that is to say, he knew almost all that was to be known in his time. The same has been said for other polymaths, such as Francis Bacon (1561–1626) and Thomas Young (1773–1829).

Today it is clear that no one could even begin to amass knowledge that comes close to knowing everything. Whether any one person has ever known all there was to know is both debatable and unprovable; however, it is clear that each person who comes into the world today is able to know a progressively smaller and smaller percentage of the world's knowledge.

More information has been produced in the last 25 years than in the last five centuries. Indeed, it has been said that a weekday paper edition of the *New York Times* contains more information than an average person living in the seventeenth century would have been exposed to in a lifetime.

The impact of the amount of information created merely in the last decade is numbing.

To see the problems that can result from this, one need look no further than the reaction of the National Archives and Records Administration (NARA) in 2009 when it discovered that the outgoing Bush administration would be turning over approximately 100 terabytes of information. That is 10 times that of what the Clinton administration generated in the same amount of time eight years earlier. To deal with the impending flood of content, NARA launched an "emergency plan." And this is an agency whose sole mission is to keep records.

In the past decade, we have created billions of pictures, documents, videos, podcasts, blog posts, and tweets. If these remain unmanaged, it will be impossible for anyone to make sense out of any of this content because we have no mechanism to separate the important from the mundane.

Going forward, we face a tremendous paradox. On one hand, we have to ensure that what is important from our time is somehow preserved. If we don't preserve it, we are doing a tremendous disservice to generations to come; they won't be able to learn from our mistakes as well as from the great breakthroughs and discoveries that have occurred in our time. On the other hand, we are creating so much information that may or may not be important that we routinely keep everything.

Key inventions and discoveries, starting with papyrus (ca. 3500 BCE) and ink (2697 BCE) but more recently photography (1839), the commercial telegraph service (1844), the typewriter (1868), the telephone (1876), xerography (1938), the DEC PDP-1 mini computer (1960), ARPANET (the military predecessor to the Internet, created by the U.S. Defense Department's Advanced Research Projects Agency, which today is called DARPA) (1969), e-mail (1971), mobile phones (1973), the personal computer (1974), and the World Wide Web (1991), have facilitated increased access by democratizing content creation and distribution.

How democratic has information become? The answer may best be illustrated by what Tim Berners-Lee, inventor of the World Wide Web, wrote in 1999 in his book *Weaving the Web*:

> Suppose all the information stored on computers everywhere were linked. Suppose I could program my computer to create a space in which anything could be linked to anything. All the bits of information in every computer . . . on the planet would be available to me and to anyone else. There would be a single, global information space.

The discoveries in the past 150 years have changed where, how, and with whom we work. They have facilitated the creation of a workforce comprised largely of knowledge workers, rewritten (or in some cases eliminated) the boundaries between work and private life, and created new workplace problems, such as Information Overload, which were heretofore considered only in theoretical terms.

Larry Bowden, a vice president at computer giant IBM, told me he knows this firsthand. "Information Overload basically slows me down because I'm interacting with information that's irrelevant and out of context and not allowing me to get to the end point to have the impact that I want."

Information Overload is causing people to lose their ability to manage thoughts and ideas, contemplate, and even reason and think. We are becoming instead, as Ted Koppel told his *Nightline* television audience in 1986, "a nation of electronic voyeurs whose capacity and appetite for dialogue is a fading memory." Active engagement, it would appear, belongs to an earlier generation. Bursts of 140 characters in the form of individual tweets seems to have replaced more thoughtful means of communication for millions of people; instead of in-depth analysis and thought, we accept brief, fleeting, ephemeral thoughts that are of little consequence and have little impact.

I spend much of my time in meetings with people who are extraordinarily tech savvy, many of them senior and top executives at large companies that either create or consume large amounts of software and information (or sometimes both). Literally every person I have spoken with has confessed how he feels overwhelmed by the sheer quantities of information he is expected to consume in a day. This doesn't even take into consideration the technologies that noisily compete for a person's attention. What no one has yet realized is, however, the tremendous economic impact that this has on organizations and the legions of knowledge workers employed therein.

If for no other reason than to make it possible for future generations to be able to access information generated by us in the present, as well as what they themselves generate, we need to take the appropriate steps to solve this problem – and we need to do this now.

How do we accomplish this? It is clear (at least to this writer) that the tools we need to find information are lacking. The amount of information we have is simply too much for individuals to manage unaided by some form of technology, yet the tools we have available to us simply can't keep up. Even the latest advances in search and discovery don't seem to keep up with the massive amount of information that piles up when we are not looking.

Technology and our use of it have evolved in the past 150 years in ways that truly numb the mind. However, man has not necessarily evolved along the same path. A computer is designed to accomplish a specific task, to compute things, but this does not mean that is an extension of how we are humans work; we do not work the same as machines. This puts us in conflict with our tools, which takes a toll, not only emotionally and intellectually but on the bottom line as well.

For all intents and purposes, we are at the very beginnings of a new Information Age, and unlike past epochs, such as the Industrial Age, we are moving at such a fast pace that mistakes are amplified. (The term "Information Age" is not new, however, even though, according to The Death of the American Telephone & Telegraph Company by James R. Messenger, AT&T coined the phrase in 1982. The first mention of the term that I can locate (thanks to Google Books) dates back to 1915, in an article entitled "The Demand for the Illustrated Information Article" although the author, A.H. Martin, had a very different sense of what was meant.)

The very notion of a modern-day corporation, something that came about once the Industrial Revolution got under way, will most certainly change as the Information Age evolves. Companies are already becoming somewhat virtual, but this trend will increase dramatically in the coming years.

A true virtual company might work more like the way movie producers in Hollywood form a production company for a single film. Workers with the right set of skills come together for the duration of the project and then move on to something else. In the coming years, smaller and more flexible organizations will be able to compete favorably with larger ones as a result of being able to draw on resources previously available only to the larger ones – as well as on some resources larger organizations simply cannot tap into.

Meanwhile, workers will be more attracted to such smaller entities because of the greater flexibility offered by such organizations for these very reasons.

Today, a virtual workforce is the calling card of a few leading edge companies. JetBlue, an airline founded in 1998, never built a traditional call center to take reservations. Each and every person in the call center works from home, a fact that few if any callers are aware of.

While many believe that all of our technological innovations and changes have done much good for humankind by increasing the standard of communications and living, these changes must be looked at critically, with the recognition that they may in fact do far more harm than anyone anticipated.

2

HISTORY OF INFORMATION

Is there anywhere on earth exempt from these swarms of new books?
—Erasmus

Today's information glut is not an accident; rather, it is the culmination of a long series of technological and societal advances.

We now have more information available to us than we know what to do with; it is interesting, however, to think back and not only imagine a world without it but ponder how what we call information came into being.

Information has existed in a nonphysical sense ever since humans began communicating with each other. Information was passed orally, through simple observations ("The saber-toothed tiger will eat you. Run quickly.") and stories, some of which eventually became myths and legends.

Orally communicated information was of a temporal nature. If one was not there to hear a story, one could not simply look it up and access it. In order to spread, it had to be passed in full from one person to the next, and there was no way to verify the validity of a story or its adherence to the original narrative.

The advent of writing catapulted information from the non-physical to physical planes, and first took the form of clay tokens used as counting aids as early as 8000 BCE in Mesopotamia. The system eventually became cuneiform ("wedge shaped," from the Latin *cuneus*, meaning "wedge"), recognized as perhaps the earliest writing form developed.

The clay tokens were marked with symbols and used to keep track of items, and eventually they were stored in clay spheres to prevent tampering. Due to the obvious inability to read the tokens that were inside a clay sphere, the outside of the sphere was marked as well to reflect what was inside. The system of markings on the outside of the clay spheres evolved into written language as the information conveyed (how many sheep) became separated from the physical item (the sheep token).

The ability to keep detailed records and capture stories via the use of clay tokens, spheres, and eventually tablets kick-started the information explosion that we endure today. Written language enabled humans to use symbols to describe their environment with text that was both hard to tamper with (relative to oral record keeping) and could be shown to others and understood without context, although poorly worded clay tablets no doubt existed.

Early texts that marked the transition from an oral history to a written one include the Instructions of Shuruppak (2600 BCE), a Sumerian "wisdom" text that served as a guide for living virtuously and maintaining one's standing in the community. The guidelines contained in the text are cited by scholars as a precursor to the Ten Commandments and the biblical Book of Proverbs. The establishment of moral codes as written doctrine, as opposed to orally passed down custom, surely set the stage for both the formalization of legal codes and the rule of law, but also the ability to share and distribute information in a form that could be referenced.

The earliest surviving written story is considered to be the Epic of Gilgamesh, an ancient Mesopotamian poem thought to have been written in Sumer around 2200 BCE about the mythological hero-king Gilgamesh. It is important to note here that there were certainly written documents prior to the Epic of Gilgamesh, but the poem represents the first story committed to text that survived.

The shift from an oral history to a written history is significant for multiple reasons. By establishing a source document, the content moves from the nonphysical and arguably looser realm of passed-down oral tradition and lore into a form that exists in a physical state, meaning it exists on its own, without the requirement of a human to relate it (literacy issues notwithstanding). Because the newly written document exists in a physical state, it then becomes necessary to create methods to organize and catalog it.

The separation of information from information-propagator (the storyteller) also meant that information could be created and recorded at a rapid rate, which in turn meant that methods would have to be developed to filter and refine it.

The Information Revolution and the Book

Unlike today, where recorded information is both plentiful and relatively accessible, until about 500 years ago most information remained largely inaccessible, and the amount of information that was being produced was fairly limited.

The first books, of course, were written on scrolls. Starting around the second century CE, a new format, the codex, where the pages are bound on one edge, took hold and eventually supplanted the use of scrolls.

The codex was a huge technological leap forward for several reasons.

First, books became more compact since text could be written on both sides of the page. Scribes usually wrote on the inside of a scroll because the text on the somewhat unprotected side of the page could smudge easily. As a result, given the same amount of papyrus, a codex could hold twice as much text as a scroll. The codex also allowed random access to any information since turning to a specific page was far more precise and accurate than scrolling through the entire document.

The codex format also made it much easier for travelers to take information with them. While a paperback book on an airplane might be a given today (as might an e-book reader, or e-reader), imagine a satchel full of rolled-up documents and how cumbersome that might have been.

An image from the Catacombs of Domitilla in Rome makes this benefit abundantly clear. It shows a *capsa* (a circular leather box) holding approximately 12 scrolls while a codex, presumed to hold the same content, is shown hovering above it.

The codex also served to fix the order of information as presented in a book. With multiple scrolls, the order was fluid. With a bound codex, the order was fixed simply by virtue of the act of binding.

Books, however, remained expensive, and most people of the day were illiterate, which meant that the information contained in these volumes was largely inaccessible.

During the Middle Ages, monks copied manuscript books in a scriptorium, or copying room. A small book could take months to produce and larger works, years, thereby limiting supply.

Shortly before Gutenberg, block books, where an entire illustrated page was engraved on a block of wood, had become popular in Europe. A similar process had been in use in the Far East for quite some time. The block book printing process was not really suitable for books that were comprised largely of text versus illustration, so their utility was somewhat limited.

Around 1440, Johann Gutenberg began developing a printing press and movable type, first in Strasbourg and then in Mainz, Germany. Gutenberg's invention revolutionized the distribution of information by making it possible to print multiple copies of a book in a short time. His process spread first to other German cities and then throughout Europe.

Thanks to Gutenberg, by the end of the fifteenth century, hundreds of books were being produced each year on wooden printing presses (one estimate shows 30,000 titles were printed in that time), and the technology to produce books did not change substantially for centuries. The only major improvement in the book printing process was the substitution of iron for wood, to make the printing press studier.

Gutenberg and his printing press promulgated a revolution in information movement and facilitated the spread of knowledge that unquestionably made a great contribution to the Renaissance and the Scientific Revolution. Gutenberg and his disciples not only printed books but made it possible to spread the sum total of human knowledge across the globe in a way never contemplated before.

Due to these technological developments, books became the first mass-produced item and turned information into a physical product. As books became affordable, literacy moved from the elite classes to the masses and provided a means of social and economic advancement. Gutenberg, more so than any other individual, was responsible for the first Information Revolution, a fact recognized by *Time* magazine, which in 1999 named him the "Man of the Millennium."

E-readers Rising

A similar paradigm shift in how books are distributed, consumed, and even written may be happening presently with the current rise in the popularity of e-readers. Amazon's Kindle has sold an estimated 3.3 million units as of early 2010 (the company does not release official numbers on Kindle sales). Additionally, Kindle e-book sales have actually outpaced traditional book sales for Amazon, with 180 e-books sold for every 100 hardcover books in June 2010. Public libraries are also participating in the move to a digital format, and many now offer online check-out of e-books that can then be downloaded to e-readers.

The electronic underpinnings of the e-book also allows publishers to develop and package extra content, such as video clips, audio, and other supplemental content, with a book. So-called enhanced e-books have the potential to boost profits, as they can be sold for more than their normal e-book counterparts, but the market for these is still in the early stages and few have been brought to market. HarperCollins, for example, has an e-book library of 8,400 titles in the United States alone, but, as of November 2010, only 11 of them were available as enhanced e-books.

According to the Association of American Publishers, the larger e-book market accounts for six percent of the total 2010 U.S. consumer book market. The growth of the e-book has been furthered by the proliferation of mobile devices such as smartphones and tablets that also function as e-book readers. For example, the Kindle iPad and iPhone App allow users to read their Amazon-purchased Kindle e-books on devices from Apple.

One of the biggest differences between purchasing an e-book versus a traditional paper book is that e-books today come with digital rights management software, a technology that can restrict access to the e-book and dictates terms of use. In practical terms, this is distinct from a physical book because typically the e-book cannot be loaned out, shared, or resold in the same manner as a physical book can.

In April 1996, I wrote an article in the *Basex Online Journal of Industry and Commerce* about what I called the LazerBook, my idea for a prospective technology for the then-nascent e-book industry that would combine the feel of a traditional book with self-service, online access. "Books are enjoyable," I wrote then. "They elicit a reaction, and the experience of reading a book is not limited to the words on a page."

At the time, many pundits were predicting that books (in the form of a codex) would disappear and would be replaced by electronic tablets. In some respects, they were correct, as the popularity of e-readers today demonstrates.

However, while e-reader users can purchase books via the device itself, and they can "carry" hundreds of books with them on trips, all contained within the e-reader's memory, clearly something is missing.

"There is a sensory experience also associated with reading a book," I wrote. "Opening a musty, leather-bound tome gives rise to a heightened sense of adventure. The binding itself adds to the reading event, as does the quality of the paper, the typeface used (and sometimes even specially designed for a particular work), and the ability to gauge the progress you are making, as the unread pages slowly diminish."

The LazerBook concept would overcome this problem by presenting the book on reusable paper, with a traditional binding. A LazerBook printer would produce the book on demand in people's homes or in shops. And because I wanted the LazerBook concept to be green, the reader would insert the book back into the device once finished, the ink would be removed, and the paper and binding could be reused for the next book.

Today, the success of the e-reader model – with its improved display and business model – makes the LazerBook perhaps seem quaint. But there are still many issues to be resolved here in terms of ensuring a pleasurable reading experience.

After the Book . . . Getting the Word Out

Until the relatively recent development of the Internet as a news source, the key means of distributing large amounts of news and information was the newspaper.

Although some news was distributed as far back as ancient Rome in *Acte Diurna*, government bulletins carved in metal or stone, government-produced news sheets called *tipao* during the Han dynasty and privately published news sheets distributed in the late Ming dynasty, cross-border trade created a need for a more modern newspaper in Europe, one with political, economic, military, and weather news. Merchants began to distribute handwritten news-letters with such information, and the Venetian government published the *Notizie scritte* on a monthly basis, selling it for one gazetta, as early as 1556.

It was the rise of the printing press in the years following Gutenberg that led to the emergence of multiple newspapers in the seventeenth century.

The *Relation aller Fürnemmen und gedenckwürdigen Historien* (*Collection of All Distinguished and Noteworthy News*), published in Strasbourg starting in 1605, is considered by many historians to be the first newspaper.

Amsterdam was a center of both trade and early newspaper publishing and the *Courante uyt Italien, Duytslandt, &c.* appeared in 1618, followed by an English-language edition, *Corrant out of Italy, Germany, etc.* in 1620, that was also the first English-language newspaper.

Newspapers arrived somewhat late in the Americas. The first and last issue of *Publick Occurrences Both Forreign and Domestick* appeared in 1690 (it lasted for one edition before the government shut it down). The first regularly published newspaper was *The Boston News-Letter*, which started publication in 1704.

By the early nineteenth century, advances in technology resulting from the Industrial Revolution allowed newspapers to greatly increase circulation and become an important means of communicating information. In 1814, *The Times* (London) deployed a new printing press that was able to print 1,100 pages per minute. By then many newspapers had cropped up in European cities as well as in North and South America.

Another advance allowed newspapers to print on both sides of the paper at the same time, further lowering the cost of the newspaper and thus increasing its circulation. The first "penny press" newspaper, the Boston *Transcript*, cost one-sixth of the price of other papers and further increased the newspaper-reading audience.

A major change in the newspaper business was the introduction of advertiser-supported papers. Émile de Giradin started the trend in France in 1836 with *La Presse*, and it was copied in Austria by August Zang in 1848 with *Die Presse*.

While newspaper circulation is on the decline now, the *Guinness Book of World Records* notes that the daily circulation of *Труд* (*Labor*), a Soviet newspaper, exceeded 21.5 million in 1990 and a Soviet weekly, *Аргументы и факты* (*Arguments and Facts*), had a circulation of

33.5 million in 1991. Today, Japanese newspapers, the world's biggest (based on circulation), are reporting a slow but steady loss in readership.

Today, the newspaper industry is in relative chaos. In the 1920s, the average household received 1.23 newspapers per day, in newspaper terms a 123 percent market penetration. According to the *State of News Media 2004*, the percentage of Americans reading newspapers began to drop in 1940, at which time the average household was buying 1.4 newspapers daily. But the population increase kept circulation figures on the rise until 1990, when actual circulation began to decline. By the year 2000, market penetration had dropped to 54 percent, and today it is less than 50 percent.

Indeed, at a speech given at the World Association of Newspapers and News Publishers Ninth International Newsroom Summit in September 2010, Arthur Sulzberger, publisher of the *New York Times*, responding to a question suggesting that the newspaper might print its last edition in 2015, said he saw no point in making such a prediction and further commented that "we will stop printing the *New York Times* sometime in the future, date TBD."

Sulzburger later clarified that he was not announcing that the *Times* has definite plans to stop printing on paper; rather, he was attempting through humor to show that it was virtually impossible to predict exactly at what point newspapers printed on paper might cease to exist.

It is, however, very likely that newspapers on paper will become rarer and rarer and will at some point be relegated to the history books.

It was the arrival of radio and television that started newspapers' decline, and the arrival of the 24-hour news cycle on cable television further sounded its death knell by transforming what was in the morning paper into yesterday's news. The Internet then emerged as the next big threat to newspapers when free classified ads (such as Craigslist) and auctions (such as eBay) replaced newspaper classifieds as the go-to medium for selling services and trading in secondhand items.

But history has shown us the media tend to adapt, rather than perish, when faced with new media predators. Radio, for example, has survived the onslaught of television and of the Internet. In fact, the Internet has perhaps broadened radio's reach by making stations readily accessible beyond traditional borders. Podcasts, which, like radio, transmit audio, are also helping support the medium.

When speaking about the effect of the Web on newspapers, it is critical to remember that the Internet itself is just plumbing; it does not by itself generate news stories. Knowledgeable reports and editorial staff, as well as an understanding of how online news presentation differs from traditional print, are still necessary for a news organization to thrive online.

While an in-depth economic analysis of the newspaper business is beyond the scope of this book, it is important to understand how Americans' newspaper consumption habits are changing, as this directly impacts the consumption of information.

Although newspapers initially feared the Internet when its popularity and use started to rise (and, today, many still do), the Internet may end up being the savior of the industry, if newspapers can adapt to the new medium.

As Eric Schmidt, CEO of Google, the search company that introduced a news aggregation service back in 2000, said at a keynote at a newspaper editors' convention in April 2010, "We're all in this together," adding that he was "convinced that the survival of high-quality journalism" was "essential to the functioning of modern democracy."

In an op-ed piece in the December 2009 *Wall Street Journal,* Schmidt announced that Google would be looking into ways to direct more revenue to the struggling newspaper industry rather than to direct it to Google's coffers.

Where is this all going? What may come out of this may be improved filtering and a better reading experience that allows readers to find the information they need or want more quickly than the current browser-based experience.

What real physical newspapers still do very well is provide a fast and simple interface for reading the news, especially when it is compared to online news sources. Even comparing the same newspaper in print and online, I can scan articles far more quickly in the print version.

One experiment in this area is Google Fast Flip, a tool that Google says should combine the best elements of print and online. Google Fast Flip allows the reader to browse through news and headlines and promises to personalize the experience by taking cues from the sources, journalists, and topics that the reader seems to seek out (based on what is selected).

While Fast Flip is fast, it does not really begin to approach the type of reading experience that people look for in a newspaper. Another experiment is the Apple iPad, the tablet computer that Apple introduced in early 2010.

Some apps for Apple's iPad may very well be the best implementation of a newspaper ever to hit a small screen. The *Wall Street Journal* iPad app, for example, brings a somewhat realistic look and feel of the print paper into the device, unlike what is achieved with the *Journal*'s Web site or smartphone apps. Thanks to its intelligent use of gestures and scrolling, I find reading the *Journal* on the iPad more enjoyable and far more informative than reading the paper version. (For that matter, I can also switch to the European or Asian edition with two taps, a feat that is not possible with paper.)

Other newspapers and magazines, most notably *Die Presse* and the *Economist*, have done similarly well in developing a superb reading experience. On the other hand, I find that reading *New York Times* via its iPad app is an exercise in frustration thanks to a poor user interface that leaves me constantly wishing I had the actual paper in front of me.

Thanks to tablet computers, we can expect further innovation in the online publishing field. Some will be successful and will provide the reader with an improved reading experience and others will fail miserably in that regard.

The *Journal* succeeds here because the metaphor of reading from a page is preserved (and somewhat improved upon) by the tablet's larger size and touch screen controls, something that is not the case in the browser or smartphone. The iPad and the tablets that will follow it add additional technology to support this metaphor, namely video, touch, and social tools that have the potential to make the tablet experience even better than the print edition.

Newspapers, especially the print editions, treat the reader like a stranger every day. For years, I wondered if I couldn't delete certain sections from a newspaper that was being delivered to my home. I could do without the sports section but I definitely want the business section. Countless trees have been sacrificed for the printing of sections that went straight into the recycling bin.

Despite the time-tested utility of the newspaper, there is little argument that publishers of the paper versions of newspapers are under pressure from their online counterparts.

According to the Newspaper Association of America, 72 million people accessed newspaper Web sites in November 2009. Those visitors read an average of 43 pages that month for a total of 33 minutes. The same association reported an average daily readership of 95 million for weekday print newspapers.

The association also reported that, as of mid-2010, print and online advertising had fallen 35 percent since the first quarter of 2008.

Newspapers in the United States, in part thanks to steep personnel cuts, lower paper costs, smaller editions, and content-sharing arrangements, have managed to remain profitable. Many newspapers are owned by companies such as McClatchy and Gannett, and they have come upon the realization that there is no need to write the same national story 15 different times for 15 different markets.

Axel Springer, publisher of newspapers including *Bild* and *Die Welt* in Germany, recorded its most profitable quarter in its history in early 2010 and announced an expansion into Poland. In Brazil, newspapers have expanded circulation by one million in the past 10 years.

While the newspaper clearly revolutionized the movement and distribution of information, its dominance as a primary source of information has in fact waned.

Newspapers' coexistence with the online world has been iffy. Only the *Wall Street Journal* and the *Financial Times*, both leaders in business and financial news, have been able to create a successful paywall model and convert casual readers into paying subscribers. From 2005 to 2007, the *New York Times* tried – and failed – to charge readers for its content. In March 2011, the *Times* erected a new pay wall that largely limits non-subscribers to 20 articles per month. But as the world looks more and more to the Internet for all of its information, newspapers (as well as magazines and journals) will find increasing pressure to monetize online content to meet their bottom line.

It is also important to note that while the newspaper is often treated as a venerable, authoritative, and trusted source of information, it is as fallible as any other source. The history of the newspaper includes the yellow journalism that marked the circulation battles in the late 1800s between Joseph Pulitzer's *New York World* and William Randolph Hearst's *New York Journal*, which included the allegations that they pushed the country into the Spanish American War, the outlandish stories presented by the tabloid press, and the ideological leanings of editors and owners. Newspapers have always gravitated toward political leanings or in some cases been outright tools of governments without even the pretense of independence.

The New News Cycle

With the advent of radio, television, and then cable television, the news cycle changed dramatically.

Traditionally, a reporter would gather news and bring it to a newspaper, where it was written, edited, typeset, and eventually printed. In the earliest days of newspapers, it could take weeks for news to travel and become known. Twentieth-century technology began to speed up the news cycle. The wide adoption of the telephone allowed reporters to call stories in; wire services transmitted news stories in minutes; live satellite technology eventually brought breaking stories into people's homes as an event unfolded through both radio and television.

Most larger cities had both morning and afternoon newspapers. The afternoon papers (which included late editions of morning papers in some cases) allowed reportage of events that took place earlier in the day, but real-time news reporting, first on the radio and later on television, gradually but not completely replaced the later editions.

Broadcast television news, although different in format, was not far removed from radio news or, in terms of information conveyed, newspapers. In its original form as introduced in 1940, a man simply read the news from behind a desk. This format was shaken up by the work of journalists such as Edward R. Murrow, who in the 1950s began to operate in a more critical manner and use the power of images to influence public opinion.

Perhaps the largest shakeup of information generation in the media world was the relatively recent shift to a 24-hour/7-day news cycle.

In 1980, Ted Turner founded Cable News Network, or CNN. It was the first all-news television channel and, more important, the first 24-hour news channel. Due to its extensive coverage of events in the late 1980s and early 1990s such as the Tiananmen Square protests, the Gulf War in Iraq, and the military action in Mogadishu, Somalia, a new term came into use in government and military circles: the CNN effect.

The CNN effect refers to the shortened decision-making time that policy makers are forced into due to round-the-clock news coverage of events as they unfold as well as the effect that real-time broadcasts of events can have on public opinion and action (such as charitable donations after natural disasters).

The effect that the 24/7 news cycle had on politics and the general civil discourse was amplified again by the rise of the Internet as an information source. Several newspapers made forays into online news in the early 1980s via videotext services, and America Online (AOL) began offering Chicago Online as its first online newspaper in 1992. By 1994, the journal *Editor and Publisher* reported that there were 20 online news services worldwide.

Today, it is virtually impossible to count the number of news services that exist online. Indeed, the challenge would not be to count them but to define what a "news source" even means in a modern, online world. People get news from a wide variety of sources that include blogs, wikis, social networks such as Facebook, and microblogging platforms such as Twitter.

Traditional news outlets have recognized the power that these platforms have in distributing news with lightning speed and have for the most part embraced the new media (although they still struggle with monetizing their content). Newspapers have blogs written by reporters, Twitter feeds of breaking news, and maintain a presence on social networking sites by link sharing, which is critical for generating page views of the original article.

Just as there is a plethora of online sources of news from traditional (and "authoritative") sources, there are near-limitless sources for information on the Web that purport to be reputable but are not.

The difficultly in locating authoritative content online is multifaceted. Primarily the problem exists because of the anonymity that the Web facilitates; it is nearly impossible to verify that the author of a random blog post is a reputable reporter using verified and reliable sources. A traditional reporter would have had to run a story by an editorial staff, which, in the interest of avoiding the embarrassment of incorrect reporting, has a vested interest in making sure that information is factual and presented in at least a relatively even-handed manner.

A blogger, however, has a vested interest in generating page views (as well as ad revenue from embedded advertisements) and thus may feel pressure to post information as quickly as possible, with less thought given to the quality of the material.

A secondary problem in determining the validity of online content relates to the previously discussed accelerated news cycle. Even with reputable news organizations, the pressure to keep up with a developing story results in information being published that is later determined to be incorrect. Since less time is available to a reporter to gather facts and analyze a story before reporting it, the likelihood of mistakes being made is greater. Oftentimes these mistakes are not corrected, and the misinformation continues to exist on the Internet, leading to unsuspecting victims who mistake it for vetted and factual information.

Online content is iterative, meaning that a new article that pops up on your RSS feed is probably the latest in a long series of other articles that establish the "facts" that form the basis for the newest piece. The iterative building of facts is not unique to online content; however, the speed at which information can be located online via a search, used in a new piece of content, and then disseminated to readers/viewers makes the consequences of using faulty information severe and long lasting.

Imagine the game of telephone, where one person whispers a message in someone's ear, who then passes it on, until the message returns to the originator. The Internet takes the game of telephone and speeds it up so that the whisperers are not even done talking before the next message is being passed on.

CHAPTER 3

WELCOME TO THE INFORMATION AGE

"There's so much in the newspapers."
"That's true – one gets dizzy merely looking at them."

—Hans Fallada

Today's Information Age had its start in the early 1980s with the breakup of the Bell System and AT&T, a move that led to a competitive telecoms environment that was able to build the commercial Internet that is somewhat taken for granted today.

This communications revolution has brought with it myriad changes in how work is done. While as recently as five years ago, much knowledge work was relatively solitary, today knowledge workers expect to be able to tap into a variety of resources – be they people, information, tools, or the collective knowledge of an organization – when doing their work.

One thing that has changed is the recognition that knowledge workers (sometimes referred to as information workers) are the linchpins of the Information Age.

We define the knowledge worker as a participant in the knowledge economy and the knowledge economy as an economic environment where information and its manipulation are the commodity and the activity (in contrast to the industrial economy, where the worker produced a tangible object with raw production materials and physical goods).

Ironically, many of the tools that support knowledge work, while having acquired significant functionality, haven't changed to better support new ways of working.

What has to happen in the workplace is nothing less than revolutionary. Software needs to adapt to the new way of working collaboratively and software development needs to support this paradigm from the ground up.

Word processing software, for example, has in many respects changed relatively little from the word processing hardware introduced by IBM in the 1960s that supported text entry, editing, and printing. This feature set was replicated in software such as MultiMate, WordStar, DisplayWrite (named after the 1980s IBM DisplayWriter hardware-based word processor), and WordPerfect, which came to define word processing at the dawn of the PC Revolution.

Even as more features were added, the way people used the tools changed very little. A Basex survey in early 2010 revealed that 25 percent of knowledge workers still print out their documents to compare the comments and edits they get from colleagues.

In part, little has changed within the enterprise because we have yet to develop a management science for the knowledge economy that managers can apply in crafting strategy, designing products, managing people, and leveraging technology. It took a good 150 years from the dawn of the Industrial Revolution until the beginnings of a management science began to take shape. Today, we are in the first quarter century of the knowledge economy, and all we can do is borrow the management science from the previous epoch and try to adapt it, an action somewhat akin to trying to fit a square peg into a round hole and one that results in great inefficiencies.

Taylorism, the management science of the Industrial Age first enunciated by Frederick Winslow Taylor, included standardizing work or replacing humans with machines and finding the "one best way" to perform tasks. Indeed, a 1974 article in the *New York Times* discusses how companies were following this course and turning offices into factories by splitting the traditional secretary's job into two parts and sending some secretaries off to word processing centers to type documents and others to administrative support stations to file papers and answer phones.

It is clear today that such "improvements" were not appropriate for knowledge work and such attempts exemplify the fact that we still have a long way to go.

It's now incumbent upon software makers to help companies find their way by providing them with tools that will support a true Collaborative Business Environment (see page 62 for a detailed explanation) and the collaborative work that will go along with it.

Is Software Holding Us Back?

Over 40 percent of the knowledge workforce (estimated to be 78.6 million in the United States alone) works on a regular basis in a nontraditional, non-Dilbertian environment several times each week. This means that a worker might not always have access to a traditional personal computer but nonetheless needs to access, edit, or create various types of information, be it a document, an e-mail, or information in another form. Previously, the same worker might have spent the majority of his day in front of his workstation in the office. Today, a multi-modal knowledge worker needs to experience the same functionality, whether in front of his own desktop or laptop, a random workstation, or even a smartphone.

Another change in the way we work may be found in the substantial increase in collaborative work. More and more documents are shared with business partners, customers, and colleagues in various and diverse ways. Managing this collaboration – and the input that comes from all directions – has become key. Many currently available technologies are not up to the challenge.

One challenge we face comes from the proliferation of features and functionality in all office software. There are hundreds of features in each application, but the right ones don't always surface when they are needed. Instead, much time is lost when knowledge workers hunt for a feature that will serve a particular need.

Another challenge comes from the vast amount of information the typical knowledge worker is presented with each and every day. To say that this has increased would be a gross understatement. Information Overload lowers comprehension and concentration levels, skews the work–life balance, and robs each and every knowledge worker of a good part of the productive day.

As a result, choosing any kind of software is far more complex today than it used to be. The ideal program will support multi-modal, collaborative work, provide an interface that makes it easier for the knowledge worker to complete a task, and will help reduce the impact of Information Overload.

Oftentimes the tools deployed within an organization to make it more efficient turn out to be the one thing holding it back. The greatest challenges companies face today are maintaining information flow and supporting collaboration among workers. Despite the technological advances of the past few decades, the flow of information in today's organizations is often one-way and of limited value. As a result, critical information is lost or goes unrecognized and unused.

Moreover, the gains promised by so-called productivity tools often have failed to deliver on their promise to improve productivity. Even when individual efficiency or effectiveness is positively affected, the overall impact on the enterprise can be barely perceptible.

The future, however, is far from bleak. New technologies are on the horizon that will allow information to flow to where it is needed, at the exact moment it is needed, and will support group- and teamwork unlike anything we have seen before.

As a result, the long-sought-after productivity gains will finally be realized, and knowledge workers finally will have access both the tools they need to do their work and the information that in fact is their work.

A variety of tools, from desktop productivity applications to customer relationship management tools, form the basis of the knowledge workers' toolset, and the selection of the appropriate tools can be critical in maximizing work efforts.

However, while all software within a given category may look as if it can accomplish the very same thing, to paraphrase George Orwell, all software applications are equal but some are more equal than others, and managers must be very sensitive to this fact.

Inside many companies, change is in the air. Slowly but surely, managers are beginning to realize that facilitating efficient collaboration among their legions of knowledge workers is a strategic priority. They are beginning to see that it is possible to decrease costs and increase productivity through the appropriate deployment of knowledge-sharing and collaboration tools.

While most managers recognize that collaboration and communication applications aren't toys, they also haven't quite figured out how to use these technologies consistently as productive work tools. Once they begin to find ways to integrate these tools into the way knowledge workers in their organizations actually work, amazing things will start to happen.

It will come as no surprise that the kind of collaboration that will succeed in the enterprise will take major cues from the consumer market. Indeed, knowledge workers want to be able to use simple, intuitive, and powerful tools that resemble the ones they are familiar with in their personal lives, such as Facebook, Twitter, blogs, and wikis.

The Tools We Use

Three of the most-used tools for creating and recording information were invented in the last 200 years. Just as the invention of the printing press and movable type by Gutenberg launched a revolution in the distribution of books (and later on, newspapers, magazines, and other printed material), several nineteenth- and twentieth-century discoveries, namely the typewriter, the photocopier, and word processing software, begat a revolution in the distribution of individually crafted documents.

These three inventions did more to shape the creation and mass distribution of information than anything that preceded them in the history of mankind.

At the same time, however, these benefits came with a price: The better the technology has gotten, the more information mankind has been able to create and distribute.

Indeed, until the era of the laser printer arrived in the 1990s (which enabled the inexpensive mass distribution of high-quality originals), creators of documents had two choices. There were those few documents important enough to warrant the investment of time and energy in setting type and printing, and there was the overwhelming majority of documents that didn't, many of them of an ephemeral nature. These were either handwritten or typed.

The photocopier closed the gap between commercial printing and low-volume copying (which was more likely to have been handled via carbon copies than anything else). It also gave knowledge workers the ability to distribute anything and everything to as many people as they wished, just as e-mail does today, albeit with less speed and efficiency.

That's not to say that knowledge workers of an earlier age didn't devote extensive time to correspondence. The great minds of the enlightenment – John Locke, Sir Isaac Newton, and François-Marie Arouet (better known as Voltaire) – exchanged tens of thousands of letters. Voltaire alone reportedly wrote more than 18,000. Needless to say, however, they did not send hundreds of copies to friends and colleagues.

The typewriter and the photocopier opened the door for knowledge workers to easily create and send documents to multiple recipients, but there were still some significant limitations compared to what is available today using e-mail. The distribution of documents within a building or campus was relatively easy and done via intra-office mail or simply by dropping off the document in the recipient's inbox. For those people traveling or in a different office or company, documents were typically sent by mail, which meant that they would not arrive until several days later.

I would be remiss if I didn't mention both telex and fax technology here for a moment, even though neither facilitated mass information distribution. Telex (which was an amalgam of TELegraph Exchange) was a popular means of business communication that used switched telegraph technology to route messages from one dedicated Telex terminal to another. Its primacy was first challenged by the advent of the facsimile machine in the mid-1970s and later by e-mail.

Today, the norm is to measure the arrival of messages and documents in seconds – and our new discoveries allow us to create more documents, more drafts and versions of the documents we are creating, as well as to distribute them to dozens if not hundreds or thousands of people with the click of a button.

That change is one of the key reasons why we have to contemplate the problem of Information Overload.

Mid-Nineteenth-Century Tools: Groundwork Is Laid

The modern typewriter, perfected (to the point of commercial use) by Christopher Latham Sholes in the mid-nineteenth century, and xerography, invented by Chester Carlson in 1938, both pale in comparison to today's software-based word processors in terms of the amount of information that they allow users to generate. Despite this, all three technologies represent tools that – at the time – supported a dramatic increase in the creation and distribution of information, which in turn exacerbated the problem of having too much information.

Pelligrino Tumi is one of multiple inventors credited with having invented the typewriter. Most of these early machines were developed not for office use but rather to enable the blind to write. By the mid-nineteenth century, the Industrial Revolution was heating up, and technology was trying to keep up with the increased pace of business communications. A stenographer could take dictation at the rate of up to 130 words per minute while a scrivener was limited to 30 at the very most.

While various inventors tried their hand at perfecting a typewriting machine (at first, the person who used the machine was referred to as a typewriter), it was not until the 1860s that Sholes and two colleagues invented what really was the first practical typewriter. In fact, the word "typewriter" comes from the first commercially successful product, the Sholes and Glidden Type-Writer.

Sholes' innovations included the QWERTY keyboard, which spaced out frequently used keys to minimize the chance that they would strike one another during fast keyboarding. Earlier typewriters were not capable of supporting fast keyboarding because of such collisions.

By the dawn of the twentieth century, typewriters were standard fare in offices and there was much standardization, including keyboard design and the use of a black and red ribbon (probably used for bookkeeping purposes at first). The first electric typewriters began to appear during this time period as well (Thomas Edison had patented an electric typewriter in 1872, but the first useable models began appearing in offices in the 1920s).

Twentieth-Century Tools: The Foundation for the Information Revolution

IBM, whose typewriters were ubiquitous in offices until they were supplanted by PCs (which, at the beginning, came from another division of IBM), entered the business in 1933 by purchasing Electromatic, a company that was then part of General Motors' Delco division.

IBM reportedly spent $1 million reengineering the company's existing machine and released it in 1935 as the IBM Electric Typewriter Model 01. The Model 01 became the first commercially successful electric typewriter in the United States.

By 1938, Chester Carlson was busy inventing the process of xerography (literally, "dry writing") in Astoria, New York, after several years of experimentation and a lifelong interest in duplication. He had been trying to create a means of duplicating a sheet of paper, such as a letter, but the only way to make copies at the time was confined to carbon paper, mimeographs, and photostats, none of which could take an existing document and copy it onto a new piece of paper without some intermediate steps or processes.

Carlson was ultimately successful by virtue of having followed a process outlined by the Hungarian physicist Pál Selényi. His work resulted in the world's first xerographic copy. It involved no chemical reaction and was a completely dry process. John Dessauer, chief of research at the Haloid Corporation, read about Carlson's invention, and Carlson (along with his agent, Batelle Memorial Institute, a technology company that was headquartered in Columbus, Ohio) entered into a licensing agreement with Haloid.

Carlson joined Haloid in 1947 and the XeroX (*sic*) Copier Model A, the world's first photocopier, was born two years later. The technology, however, was difficult to use as each copy required 39 steps. Other companies, including 3M and Kodak, introduced easy-to-use copying machines in the following decade, although these machines used an inferior process and did not copy onto plain paper. This put intense pressure on Haloid to perfect its machine, a process that took well over 10 years.

In 1944, IBM introduced the Executive typewriter, the first machine with proportionally spaced type. Since knowledge workers of the time were used to monospaced type, pages typed with the Executive typewriter appeared to have been typeset. This was another key advancement in terms of improving the readability and quality of typed material.

In 1948, IBM unveiled the Model A Standard Electric Typewriter, promising users "a new feeling of comfort and control" thanks to fingertip touch controls for carriage return, backspace, tabulator, and shift key. These machines were virtually indestructible and lasted for decades. However, this presented IBM with a dilemma: Since the machines never wore out, it was difficult to convince customers to purchase new ones so IBM had to continuously innovate by adding new features and functionality to its typewriters, a tradition that continues today in the computer industry.

A significant improvement in tools for mass information distribution was the automatic or repetitive typewriter from the M. Schultz Company. Introduced in the 1950s, the device, which used punch cards that operated the typewriter in a manner reminiscent of a Pianola piano-player (the automated musical instrument, not the individual), allowed knowledge workers to create templates that were then used for the mass production of letters and documents. This was the first volley in the creation of word processing, although the term was to appear in the lexicon only in the following decade. It was the translation of the German *Textverarbeitung*, a word coined by Ulrich Steinhilper, an IBM engineer, in 1955, who conceptualized electronic word processing as a counterpart to data processing, which was already quite common at the time. Steinhilper received a World Achievement Award in 1972 from IBM in recognition of his creation of the term.

Breakthroughs in Productivity

One of the most significant breakthroughs in office systems came in 1959 with the introduction of the Xerox 914, the world's first modern photocopier. The fact that the Xerox 914 made its copies onto plain paper made it unique – and highly sought after. The 914 was also unique in that it came with what Xerox called a "scorch eliminator," or fire extinguisher, necessitated by the fact that the machine had a propensity to self-immolate.

Up until that time, photocopiers made copies onto coated paper that tended to curl and fade. As a result, they were not very useful, and they also looked nothing like the original.

Just as Gutenberg's printing press revolutionized man's ability to spread information in geometric proportion, Carlson's Xerox 914 had a similar effect, largely, at least at first, on knowledge workers in offices.

Office life got a lot easier, in many respects, thanks to Carlson, but one could also look at the photocopy as one of the first instigators in the dramatic increase in information production and disbursement that has led to the problem of Information Overload.

A 1961 ad for the Xerox 914 put it succinctly: it "makes copies of anything . . . on ordinary paper . . . even pages in a book."

Meanwhile, while IBM had introduced multiple innovations into the design of office typewriters over the decades, the one with the greatest impact was the launch of the IBM Selectric typewriter in 1961.

The Selectric used a "typing element" (which resembled a golf ball with characters on it) instead of individual keys for the letters. The element moved laterally in front of the paper instead of the carriage and paper moving across the print position, as had been the standard.

The Selectric elements were interchangeable, and users were able to purchase them with a wide variety of fonts. As a result, IBM can be credited with having introduced the first desktop publishing tools with the Selectric. While it is true that few users used multiple fonts (I was one of them), it was indeed possible to achieve a typeset look thanks to the high quality of both the fonts and the Selectric's output, especially when using a film rather than a cloth ribbon.

IBM Selectrics (including the Selectric II introduced in 1971 as well as the Correcting Selectric) accounted for 75 percent of the typewriter market until the word processor almost completely replaced them in the office.

Online Collaboration Makes Its Entrance

Imagine a world without the collaborative tools we take for granted today. Decades before the emergence of the Internet and World Wide Web, computer pioneers were building Plato, a system that pioneered chat rooms, e-mail, instant messaging, online forums and message boards, and remote screen sharing. These collaborative tools began to make their appearance in 1973 (Plato was first built in 1960 as a computer-aided teaching system at Computer-based Education Research Lab at the University of Illinois). That year, Plato got Plato Notes (message forums), Talk-o-matic (chat rooms), and Term-talk (instant messaging).

Plato was also a breeding ground for today's technology innovators. Ray Ozzie, the creator of Lotus Notes and more recently Microsoft's chief software architect, worked on the Plato system in the 1970s as an undergraduate student at the University of Illinois at Urbana-Champaign. Don Bitzer, credited by many as the "father of Plato," is the co-inventor of the plasma display and has devoted his career to focusing on collaborative technologies for use in the classroom. And there were many others, too numerous to detail here.

Enter Charlie Chaplin

The PC Revolution changed everything.

Leading up to the PC Revolution were multiple innovations. IBM began using the term "word processing" in the 1960s, but it referred to a typewriter-like system with limited storage, the IBM Magnetic Tape Selectric. Other key developments included IBM's MagCards (1969), magnetic cards that recorded what was being typed on paper, the display-based word processing systems developed separately by Lexitron and Linolex (1972), IBM's floppy disk (1971), and the first word processing programs (1976).

Modern word processing software made its appearance in 1976. NBI introduced the first microprocessor-based word processor that year, and Michael Shrayer, a programmer at Altair, an early computer company, created the Electric Pencil word processor, primarily to facilitate the creation of manuals for the computers he was working on.

In addition, two computer companies, Digital Equipment Corp. (DEC) and Wang, also introduced software-based word processors that year. Only the DEC WPS-8, however, worked on a general-purpose business computer as opposed to a dedicated platform for word processing.

I spoke with Dan Bricklin, the co-inventor of VisiCalc, who was on the team at DEC that developed WPS-8 in the mid-1970s.

> When we first started to look into developing word processing software, our team, which was led by Jack Gilmore, looked at the history of word processing, including such innovations as the player-piano-like M Schultz repetitive typewriter and the MagCard Selectric. There were dedicated boxes on the market from NBI and Lexitron (Wang was not yet in the business), but no one was offering software for a general-purpose business computer.
>
> That was to be what we developed. The eventual system supported a lot of features which we today still take for granted, such as bold and underlined printing, background printing, document-oriented editing with widow detection, and the embedded ruler, which we had to "invent" for ourselves.

The result was the WPS-8, which ran on the DEC 310w, a special version of the DEC 310 which had a video display terminal of our design to support word processing.

WordStar was introduced by MicroPro International in late 1978 and became the best-selling software program of the early 1980s. It was designed to run on any CP/M PC (CP/M, which stood for Control Program for Microcomputers, was an early operating system for PCs).

Word processing became an important part of the Information Revolution with the introduction of the IBM PC in 1981.

The IBM Personal Computer, typically referred to as the IBM PC, was introduced on August 12, 1981, with Charlie Chaplin's tramp as its spokesman. At the time, the personal computer market (the term "personal computer" was used as early as 1972 to denote the Xerox Alto) was dominated by such machines as the Apple II, the Commodore Pet, and computers from Atari and Radio Shack's TRS-80 line. Designed to reduce time-to-market under the leadership of IBM executive Don Estridge, the IBM PC largely used off-the-shelf components, and competitors were able to develop IBM PC–compatible models by 1982. The decision not to use a proprietary architecture was without question the reason that the IBM PC became the dominant standard in computing for several decades.

While WordStar introduced an IBM PC–compatible version, it was WordPerfect, a package offered by Satellite Systems International, that defined word processing on the original PCs.

The original version of WordPerfect was written for Data General minicomputers, and the PC version was first launched in 1982 as WordPerfect 2.20 (the company continued the version numbering from the DG series).

WordPerfect 4.2, released in 1986, overtook WordStar as the market leader and WordStar faded into oblivion. WordPerfect 4.2 offered multiple innovative features, including automatic paragraph numbering (which made the package quite beloved by law firms) and the ability to split a lengthy footnote across pages. WordPerfect 5.1, released in 1989, included pull-down menus and added support for tables, giving it spreadsheet-like functionality.

It's important to acknowledge the original spreadsheet program, VisiCalc, created by Dan Bricklin and Bob Frankston in 1979 for the Apple II computer. VisiCalc was the original killer app, meaning that it actually drove sales of the Apple II to the point that customers were coming into Apple stores asking for a VisiCalc machine. This lasted until the introduction of the IBM PC, which was quickly followed by the launch of Lotus 1–2–3, an IBM PC–compatible spreadsheet tool from Lotus Development Corp., a company started by Mitch Kapor, a friend of the VisiCalc developers. Lotus 1–2–3 quickly became the new standard in this market.

The 1990 launch of Microsoft Windows 3.0, a graphical user interface for the PC platform, changed the face of word processing software, as well. WordPerfect (which was by now the company name, too) was slow to release a Windows version (the first Windows version, WordPerfect 5.1 for Windows, released in 1991, would not install from within the Windows environment and was not very stable).

Microsoft, however, had already released Word for Windows in 1989, prior to Windows 3.0's launch, and it soon replaced WordPerfect as the preferred word processing platform in most organizations.

Enter the Office Suite

Almost 10 years after the PC Revolution, the word processor began to change and appear in the form of so-called office suites. In 1989, Microsoft introduced the first such offering with Microsoft Office on the Macintosh platform (a PC version followed in 1990). It probably didn't occur to the early designers that they were taking the first steps to integrate functionality that would – a few years later – start to positively impact the efficiency of hundreds of millions of office workers as well as sow the seeds for a massive increase in the creation of information.

The concept of an office suite was originally more marketing than technology. Bundling a word processor (the most popular desktop application) with a spreadsheet program (the second most popular) and presentation software would capture three "sales" all at once.

Before Microsoft Office, software used for desktop productivity purposes, be it processing words or calculating figures, was decidedly single purpose for much of its history, as we have seen. At some point in the early 1990s, after PCs and networks became the de facto means of managing documents and finances, it occurred to Microsoft's developers that they should share certain functionality, such as a spell checker, across multiple programs.

Then OLE (object linking and embedding) technology was developed. This allowed other programs to provide limited functionality within a host program, such as the generation of a chart or graph in a word processing document.

Today knowledge workers take office suites for granted, and Microsoft Office (in all of its iterations) has become the most widely deployed software application in the world, with, according to Microsoft, an estimated 600 million users worldwide as of 2010.

In 2003, Microsoft introduced Microsoft Office System 2003, a comprehensive set of programs, servers, and services that started the process of integrating the traditional suite of Office products (Word, Excel, PowerPoint) with a coordinated set of tools. The ultimate goal was for these tools, when implemented together, to facilitate collaboration and knowledge sharing.

Microsoft Office System 2003 also represented a substantive change for the company as well as for desktop productivity tools, as it set out to meet a different set of customer requirements and challenges that the extant versions of the now-ubiquitous Microsoft Office suite didn't address. Until then, Office developers had focused on making individuals more productive by adding feature after feature. But users rarely used more than a small subset of these features, and adding more features without greater coordination between them did little to make workgroups and teams more productive.

Four years later, Microsoft introduced the 2007 Microsoft Office system, a product that it invested an estimated $2 billion in developing. While the 2003 version offered improved functionality and incremental improvements in functionality, the 2007 version was completely redesigned. Here Microsoft not only improved on how the different applications in Office worked together, but it also introduced a new user interface for the suite's main components (word processing, spreadsheet, and presentations). But the company didn't stop there. A new version of Office was already in the works by the time Office 2007 was released.

An Office for the Twenty-First Century

In 2010, Microsoft introduced Office 2010, an update that also cost the company upward of $2 billion in development costs. The company conducted extensive research and studied how actual knowledge workers work in order to improve their experience with software as well as their ability to handle increasing amounts of information.

More important, Microsoft began to explicitly acknowledge and address the problem of Information Overload as it launched Office 2010 and its e-mail and collaboration platform, Microsoft Outlook 2010 and Exchange Server 2010. The company added features to reduce Information Overload and improve collaboration.

Co-authoring is one feature that may help some knowledge workers combat Information Overload. Microsoft has added Co-authoring to Word, PowerPoint, Excel, and OneNote. The feature requires SharePoint Server 2010 or a Windows Live account to link the applications and store documents.

Co-authoring allows people to work on a document concurrently, so that one person could be working on introductory text while a subject matter expert fills in details on charts. Areas that are being accessed for edits are locked to prevent conflicts; the locking is possible on multiple levels, including sentences, paragraphs, objects, textboxes, fields, headers, and footers.

When entering a document, the user is alerted to other authors who are working on the document via a notification box on the bottom of the screen. When a user hovers over the box, he can see the authors who are working on the document at that time, with contact information so that communication by phone, instant message, or e-mail can be initiated with a click.

If an author is working on a section, it is locked to prevent simultaneous edits by others. Changes and additions are shown to other authors only when the document is saved. If changes have been made to the document, bubble notifications appear to show other users what edits have been made and who made the changes.

People expect the knowledge economy to run on twenty-first-century time, which means that knowledge workers need immediate feedback on documents from multiple collaborators at once. Co-authoring may not be for everyone, as some knowledge workers prefer to write as a solitary exercise, but the new functionality does an impressive job of supporting faster movement of information while improving what today is a grossly inefficient and error-prone process.

In addition to what was added to Office, multiple productivity-enhancing features have been added in the 2010 release of the

Microsoft Outlook e-mail client, including MailTips, an alert system that notifies the user when he is about to send a message that violates e-mail usage etiquette or formal rules, and Quick Steps, which provides one-click buttons to automate common and recurring tasks. Outlook 2010 also features deeper integration with OneNote and Office Communicator.

Within Office 2010, Microsoft recognized and began to address the inefficiencies that exist today in terms of how knowledge workers interact with documents. The new version allows workers to collaborate in a richer environment around documents and also streamlines document processes for knowledge workers.

In 2006, Google introduced a cloud-based office suite that provides some of the basic functionality that Microsoft delivers in its traditional software suite. Although the number of users is relatively small compared to Microsoft's (at the most, Google has 25 million as of 2010 compared to 600 million for Microsoft Office), Google Apps does offer some features and functionality that address the problem of Information Overload.

Google Apps applications include Google Docs, Gmail, Google Calendar, Talk, and Sites.

Google Docs provides basic document functionality but is limited in terms of more advanced features. It is a set of browser-based applications including software for word processing, spreadsheets, presentation generation, diagram and chart creation, form management, and file storage. Users can co-create and co-edit documents with others in real time as well as share documents with other users and set permissions to view or edit.

Google Docs supports collaborative real-time editing for up to 50 users, with changes reflected in real time as they happen in the document, with no need for page refreshing or manual saving. Users can also leave comments around text that is being worked on without disturbing another author's writing and see who is working on what text via a name tag that is attached to that user's cursor in the text.

Non–Google Docs users can collaborate in editing documents with registered Google users.

The word processor is based on Writely, a product Google acquired in March 2006 when it purchased software company Upstartle. The technology for the spreadsheet came from the XL2Web product by 2Web Technologies; it was originally known as Google Labs Spreadsheets. The presentations tool incorporates technology created by Tonic Systems, released in the summer of 2007. The word processor and spreadsheet programs were merged into one program in June 2006.

Google Docs offers smartphone-optimized access via a mobile device's browser that supports viewing and editing spreadsheets and viewing of text documents. Presentations and PDF files are not accessible. Google Doc applications for iPhone and Android smartphones enable one to view presentations.

Gmail and Calendar don't really integrate into the other offerings, and their user interfaces are somewhat different as well. Google Docs requires one to be connected to the Internet for full functionality, although Google has stated that upcoming releases will replicate the offline functionality that was previously possible via Google Gears.

Gmail has had numerous and very public outages during its short lifetime (in a 12-month period ending September 2009, Gmail was down at least seven times). Regardless of the wisdom of using a free service, more and more people are doing just that, using Gmail for business purposes. When it fails, Gmail users go crazy. When Gmail went down in September 2009, for example, a senior executive at a large retailer told me that he wanted to "strangle someone." All I could say was "I told you not to outsource your mail to a free service."

One side benefit of Google Docs is that it has prodded Microsoft into recognizing the fact that knowledge workers will – in some cases – use cloud-based word processing and spreadsheet applications. As a result, with the Office 2010 release, Word is also available as a new Office Web Application, thereby enabling browser-based access to documents stored in SharePoint document libraries or in SkyDrive, a free online storage space linked to a Windows Live account.

The Problem with Documents

Despite the massive amount of technology we have created, all is not well on the information front. Indeed, today, the document process is broken.

In 2009, Basex surveyed 295 knowledge workers and asked questions in an effort to develop a clearer picture of how we are dealing with documents in the workplace. The questions ranged from general, such as "How many documents do you create on an average day?" to specific, such as "Do you avoid including specific people in a document review cycle because you know they will take too long to complete a review?" It turns out that half of those surveyed actually have left people out of review processes because of past tardiness, and an additional 11 percent do not do so but want to.

What we were looking for was an understanding about the relationship between the knowledge worker and the document creation and review process, which takes up a significant amount of the knowledge worker's time. (A separate Basex survey shows that creating and reading content, which includes document creation and review, takes up 48 percent of the workday.)

The prevalence of word processing tools and e-mail have made it easy, some would say too easy, to send documents anywhere and everywhere for input from colleagues, business partners, customers, and suppliers.

A mere 25 years ago, document review was very different. Fewer documents were being generated overall so there were fewer to review. The review process was paper based, documents were typically stored in file cabinets, and, since making corrections and revisions often meant retyping a document, people only made important corrections and tried to get it right the first time around.

Some of what we found when we analyzed the results was expected, but some findings were particularly scary.

There was little surprise when we saw that almost all (95 percent) of knowledge workers create and review documents on a regular basis. In fact, we wondered what the other five percent was doing.

It was also not surprising to find out that the typical knowledge worker creates at least one to two documents of one to two pages a day and receives three to five documents of three to five pages for review each week.

Our survey respondents told us that each document that a knowledge worker creates is typically reviewed by two colleagues and will come back with multiple edits and comments – again, not a big surprise.

What was surprising and alarming was how inefficient we (and they) are in working with these documents. If anything, it's these very inefficiencies that keep the number of documents we manage relatively low.

More specifically, the typical knowledge worker uses an inefficient process to review documents. While it is impossible to access the actual cost, anecdotal evidence suggests that a knowledge worker loses several hours per week because of inefficient document review methodologies and technologies.

When asked how they conduct document reviews, 60 percent of knowledge workers reported that they e-mail the document as an attachment to several reviewers at once. This is poor practice since it creates multiple versions of a document which then must be resolved in some fashion, most likely in a time-consuming and error-prone process. Even more worrisome, 20 percent reported that they print out hard copies of documents to send to reviewers.

To apply edits and changes, 46 percent report that they compare edits and comments manually once they have received a document back from reviewers.

As a result, only 48 percent of knowledge workers receive document reviews back in a timely fashion. Another 25 percent say that they intentionally leave people out of the review process for fear of slowing it down. In addition, almost 40 percent say that they miss others' edits and comments in the documents they get back from review.

Today, document review is a time-intensive process that takes a huge toll in terms of its cost, in both financial and human terms.

We spend a great deal of time managing each and every one of our own review processes, not to mention the time we expend on reviewing the documents of others.

Not counting the work entailed in creating a document, the time-consuming steps include sending out documents to the next review after they come back and compiling what are often significant edits and comments.

As you can see, a typical document can require several hours of management time aside from authoring and review time. All of these inefficiencies come with a significant cost to the bottom line. Errors in documents that are overlooked can result in lost sales and lower profits. The multiple hours a typical knowledge worker spends each week trying to manage the review process could be put to far better use.

In 2009, I came across a small start-up in Sweden called Nordic River, whose founder, Tomer Shalit, had come up with a tool, TextFlow, that allowed knowledge workers to send a document to multiple reviewers at once and then to quickly compile edits and comments as reviewers reply.

Using TextFlow, a typical document requires just minutes of management time (not including authoring and review time).

It's small, individual efforts such as this that can make a difference in the fight against Information Overload. We may not reduce the overall amount of information that we deal with, but we certainly can reduce the high management time cost associated with it.

The Collaborative Business Environment

In order to better explain how knowledge workers should work with information, Basex president David Goldes and I developed a model called the Collaborative Business Environment around the year 2000. Our goal was to promulgate a new way of looking at the knowledge worker's electronic workspace. Many of the ideas we espoused have since been adopted by the software industry (perhaps even in part thanks to our model).

A Collaborative Business Environment (CBE) is a workspace designed for the knowledge worker and knowledge organization that supersedes the traditional desktop metaphor of separate and distinct tools. Once deployed, a properly designed and implemented CBE should facilitate and significantly improve knowledge sharing and collaboration.

Given the recent economic downturn, managers are always on the lookout for anything that will give their organization a competitive edge. One such possibility is building systems that allow knowledge workers to have the correct and most current information when and where it is needed. Being able to locate knowledge and people resources will ensure that fewer opportunities will be missed. And knowing when an event must occur – be it a phone call or document approval – will speed reaction time throughout the enterprise, increasing productivity and lowering the cost of doing business.

Max Christoff, a managing director at Morgan Stanley, believes that the competitive advantage we gained from getting more information faster is starting to disappear. Companies, according to Christoff, need to focus on how to provide more relevant information where it's needed.

Studies conducted by Basex starting in the 1990s have continuously demonstrated that giving knowledge workers access to all applications in one place – with a common interface – greatly increases efficiency and effectiveness. Creating a more efficient work environment and bringing workers together – both synchronously and asynchronously – allow the enterprise to run on twenty-first-century time.

But why doesn't every organization have even a rudimentary CBE at this point in time? The primary reason is that few managers truly understand how different tools interact and work together, and they therefore fail to recognize the various codependencies and overlapping capabilities among these tools. As a result, they end up investing in redundant technologies, which in turn creates Technology Sprawl, a term I coined to describe the phenomenon that occurs when companies have multiple applications duplicating functionality (e.g., multiple content management systems, multiple nonfederated search systems, etc.).

Companies that do undertake the creation of a CBE will be able almost immediately to leverage their people and knowledge while creating environments that actually facilitate how people do their work on a daily basis.

Collaborative Business Knowledge tools and services are used to build CBEs and cover these related areas:

Blogs	Expertise location
Business intelligence	Knowledge-enabled CRM
Business process management	Knowledge management
Collaboration tools	Mobility and wireless
Community software	Portals
Content	Search and categorization tools
Content management	Social software
Distributed workforce	Telecommunications
Document management	Unstructured data management
E-learning	Wikis
E-mail messaging	Work flow

Managers who recognize that they have to start building infrastructure for the knowledge economy can follow the three tenets of the CBE to help prepare their organizations properly for the challenges that the knowledge economy will present.

The three tenets are:

1. **The One-Environment Rule.** The more a knowledge worker can remain in one overarching environment for work, the greater the likelihood that the knowledge worker will be productive and that the tool will be successful. A well-designed CBE will allow the knowledge worker to focus on the work at hand without having to leave the environment to find information or use applications.
2. **Friction-Free Knowledge Sharing.** Too many tools used by the knowledge worker cause unnecessary friction, defined as a force that resists relative motion. Such friction could be at the point of knowledge creation, where tools require categorization, sorting, slotting, and development of metadata to the point of turning a knowledge worker into a knowledge engineer.
3. **Embedded Community.** The term "embedded community" implies deploying community and collaboration tools, such as e-mail, instant messaging, presence, and awareness, within CBEs. In short, it means bringing these tools deep into environments where knowledge workers perform their tasks, linking knowledge work and collaboration, and knowledge workers with each other.

A Collective Business Environment can be viewed from multiple angles:

- **Architecture and Application Integration.** Applications in office suites take many forms, ranging from core applications such as word processing and spreadsheet to database and unstructured data management. How unified is the interface? How integrated are the applications? How well do they work together? What happens when some functionality is missing?
- **Desktop Productivity.** Collecting, managing, and publishing information is critical to any organization. How well do the office suites address the new role of collaboration and collaborative work? Do they alert workers to perform specific tasks, such as approving a document or sending an e-mail?
- **Embedded Community.** Knowledge workers need their tools to leverage both internal and external relationships

and resources. How well does a particular office suite facilitate collaboration and support a variety of communication pathways?

- **Knowledge Management.** Functions such as search, which should expose the knowledge worker to a variety of appropriate resources; expertise location, which connects individuals with subject matter experts; and reporting, which summarizes information so it is easily understandable, are key to how well a particular office suite facilitates and encourages effective and efficient work. How well does a suite deliver in these areas?

A true CBE will enable an organization to be much more effective in all areas of business operations than it could otherwise be. There are tangible cost savings, including reduced costs of training, travel, content creation and distribution, and, most important, a reduction in the continual reinvention of the wheel.

The CBE model has the added benefit of significantly reducing Information Overload by its very nature, in that it improves search and searching by making everything accessible under one virtual roof.

4

WHAT IS INFORMATION?

*To know that we know what we know, and that we do not know
what we do not know, that is true knowledge.*
—Henry David Thoreau

The discussion around Information Overload thus far has seemingly ignored the large elephant in the room, namely, what exactly we mean when we talk about information.

While most people take it for granted, few can define the term. The fact is the word "information" in English is rather flexible, and it means many things to many people.

To borrow from Justice Potter Stewart, who was writing about the difficulty of defining "obscenity," I know information when I see it.

The reason information is important is because human beings have had to communicate with one another since the dawn of civilization. From cave paintings and oral history to the beginnings of a written tradition, mankind has documented and recorded that which is important and left it for future generations.

An increase in the human population, combined with improved tools for sharing information (starting with the tablet, paper, movable type, and going all the way into the computer age), has resulted in more information being created today than perhaps anyone had ever anticipated. What haven't been developed in lockstep with this are tools that allow us to filter information so we get both what we need but also what we can absorb.

Despite great technological advances, we actually understand very little about how to manage information. Until we do learn more about managing what has become a flood of information, all we can do is try to cope with the reality of Information Overload.

If we are going to discuss the problem of Information Overload, it's incumbent upon us to have a solid understanding of the concept of information as well.

A brief look at the roots and origin of the word "information" also helps us better understand it. The term entered English from the Anglo-Norman with a fairly narrow meaning, namely accusatory or incriminating evidence against a person. According to the Oxford English Dictionary (OED), by the 14th century, "information" started to mean a "piece of information" as well as data or knowledge, that is, its meaning was similar to how we use it today. Its etymon in classical Latin meant the formation (of an idea) and in post-classical Latin, the meaning expanded to include teaching and instruction.

"Information" today has several specific meanings. It is understood to mean knowledge one gains through study, research, and instruction (such as by attending a class or researching a specific subject matter). It can refer to facts and data, and it also can have industry-specific meanings, such as in the telecommunications industry, where one dials "information" to obtain a phone number. There are information kiosks (with volunteers or employees stationed there) to provide information to the public at venues ranging from airports to museums.

"Information" also has multiple synonyms, according to the OED, including instruction and teaching. While an in-depth discussion of the word "information" is worthy of a book on its own, it is perhaps best for me to refer the reader to the December 2010 update of the OED, which has an excellent and wide-ranging entry for "information" that covers the communications-based uses of the term as well as the educational, legal, mathematical, and religious meanings.

Indeed, the three trickiest words in the English language may very well be "information," "knowledge," and "wisdom," not to mention "raw data," precisely because their meanings as well as the concepts behind them both overlap and are intertwined.

This wide-ranging definition of information is part of the problem and may serve as a clue as to why Information Overload is the problem that it is.

Defining "knowledge" is no easier a task. Its definitions range from cognition to familiarity with a subject or branch of learning. "Knowledge" is a state of knowing and a familiarity with a particular subject or topic. It could also be the sum total of what has been discovered or learnt.

Where "knowledge" and "information" overlap is that they both mean a body of facts and something that is known.

The two words can be used interchangeably in sentences such as "She sought knowledge/information of her manager's activities."

There are some differences. While "knowledge" can refer to expertise and skills, "information" cannot. In usage, a reference book (such as a dictionary) may contain information, but it does not contain knowledge. The knowledge is derived from the actual use of the information.

Both knowledge and information are often comprised of data, the plural of datum, and "information" is sometimes synonymous with "data" as well.

What is data? In a 2002 report, *Carpe Data*, I defined "data" as raw numbers or unstructured facts and differentiate further between information and knowledge. Raw data matures into information by virtue of its being placed in context. Then, with the application of human interpretation and understanding, information becomes knowledge.

Put simply, once data is organized and put into context, it becomes information or knowledge.

Dictionary.com explains a further difference:

> Today, DATA is used in English both as a plural noun meaning "facts or pieces of information" (*These data are described more fully elsewhere*) and as a singular mass noun meaning "information."

As we have seen, the concept of "information" is a wide-ranging one. Depending on context, it could mean raw data, facts, intelligence, or knowledge – or all of the above.

Quantifying Information

The way we measure data gives us an idea of how much there is. It doesn't necessarily tell us how much we are consuming, however.

Researchers at the University of California in San Diego studied the flow of data to households in the United States and found that, in 2008, the average household received 3.6 zettabytes of information, which translates into 34 gigabytes per person per day. Much of this was indiscernible to the individual as it came in the form of television and video games. Actual text comprised less than 0.1 percent of the total.

Much of the world's information is seen largely by machines so it causes little harm to humans. For example, in 2000, the telescope from the Sloan Digital Sky Survey collected more data in its initial few weeks of service than astronomers had collected since astronomy began. Google collects vast amounts of data on its users, which it uses to refine its ad targeting and search engine. It is extremely unlikely that an actual human will look at the data that Google has on you; more realistically it is an algorithm that will determine what you are most likely to be searching for or what brand of car your demographic covets.

Why Information Is Exploding

Technology has been the driver for the information explosion since the mid-nineteenth century, when the invention of the telegraph, followed by the telephone and radio, led to new avenues with which to distribute it.

But, as we saw in Chapter 2, each earlier Information Age has also had a kind of explosion, whether it was the number of books published after Gutenberg or the number of Web sites that appeared as the Internet became mainstream.

The PC Revolution, which started in the early 1980s, followed by the Internet Revolution (which resulted from the commercialization of the Internet) of the mid-1990s and the Online Revolution (the point at which people started spending substantial amount of time online) of the early 2000s, inexorably changed the face of information.

Society has always generated too much information relative to its ability to consume it. But the ratio of consumable versus unconsumable information is changing dramatically, and not for the better. Today it is outstripping our cognitive abilities to deal with it.

How Information Is Going beyond Network and Storage Capabilities

Moore's Law, named after an observation by Intel co-founder Gordon Moore in a 1965 paper in *Electronics Magazine*, states that the number of transistors that can be inexpensively placed on an integrated circuit will double approximately every two years. Many technologies are linked to Moore's Law, including processor speed and memory capacity. The trend has continued well over half a century and may continue for the foreseeable future.

Moore's Law is sometimes incorrectly presented as the capacity of chips doubling or their prices halving every 18 months, but the time period is less relevant than the phenomenon.

There is no equivalent law for data or information yet the amount of information we create exceeds the network's ability to carry all of it. In June 2009, Cisco, a maker of network gear, predicted that the yearly amount of traffic that flows across the Net will reach 667 exabytes by 2013; in 2010, it predicted that by 2014, traffic will reach 767 exabytes. For comparison, in 2008, the yearly traffic was a mere 10 exabytes.

Structured versus Unstructured Information

Most of the world's information, perhaps as much as 80 percent, is unstructured. Unstructured data typically is found in such sources as Web pages, news content (including RSS feeds), social network pages, e-mail, text files, PDF files, and word processing files, while structured sources may be found in databases, business applications, customer relationship management (CRM) applications, and information portals. The information that we create as we move through our day is, except in rare cases, unstructured, and thus hard to find when we need it.

Without question, search is the Achilles' heel of knowledge work and Information Overload. As you will see in Chapter 15, 50 percent of all searches fail outright and 50 percent of the searches that knowledge workers believe to have been successful also fail in some manner (i.e., outdated information, second-best information, or content that is just outright incorrect).

Obviously, failed search is a major issue and large contributor to Information Overload. Part of the problem is not the search technology per se but the selection of the source that provides the results. If a search only looks through unstructured data, it ignores the valuable information that exists as structured data. Search tools need to look at all information sources in order to not only return complete results but to rank results from disparate data sources accordingly.

For reasons that are unclear to me, many companies have failed to deploy search tools that examine every nook and cranny of a company's information assets – that is, structured as well as unstructured information – although a few smart companies have indeed done so. Exercising due diligence in searching can avoid failures that result from searching in a partial source set.

Given the amount of time knowledge workers spend searching for information, and the fact that the odds of finding what they are looking for are against them, improving search tools would appear to be a significant step ahead in the war against Information Overload. Most tools in a company simply don't search in enough places, and because of technology sprawl, knowledge workers are just as likely to have stored critical information in a vat that is not touched by the search system as one that is.

Data Mining to the Rescue?

Data today is woefully underutilized. In many organizations, managers assume that, once a transaction is complete, the data, now organized as structured information, is no longer relevant, so it then sits in a data silo and rusts. (Some observant readers may point out that data cannot actually rust but in reality simply gathers dust.) Data mining attempts to reclaim this unrecognized information from oblivion. Even 10 years ago, I estimated that the sum total of the value of unrecognized information could be as much as $3.5 trillion on a global basis. Today, that number is far higher.

How do we best push data through the purgatory of information to turn it into what some call actionable knowledge, or knowledge that is ready to be put to use?

One answer may be through the use of data mining. Data mining is the process of extrapolating relationships from data. It is generally considered to be part of a data processing troika, which includes analytics and business intelligence. Analytics is the process of analyzing data (generally about customers) so that services to the customer can be enhanced. Business intelligence is the start-to-finish process of collecting, storing, and using data to improve business decisions. These are the three main uses of data within the business context. All three of these center on building models based on the data. With data mining, a company's raw data is turned into a form of knowledge through the use of models. These models, in turn, lead to the implementation of strategies that are designed to improve the corporate bottom line.

The technology that has led to what we refer to as data mining today has evolved slowly over the last few decades. In the 1960s, large-scale data collection was automated; mainframes allowed companies to record their sales and other relevant data. By the 1980s, access to such data had become ubiquitous; relational databases and database languages such as SQL allowed desktop access to much of that information. In the 1990s, data warehousing took off; this data could now be analyzed and broken down as needed. It is data mining that allows enterprises to predict what will come next. Data mining is not historic but forward-looking; it makes history predictive, discovering new patterns that are invisible to the naked human eye.

Data mining works through building analytic models. An analyst builds a model that is based on one scenario and is then applied to others. The resultant model is then applied to vast stores of data in order to obtain a direct course of action, such as a highly targeted direct mail marketing campaign. A model may predict, for example, that men between the ages of 24 and 36 and who live in New York are the most likely Americans to buy toasters and that they will spend $65, on average, for each one. Analysts take the methods that produce a good answer and apply the model to situations in which the answer is unknown.

New uses of data mining include the emerging field of digital humanities, which is using this technology along with digital mapping, geographic information systems, and online preservation to reveal patterns and trends that otherwise remain undiscovered.

Data mining is part of the ever-growing pattern to quantify and track what was previously unquantifiable and untrackable. Data mining is, in some respects, knowledge management taken to the next level: It gets the right predictions, to the right people, at the right time. It also automatically updates the predictions as the data changes. All of this is leading not only to more efficient business processes but to a new world, a world in which every bit of data is tracked, mined, and predicted upon.

CHAPTER 5

THE INFORMATION CONSUMER

A wealth of information creates a poverty of attention and a need to allocate that attention efficiently among the overabundance of information sources that might consume it.

—Herbert A. Simon

When thinking of the consumer experience, we generally think about products such as food, televisions, cars, or clothing. Today, the consumer is as much an information consumer as a consumer of physical goods. Consumers, along with the media companies that provide information, are beginning what will undoubtedly be a long process of adaptation to the online world and the rise of information as a product.

The challenge that we, as information consumers, all face is not really technology but how technology has altered our media diet and habits. We aren't able to multitask – focusing on more than one thing at a time is a myth – but the term does describe our behavior at times, especially with respect to information consumption.

We watch television and at the same time post comments on social networks about what we are watching, while we also text our friends and surf the Web. There is a certain adroitness that information consumers are acquiring in this respect, although it may not be a healthy one.

At the same time, our attention spans are evolving – perhaps not for the better. They are becoming shorter and shorter, and the ability for many people to read and digest longer works is starting to disappear as we constantly face temptations from e-mail and social networks and other tasty treats. Don't know a word? Look it up online. Curious about the meaning of a particular passage? Look that up online also or perhaps engage in an invigorating (online) discussion with (real or virtual) friends about it.

A look at my own media diet, how it's changed over the past 20 years, as well as my ability to consume information, is somewhat revealing as we examine the problem of Information Overload.

Twenty years ago (that would be 1990), most of my news still came from printed material or television and radio since few alternatives existed. I was a loyal subscriber to the weekday and weekend editions of the *New York Times* at home and barely glanced at the *Times'* Web site after it launched in 1996 except to check for breaking news. Even after I became accustomed to the Web site, I preferred to read anything long in the print edition.

News reached people far more slowly then, and the news cycle itself was much slower.

A copy of the *Wall Street Journal* would be waiting for me at the office, and I typically glanced through it while having coffee and planning my day. If there was something really interesting to read, I would take it home.

I subscribed to several business and news weeklies, including the *Economist* and *Business Week*, the latter being a habit I inherited from my father.

The *Economist* was a habit I picked up while attending university in Munich. I found it then (as I do now) far more balanced in world coverage than *Time* or *Newsweek* and far more insightful. It is also not written in language intended for eighth graders.

I didn't always have time to read the entire *Times* in the morning – but by the time I went to sleep, I had gone through all of the sections that interested me. I eagerly awaited the *Economist* and *Business Week* on Fridays and had finished reading them both by the end of the weekend.

Back then, I also read *Wired*, which covered the early days of the new media age, and several tech weeklies, such as *PC Week*, a weekly magazine chronicling enterprise desktop computing news, as well as monthlies such as *Byte, PC World,* and *PC Magazine.* Despite the lag time in getting a print edition out the door, these publications were major sources of technology news for many people, including myself.

I also read four monthly car magazines (*Motor Trend, Car & Driver, Automobile,* and the *Roundel*) on a regular basis, given my love for the automobile.

To round out my media diet, I also watched the evening news at least a few nights a week (I was an equal opportunity television viewer as I alternated between CBS, NBC, and ABC), and I listened quite a bit to WCBS NewsRadio 88, a 24-hour news station. The radio station was, in effect, a real-time stream of live news, and I was – even then – an information junkie.

All-news radio itself is an interesting phenomenon. While the first all-news radio station started broadcasting in 1959 in San Francisco, the KFAX 1100 experiment did not last very long. New York in 1990 had two all-news radio stations (WCBS and WINS) and would soon have a third, Bloomberg Radio, WBBR.

At the time, I received between 50 to 150 e-mail messages per day. The interesting thing about these e-mails is that the number of those that were relevant to what I was working on was much higher than today, and the quantity really didn't seem to really interfere with my work.

Even at that time, however, people were noticing an increase in the information flow, and an occasional article or television segment would make mention of it.

Despite having all of this information at hand, I managed to finish all of my work, all of my e-mail, read the paper, and stay current on information for my work.

Ten years ago, as the twentieth century drew to a close, things had already begun to change in my information diet. I noticed that I was reading the *Times* online more – and eventually the paper edition began to bore me, as all it offered were articles I had already read online. Indeed, some articles were online a full day before they hit the paper edition. Some days I barely touched the actual paper edition. Still, I continued to receive the paper every day along with the *Wall Street Journal* (which by that time I was receiving at home as my telecommuting had increased when not traveling).

I found I was no longer reading any personal computer-related publications. At the office, we had started to receive real-time feeds of news releases from the IT industry so anything that came out in print was old news.

I still enjoyed the car magazines but more for their reviews and road tests. Automotive news was increasingly available online, largely through blogs and, later on, through Web sites run by the car magazines themselves as they began to compete with bloggers for eyeballs.

Despite my increased online information consumption, I was not even scratching the surface. The amount of content on the Web was growing rapidly; in fact, one could easily see how people were getting lost in a sea of information on the Internet.

Although the effort to catalog the Web is really as old as the Web itself, the Yahoo Directory, created by David Filo and Jerry Yang in 1994 to organize their favorite Web pages, became the first truly useful and searchable directory. Yahoo's search function used this directory to help people locate Web sites, instead of searching full-text indices of Web pages. Yahoo also allowed users to browse its directory structure instead of doing a keyword-based search.

Around the same time, WebCrawler, Lycos, and InfoSeek began to catalog the Web and offer relevance-based searching. But it was AltaVista, launched by researchers at Digital Equipment Corp. (DEC), that offered true innovation, such as natural language queries and advanced search techniques.

Google first came into prominence on the Web around 2000, although it began as a research project at Stanford in 1996. Thanks to an innovation known as PageRank, an algorithm that ranks Web pages based on the number and PageRank of other Web sites and pages that link to the site in question, Google was able to provide better and more accurate results than the competition. Google's minimalist home page was also attractive to users, compared to the portal-like environments most search engines presented to the user.

The first decade of the twenty-first century was a time of great change in my information diet. The changes I was making were in a sense a reaction to the impact that the Information Revolution was having on both the quantity of content and where it was consumed.

A little less than three years ago, I canceled my subscription to the *New York Times*. I didn't do it lightly. I reasoned (with myself) that I was saving paper; indeed, most of the newspaper was going "unread" because the articles I was interested in I had read online.

I did enjoy the weekend sections, but those weren't time sensitive and I could get those from my parents after the weekend was over.

Today, I read the *Wall Street Journal* on my Apple iPad (which I find to be a superior reading experience, as discussed in Chapter 2) and I no longer get the paper edition delivered to me at home. I also have begun to read the *Economist* on the iPad and find that I enjoy that reading experience very much. I haven't subscribed to *Business Week* in well over a year and, quite frankly, I don't miss it. *Business Week* had lost its focus a few years back and seemed most weeks to aspire to be a technology publication as opposed to a magazine dedicated to important business news and insights.

Out of all of the car magazines I used to get, the only one I still receive (and enjoy reading) is the *Roundel*, which is a benefit of membership in the BMW Car Club of America.

As for my *New York Times* habit, something that started in grammar school, I read the paper either on the Web or, less frequently, on the paper's iPad app (the interface for which leaves me cold). Out of the entire paper edition of the Sunday *New York Times*, which can reach a height of three inches or more and whose articles sometimes appear online as early as the preceding Wednesday, I find myself reading on paper only the magazine, Arts and Leisure, automobile, and real estate sections. There is something to be said for sitting back, relaxing, and reading the Sunday paper, and it still works best with the paper edition for these particular sections.

WHAT IS INFORMATION OVERLOAD?

There is much pleasure to be gained from useless knowledge.
—Bertrand Russell

"Information Overload" describes an excess of information that results in the loss of ability to make decisions, process information, and prioritize tasks. Peter Miles, executive vice president of BMW of North America, told me that "it's a scourge of modern day society."

Larry Thaler, at the time a vice president at NBC Universal, described to me how he was trying to cope. "I was working on a process map. The process map had a lot of little boxes . . . on the screen. And while I'm doing this, little e-mails are popping up breaking my concentration, driving me bananas. I couldn't believe how much I would lose my place. I had to turn off the function and ultimately I realized how distracting all of this is."

Information is the new currency of our society (at one point in civilization, it was salt) yet, instead of being scarce, workers are drowning in an overabundance of it. A typical worker on a typical day gets hundreds of e-mails, instant messages, phone calls (office phone and mobile phone), and text messages, not to mention the vast amount of content that he has to contend with that arrives in other forms.

Amy Wohl, a leading thinker and pundit in office automation and knowledge work who knows more than most about e-mail and information management, has also been impacted. "Information Overload impacts me by making it absolutely impossible for me to ever get through all the information I get."

Information Overload decimates work-life balance, decreases knowledge workers' effectiveness and efficiency, and causes diminished comprehension levels, compromised concentration levels, and reduced innovation. It can also further exacerbate health issues that are starting to become common among knowledge workers. According to a 2008 Basex survey, 35 percent of knowledge workers experience work-related back and/or neck pain, carpal tunnel syndrome, eyestrain, headaches, or stress-related symptoms.

The problem of Information Overload is multifaceted and impacts each and every organization, whether top executives and managers are aware of it or not. In addition to e-mail, Information Overload is an outgrowth of the proliferation of content, growing use of social networking tools, unnecessary interruptions in the workplace, failed searches, new technologies that compete for the worker's attention, and improved and ubiquitous connectivity (making workers available anytime regardless of their location). Since almost no one is immune from the effects of this problem, when one looks at it from an organizational point of view, hundreds of thousands of hours are lost at a typical organization, representing as much as 25 percent of the work day.

It's not just a case of too much e-mail, too many interruptions, too many projects, and too much content. It's all these things clashing – sometimes like an orchestra without a conductor. It's also enough to make the individual knowledge worker feel like Lucy Ricardo in the chocolate factory in *I Love Lucy* episode 39 entitled "Job Switching," where Lucy and pal Ethel are overwhelmed by the amount of chocolate coming down the assembly line that they have to package.

We have created billions of pictures, documents, videos, podcasts, blog posts, and tweets, yet if these remain unmanaged, it will be impossible for anyone to make sense out of any of this content because we have no mechanism to separate the important from the mundane. Going forward, we face a monumental paradox. On one hand, we have to ensure that what is important is somehow preserved. If we don't preserve it, we are doing a disservice to generations to come; they won't be able to learn from our mistakes and from the great breakthroughs and discoveries that have occurred. On the other hand, we are creating so much information that may or may not be important that we routinely keep everything. If we continue along this path, which we will most certainly do, there is no question that we will require far superior filtering tools to manage that information.

For better or worse, millions of people now use a variety of social networking tools to inform their friends – and the world at large – about their activities, thoughts, and observations, ranging down to the mundane and the absurd. Not only are people busily engaged in creating such content, but each individual's output may ultimately be received by dozens if not thousands of friends, acquaintances, or curious bystanders. Just do the math.

An interesting way of measuring Information Overload presented itself during an in-depth conversation I had with Jim O'Donnell, CEO of a BMW of North America, in 2009.

"We send our dealerships," he told me, "about a foot or so of information every day. There's no way anyone can digest all of it." How did he measure this? The company printed out every piece of paper that goes out to the many dealerships around the country, and that's how high the average stack was.

This reminded me of an experiment conducted by Dave Stemmer, who, in the 1980s, was EDP (electronic data processing) manager at National Cold Storage, a refrigerated warehousing company. He noticed that the various departments were requesting printouts of dozens and dozens of reports each day and wondered how many were actually being read. So he stopped printing the reports and waited for the phone to ring with someone requesting them. Apparently only 10 percent of the reports were re-requested so the waste in computer time (when this was a valuable commodity) and paper was huge.

Stemmer's experiment, while less focused at the problem of Information Overload and more on the use of scarce computer resources, does demonstrate man's proclivity to create too much information that will subsequently go unused.

In the case of BMW, the amount of information was a wake-up call. Today the company is not only looking to reduce the amount of information sent to its dealerships but also looking to find ways of making that information more useful and relevant.

Meetings: Too Much of a Good Thing?

A component of Information Overload is meeting overload. Although meetings were common decades ago, they have proliferated in an age of easy communication. Conference calls (and even video conference calls) with far-flung colleagues, a host in Chicago, participants in Vienna, Sydney, and Jerusalem, among others, are not uncommon. What is crucial here is the information that is missing in these calls.

Participants in such meetings may believe that they are communicating far more information than they actually are. Over 40 years ago, Ray L. Birdwhistell in his book, *Kinesics and Context*, stated that "no more than 30 to 35 percent of the social meaning of a conversation or an interaction is carried by the words." The rest is communicated with kinesics, non-verbal behavior, commonly called body language, such as facial expression and gestures.

Such body language might convey many specific meanings, and their interpretation may be both context-based and culture bound. Without the ability to see and interpret kinesics, there is a significant risk of misinterpretation, particularly in intercultural communications.

In addition, many knowledge workers today are called upon to attend more meetings than would be necessary to do their jobs. Many tend to invite more colleagues than necessary to meetings, a process reminiscent of the overuse of the copy function in e-mail.

Ever since AT&T (at the 1964 World's Fair in Flushing Meadows, New York) unveiled the Picturephone, companies have been promoting videoconferencing systems to replace face-to-face meetings. The technology today is greatly improved, with systems that emulate an in-room experience using large-screen displays and technology that eliminates jerky video, but they are too costly to be placed into service for the hundreds of thousands of meetings that take place every day among knowledge workers.

Meetings are, of course, necessary, but as Rosalind said in *As You Like It*, there can be too much of a good thing.

But companies are doing something about the problem. IBM introduced ThinkFridays across the company in the mid-1990s. Friday afternoons everywhere are to be free of nonessential meetings and interruptions. The practice was informally begun by IBM programmers, who used the time to conduct research or write papers in relative peace. Similarly, Dow Corning sponsors a no-meetings week once each quarter, banning nonessential meetings. Despite all of these efforts, meetings remain a large contributor to Information Overload.

How Long Has This Been Going On?

We may think Information Overload is a new problem, but it isn't. Information Overload was very much on the minds of thought leaders of an earlier Information Age centuries ago, including Roger Bacon, Samuel Johnson, and Konrad Geßner, whose 1545 *Bibliotheca Universalis* warned of the "confusing and harmful abundance of books" and promulgated reading strategies for coping with the overload of information. Even the Bible warns of it: "Of making many books there is no end; and much study is a weariness of the flesh."

Socrates cautioned his fellow Athenians against writing, preferring to remain a champion of oral communication. Writing, according to Plato's Socrates in *Phaedrus* in 500 BCE, destroys memory and weakens the mind. It is "an inhuman thing."

Even the study of Information Overload is not new: In 1997, Reuters, an information provider, announced research that showed that 54 percent of workers claimed to get a "high" when they found information they had been seeking, 53 percent of managers develop cravings for information, and more than one-third believed their colleagues were obsessed with gathering information. The research was conducted in conjunction with a marketing campaign for Information Fatigue Syndrome, a term the company coined to point out that it had information solutions that would lessen the problem.

Information, in the form of e-mail, instant messages, text messages, Web pages, discussion forums, RSS feeds, wikis, blogs, phone calls, letters, magazines, and newspapers, keeps piling up. In fact, we have become far more proficient in generating information than we are in managing it. Just ask Andy Chew, a senior vice president at Siemens, who told me that "there's no question that the amount of information I receive makes it hard for me to prioritize and means that I've got to put a greater amount of time in just to manage it."

But what can we do about it? You've made it this far without being interrupted, so please keep reading.

More Information – Isn't that What We Wanted?

We are drowning in a sea of information. The sheer volume – we have added tweets, Facebook and Foursquare updates, video calls, RSS, always-on netbooks and smartphones, and Hulu to a life that was already full thanks to e-mail, instant messages, text messages, Web sites, and phone calls – seems more than one could possibly ever manage.

But isn't more information what everyone wanted and even dreamed of?

Yes it is, and it is also a kind of inverse Malthusian trap: Rather than seeing man's consumption outpace his resources, man's resources would instead outpace his ability to consume them.

For thousands of years, most of the earth's population in pre-Industrial Revolution society lived in poverty. Thomas Malthus demonstrated the tendency of the population to grow faster than the food supply, leaving most people in abject poverty throughout.

Only at the dawn of the Industrial Revolution, which started in England in the mid-to-late eighteenth century, did enough changes in human behavior come about to result in an end to the Malthusian cycle.

But Information Overload itself is not merely a function of the sheer volume of information that exists. Rather, it manifests itself when the volume of information outpaces the capability of the tools we have to assimilate and manage that information.

When e-mail first started making significant inroads within larger companies in the early 1990s, my entreaties to be aware of its dangers were thought to be mildly eccentric. Everyone was so giddy about the fact that they had e-mail that no one could fathom that there could ever be too much.

The problem of too much information clearly isn't new – but interest in it seems to come in waves. Reuters' Information Fatigue Syndrome campaign, for which the company even brought in a psychologist to produce a research report to add credibility to the marketing campaign, was followed by a 1998 story, "Is Information Making You Sick?" (a story that was written by Reuters, of course).

Also in 1999, Autonomy, an information management company, issued a news release for "victim[s] of Information Overload syndrome."

In 2009, Xerox released a marketing campaign around Information Overload Syndrome, the result of trying to manage the 281 exabytes of information available online (as of 2009) compared to five exabytes of data online in 2002.

So what exactly is the problem?

People have become information junkies, and the very tools that cause Information Overload are also the tools that feed their habit.

Fifteen years ago, IBM and Microsoft were also promising tools that would reduce Information Overload. Lotus Notes 4.0 promised that software agents would help users zero in on critical data, and Microsoft was about to release Exchange Server, promising filtering and routing that would serve a similar purpose.

And yet, despite the promises of the technology companies, we are still overloaded today. *Plus ça change, plus c'est la même chose.*

Take me, for example. On a typical day, I get approximately 140 e-mail messages. Out of the 140, I would say that 10 percent were truly important and required my attention. I also get at least 50 instant messages (I'm counting each individual message here, not sessions), five phone calls, 100 text messages, and 20 BlackBerry Messenger messages. I have to look at our news release feed (our system gets about 2,000 news releases per day but filters that down into about 100 headlines that someone has to look at, sorted by category and the reason they surfaced in the first place), I read headlines from the *New York Times* on the Web and the *Wall Street Journal* and *Die Presse* on the iPad.

This is all before I start doing my actual work, which is searching through information to write reports, studies, and analyses. Are you beginning to see the problem here?

Information Overload and the Tragedy of the Commons

A commons is any shared resource, which in this day and age might include our time and knowledge. According to a theory first voiced by Garret Hardin and published in *Science* in December 1968, the tragedy of the commons occurred when cattle herders would overuse a village commons, or pasture, that became depleted because no one herder had an incentive to moderate the size of his own herd.

Today, the "tragedy of the commons" refers to a common resource that is despoiled by overutilization or abuse. Hardin later commented that he should have entitled his article "The Tragedy of the Unregulated Commons."

Free access and unrestricted demand for a finite resource, in this case the time of the knowledge worker, will ultimately doom the resource. The benefits of such exploitation accrue to individuals as opposed to the organization at large, and each is economically motivated to maximize his use while the costs of such exploitation are borne by everyone.

Demand for the resource, the knowledge worker's time, is consistently increased until the resource is exhausted. All of this is relative, of course, as the rate at which the resource becomes exhausted will depend on the number of users relying upon the commons, the amount of the resource they consume, and the robustness of the resource.

This scenario is applicable to fisheries, to the extent to which they are not overfished, and to automobile traffic, where drivers choose SUVs in order to see over other traffic. Most people do what is in their own best interests, which results in the depletion of fish stocks and an excess of overly large vehicles on the road.

The tragedy of the commons is, in some respects, the inverse of Metcalfe's Law, which, as formulated by George Gilder in 1993, states that the value of a telecommunications network is proportional to the square of the number of connected users of the system (n^2). (Metcalfe's Law originally concerned itself with "compatibly communicating devices" on a network, not with users per se, when it was presented in the early 1980s.)

Metcalfe's Law is frequently illustrated using a telephone or fax machine; a single phone or fax machine is, of course, of no value, but the value of the device increases as the total number of devices in the network increase, because the total number of people with whom each individual may interact increases.

While Metcalfe's Law encourages people to use resources more fully, the tragedy of the commons seeks to find an optimal level of usage, beyond which the commons will be depleted.

As more people generate more content and disperse it through more devices, creating more and more Information Overload, the human commons is becoming sorely depleted.

The Ephemerization of Information

Every day, 15 petabytes of new information are created, and much of this information is then distributed to hundreds if not thousands of people with the click of a few buttons. Two hundred years ago, in order to create distributable content, one needed a printing press. At the turn of the twentieth century, a Gestetner stencil duplicator would do the trick. By the 1960s, a photocopier was all that was needed.

These methods all had one thing in common: paper, a medium that then had to be physically distributed to the reader. Paper, until recently, has occupied a unique and historic role. It fought for change alongside countless revolutionaries.

Thomas Paine greatly influenced the American Revolution with his widely read pamphlet, *Common Sense*. Hans and Sophie Scholl, members of the White Rose (Weiße Rose), distributed six anti-Nazi political resistance pamphlets in 1942 and 1943, a deed for which they were executed.

Today, getting content to potential readers, even for revolutionaries, is easier than ever. Eighty percent of the newly created information is what we call unstructured data (compared to structured data, which is stored in fielded form in databases). Much of this content is comprised of e-mail messages, but an increasing amount is formed by documents, images, rich content (audio including podcasts and video), and ephemeral content such as blogs and microblogs.

Unlike access to a printing press, which is somewhat restricted due to a variety of factors, including cost and the need for extensive training, today virtually everyone has access to what may be the modern-day equivalent, the World Wide Web. Once on the Web, one can create unlimited quantities of content, which is then accessible, potentially, by millions of people.

To understand how much content creation has increased in recent years, one only has to look at the growth of the Web. By 1998, Google had reportedly indexed 26 million Web pages. That number reached one billion by the year 2000. As of July 2008, Google said it has indexed over one trillion unique Web pages, and that the number is growing by several billion per day.

Much of the content that is created on the Web is ephemeral; that is, it is of a brief and evanescent nature. This content can range from the absurd (there is even a blog devoted to absurd ideas) to the mundane (tweets such as "I am now having breakfast at the diner and the waitress just brought the coffee"). Although much of this content may seem to be of limited value, at times ephemeral information merits the transition to a more permanent state.

By nature of the mass quantity of ephemeral content produced, the likelihood of relevant content surfacing increases, with the caveat being that we must have the tools and methods to do find it. Additionally, due to the short temporal relevance of ephemeral content, it is critical to stay up-to-date; blogs and tweets must be monitored (perhaps in an automated fashion) daily if not hourly to take advantage of the stream of potentially valuable and fresh information.

Contrast this with an academic journal that arrives in your mailbox monthly, with the past month's news and relevant studies summarized, peer reviewed, and printed. Yes, the content in the journal is far more authoritative; however, it is not nearly as fresh and fast moving as the ephemeral content, and, indeed, much of the journal's content may have been available elsewhere weeks before it arrived in hard copy on your doorstep.

We refer to the phenomenon of mass quantities of information being presented this way as the ephemerization of content. To put this in content, a few definitions are in order.

"Information" has many definitions. It has been defined both as data that is being processed and important or useful facts that are obtained by virtue of the processing of data. For a complete discussion of the pitfalls of defining terms like "information," "knowledge," and "data," see Chapter 4.

I further define "information" as a unit of communication. It can therefore include data, explanations, a databank, evidence, statements, disclosures, reports, messages, and news. Information used to be comprised of matters of relative importance. Now it's far more complex.

"Ephemeral content" is that which is intended to be short-lived. In fact, Twitter is perhaps the epitome of content ephemerization in that it is a virtual chorus of individuals creating short-lived little bits of content, much of it trivial in nature. (In a delicious twist of irony, Twitter, on its Web site, claims it is "a modern antidote to Information Overload.")

Social software, that is to say blogs, Twitter, Facebook, MySpace, and YouTube, among others, makes would-be publishers out of everyone and anyone. The popularity of such software has dramatically increased the amount of content that is created every day. While the Web gave even a dog the opportunity to be someone on the Internet (at least in the *New Yorker* cartoon by Peter Steiner from 1993 showing a dog sitting in front of a computer with the caption "On the Internet, nobody knows you're a dog"), creating and maintaining Web pages required some degree of technical skill.

Such social publishing tools are no longer just for kids or early adopters; rather, they have become mainstream, attracting users across all age groups to a partially online life, taking a hint perhaps from life in the Metaverse as envisaged in Neal Stephenson's epic science fiction novel, *Snow Crash.*

Another area that generates a tremendous amount of content is online reviews. Today, everyone has become a reviewer. Books, cars, and electronics are among the many product and services categories that can easily generate thousands of reviews. These can appear on the Web site of an online retailer such as Amazon.com, an automotive discussion forum, or a third-party review site such as epinions.com.

Many more shoppers check and rely upon online reviews before heading off to make a purchase. The newfound ease of publishing on the Web has blurred several lines that historically were quite clear. Many companies regularly pay bloggers for "positive ink," according to an April 23, 2009 story in the *Wall Street Journal,* a practice that can deceive readers into thinking that they are reading an unbiased review where in reality they are reading a paid promotional pitch.

What's more, the line between reviews and discussion has blurred significantly, as product review blogs such as Gizmodo proliferate.

The result is more information about products and services than ever before. Case in point: If a laptop or book already has hundreds of reviews, why do people bother to write yet another one? The book *The Catcher in the Rye,* by J. D. Salinger, already has 3,031 reviews on Amazon.com as of December 2010. Two versions of the book *Night,* by Elie Wiesel, have a combined 1,647 reviews on Amazon and many more elsewhere. Will the 3,032nd review of *Catcher in the Rye* or the 1,648th review of *Night* enlighten a potential reader or merely add to the clutter? Clearly, the answer is "it depends," but only a few Web sites, such as Amazon, allow visitors to rate reviews and allow the most "helpful" to rise to the top.

With so many people tweeting, blogging, linking, reviewing, and posting, how do you separate the important from the mundane and find useful and helpful information? More important, how do you escape the mundane? The millions of pages of content that are published every day contribute to an increase in information's ephemerization as the amount of less important and evanescent information can effectively crowd out important information that someone is looking for.

The ephemerization of content brings with it concomitant problems. Compared with what may be referred to as "authoritative" content, much of this rather ephemeral content is of interest to a very small group of people. In addition, this nonauthoritative content is frequently riddled with errors or quickly becomes out of date as it is only intended to be short-lived.

Clearly, the ephemerization of content will continue to increase. The only way to counter it is to build better, smarter tools that allow people to find the information they truly need and that is truly correct.

7

THE COST OF INFORMATION OVERLOAD

We're drowning in information and starving for knowledge.
—Rutherford D. Rogers

The dirty little secret of Information Overload is that it has become a significant problem for companies of all sizes. The problem is that they simply don't know it.

Even smaller companies lose tens of millions of dollars each year in lowered productivity and hampered innovation, while the world's largest corporations each face an exposure of a billion dollars or more. In 2010, Basex estimated that the total cost of Information Overload to the U.S. economy was $997 billion.

My colleagues and I arrived at this figure by determining the total number of knowledge workers, based on recent data derived from the Bureau of Labor Statistics (BLS). We found that the number of knowledge workers working full time, or 2,000 hours a year, was 78.6 million.

As the BLS does not maintain a separate category for knowledge workers, we had to create our own classifications to group the 711 occupations that the BLS recognizes to determine who the knowledge workers were and what characteristics they displayed.

We came up with four groups based on the number of skills required and the level of independent thought and action needed.

The top level of worker we found to be Highly-Skilled Knowledge Workers, those who posses multiple skills with a high level of independent thought and action. Examples of Highly-Skilled Knowledge Workers include those in management roles, teachers, doctors, scientists, engineers, pilots, and many more. We found that there were 36,090,720 of these workers in the United States, with an average wage of $33.42 an hour.

We did not limit this group to those who primarily are found in front of a computer all day, because it must be recognized that technology itself is not a defining characteristic of knowledge work. Knowledge work is exemplified by the use of knowledge to perform a task – that is, the application of skills that have been learnt over time to a specific situation. Highly-Skilled Knowledge Workers have to take their years of learning and adapt to changing circumstances by applying independent thought and action. For example, those in management roles are considered highly skilled, due to the variety of skill sets and independent thought that is required, while sales representatives, although still knowledge workers, have a narrower required skill base and capacity for independent action.

The next group of workers we identified was Skilled Knowledge Workers, those who posses multiple skills with some level of independent thought and action. This group is made up of 29,304,600 individuals, who receive an average hourly wage of $20.43. Nurses, office managers, programmers, and many more fall into this category.

The third group of workers is the single-skilled contingent. Single-Skilled Knowledge Workers are those who are proficient in a single skill, with very little need for independent thought and action, such as computer technicians, telemarketers, clerical workers, and others. Essentially, they are rudimentary knowledge workers, but knowledge workers nonetheless.

Finally, rounding out the classifications are two groups of workers that are not in the category of knowledge worker. Semi-Skilled Workers are those workers who perform a skilled task, such as a security guard or a gardener, but do not typically work with information. Unskilled Workers are those who engage in manual labor or repetitive tasks, with no need for independent thought or action, such as dishwashers, cashiers, and laborers.

After sorting occupations into these categories, we were able to calculate the cost to the economy, based on research conducted by Basex from 2004 to 2010 that shows that the average knowledge worker loses approximately 25 to 30 percent of the day due to Information Overload, including unnecessary interruptions and recovery time.

Indeed, $997 billion is at the low end of our estimate, and represents the cost of the total number of knowledge workers in the United States losing a mere 25 percent of their day to Information Overload.

In order to better understand the implications here, we need to look at what is generally referred to as "productivity."

"Productivity" is a term you may hear on a daily basis, but have you ever stopped to consider its meaning, especially within the context of knowledge work and knowledge workers? It probably isn't what you think it is. If you listen carefully, you will hear almost every software vendor use the term "productivity" in its message. Everyone's software, it turns out, makes knowledge workers more productive.

While promises of productivity increases frequently come from technology vendors in the course of promoting their offerings, few, if any, appear to be able to explain exactly what they are promising, leaving one to wonder if one might therefore type faster, have more meetings, hold more efficient meetings, or write more memos and e-mail messages. In a more serious vein, however, this is a very complex question: What exactly do we mean when we use the "p" word?

That's not to say that the software doesn't necessarily enhance productivity. But that's not what the software companies really mean to say. Their software is intended to make workers more efficient. Once the workers become more efficient, they can become more productive. But productivity doesn't necessarily follow in the steps of efficiency.

Productivity is defined in economics as the rate at which goods or services are produced. We tend to view this as output per unit of labor. When the workforce was still largely industrial, we knew exactly what productivity was: how fast we are able to make widgets and how many go flying out the factory door. To make them quickly, however, had little to do with productivity and everything to do with efficiency.

The *American Heritage Dictionary of the English Language* defines productivity as "the rate at which goods or services are produced, especially output per unit of labor." The BLS uses the definition "output per man-hour" to indicate productivity. When applied to knowledge work, however, it seems that all bets are off. So how exactly can one measure knowledge worker productivity in a quantitative fashion?

In Search of a Management Science

It took 150 years from the dawn of the Industrial Age until the beginnings of a management science began to develop. Unfortunately, there is little applicability of the Industrial Age's management science to a knowledge economy setting. Indeed, today we are in the very early stages of developing a management science for the knowledge economy, and it will probably be decades before we fully understand even what questions have to be asked. The wide range of tasks that knowledge workers undertake, combined with the fact that there are different levels of knowledge workers, ranging from those with a single skill to highly-skilled workers who exercise independent thought and action most of the time, makes the task of defining productivity and developing a management science somewhat tricky, to say the least.

The BLS measures productivity by comparing the amount of goods and services produced with the inputs that were used in production. Labor productivity is the ratio of the output of goods and services to the labor hours devoted to the production of that output. The broadest measure of productivity published by BLS is for the U.S. business sector, which is responsible for 80 percent of the value of the gross domestic product (as of 2010).

The term "efficiency" refers to accomplishing a job or task with a minimum expenditure of time and effort. In industrial settings, companies have developed processes, such as just-in-time manufacturing and factory automation (think robots), that are more efficient than older methods.

It is possible to be very efficient without producing something even nominally useful. E-mail is innately efficient, but if an e-mail exchange takes three weeks to cover the same ground that a five-minute phone call could have achieved, one isn't being efficient at all.

So how exactly does one measure productivity for knowledge workers? For the knowledge economy, the first question might be: What is output? The answer is not as straightforward as determining what good or service we are producing. Is it the actual document or design – or the thinking behind it? Is it crossing things off one's to-do list and getting things done? One can be quite busy being efficient without having much to show for the effort.

Software companies make tools designed to make knowledge workers more efficient. Improvements in efficiency will (one hopes) lead to improvements in productivity. This is far from straightforward, however, and we'll need to do a lot more work to answer this question.

I recall a comment made to me years ago by the chief financial officer of Valentino, a fashion company, while we were standing outside the bookkeeping department, which was filled with many very busy bookkeepers. "What are all these people doing?" I had asked. His reply: "I don't know but they are always very busy doing it."

CHAPTER

WHAT HATH INFORMATION OVERLOAD WROUGHT?

We have reason to fear that the multitude of books which grows every day in a prodigious fashion will make the following centuries fall into a state as barbarous as that of the centuries that followed the fall of the Roman Empire.

—Adrien Baillet (1685)

While the inventions of paper (in the year 105) and ink (2697 BCE), the quill pen (ca. 700), and movable type (ca. 1440) increased mankind's ability to generate and distribute information, it was the advent of commercial telegraphy (1844), the stock ticker (1870), the telephone (1876), and xerography (1938) that truly changed how we create, move, manage, and interact with information.

With these inventions, mankind gained 1.) the ability to send information to others, regardless of distance, in real time, and 2.) the ability to create multiple and exact duplicates of documents without a printing press. More recently, advancements that followed the advent of the Internet conflated these two capabilities into systems that allow exact duplicates of documents to be sent in real time to others.

The tools and technologies used to share information may have changed over the years, but the underlying questions (not to mention organizational requirements) haven't changed terribly much. What has changed is how and with whom people work, enabled by the creation of new tools that are capable of moving more information than anyone in previous generations had imagined could exist.

Now it is possible not only to record content and send it to one another but to create the content collaboratively with others from different geographic locations in real time. In terms of information and how it is created, shared, and utilized, the meaning of time and space has changed dramatically, in effect heralding the "death of distance" (a term memorialized by *Economist* editor Frances Cairncross in her 1997 book of the same name).

The way we interact with content increasingly resembles what Marshall McLuhan in the early 1960s dubbed the "global village," a world where communications are not restricted by borders. In his 1967 book *The Medium is the Message: An Inventory of Effect,* he wrote, "'Time' has ceased, 'space' has vanished. We now live in . . . a simultaneous happening."

It would have been uncommon, 20 years ago, for a project team to include members in Los Angeles, New York, Munich, and Mumbai. Most teams would have been formed in the same office; indeed, membership in a team might have necessitated the relocation of one or more team members to a different city or country. Today time zones and language barriers have largely been overcome, and managers can build teams that are comprised of the most qualified people, regardless of location, as opposed to the most proximate.

Where work is done is less important than having the best people on the team. The death of distance means that colleagues can collaborate from far-off regions; electronic proximity can and has indeed replaced face-to-face meeting time – especially if it benefits the team and the organization.

While this trend is not exactly new, it was perhaps first recognized by Cairncross, who explained what happens in a world where distance no longer controls the cost of communication. This change, Cairncross predicted in 1997, would reshape the globe. Cairncross correctly foresaw that the death of distance would be both democratizing and liberating. She also envisaged a world where the line between home and office would blur, with increased mobility and with a deluge of information.

Where we once accepted the need to wait for a letter to come in the post, now we expect that an e-mail will reach us within seconds. Distance was once geographically rooted in that colleagues in different countries could not work together in real time on a project because they could not exchange information fast enough for that to be efficient; however, today that is no longer the case. Consequently the spatial element that had limited collaboration has almost vanished.

The end result is that countries will compete for citizens by offering superior services. Time zones and language will supplant distance. Smaller companies will compete favorably with larger ones, and more organizations will take on "virtual" characteristics.

All of this is being enabled by technology and information, which although now ubiquitous, have maintained an uneasy relationship with one another.

Aspects of Information Overload

Information Overload has its fingerprints on almost everything in the enterprise. Here are some of the far-ranging ways in which Information Overload impacts the knowledge worker and the knowledge organization.

Failed Searches

The knowledge worker spends 10 percent of his day searching for content, according to a survey conducted by Basex in 2010. More often than not, this is not time well spent.

It is by now axiomatic that 50 percent of all searches fail. This figure, however, tells only part of the story: Through research conducted by Basex in 2007, we learnt that 50 percent of the searches that knowledge workers believe to have succeeded also fail in some manner. This can occur when an incorrect response or a response that is somewhat correct but not the "best" response is accepted and used.

We look at this problem in greater depth in Chapter 15, "The Googlification of Search," but here is a quick overview.

The root cause of the search problem is that search requests return correct results – content that matches the literal criteria of the search – but this does not mean that the correct answer was supplied. Indeed, because search tools return a list of results (sometimes in the tens or hundreds of thousands) instead of a more precise answer or small selection of answers, choosing the correct "result" has become somewhat of a guessing game as well as a game of chance (i.e., the knowledge worker either guesses or picks a result he thinks may be the right one).

This approach is sufficient for some applications; full-text searching, for example, is a moderately effective tool for finding content in a database or an e-mail in an overflowing inbox. However, for such purposes as business intelligence and medical research, fields that rely on having the most current and relevant information, even tools such as semantic and natural language searching may fall short of the mark. Simply put, correct results do not equal correct answers and, when trying to stay abreast of current information, be it medical research or shifts in the world market, outdated or irrelevant information is a serious obstacle.

The problems here include inferior search technology, flawed taxonomies, failure on the part of the knowledge worker to construct a "proper" search query, and the mountains of information that a standard search returns – indeed, the list goes on and on and is beyond the scope of this chapter.

Setting aside the factors that lead searches to fail, the detrimental effects of failed search are myriad. It's not just a question of not finding something; rather, it's what happens *after* something is either not found or when the searcher uses incorrect or out-of-date information believing it to be correct.

For example, a knowledge worker might spend hours, if not days, re-creating a document because a suitable document (or portions thereof) could not be found – even though it does in fact exist. Moreover, if the knowledge worker believes he has found something but that information is incorrect or inappropriate and he doesn't recognize this fact, it can result in a chain of problems or errors down the road.

Often, the knowledge worker is searching for answers from an expert in his own organization, which presents a whole new set of complications. There are generally two ways that experts are located: by asking a few close colleagues and getting a limited number of answers, or by sending an "all-hands" query e-mail to hundreds or thousands of colleagues.

Of course, the all-hands method is a poor search technique and is very disruptive and only adds to the problem of Information

Overload. An e-mail query that should have gone to only a handful of colleagues but went to 500 would cost a company 1.7 days (approximately 40 hours) in lost man-hours when one calculates the impact of the interruption to 488 people who didn't have to receive it. That e-mail dance probably happens multiple times a week despite the results of this search technique being modest at best.

Another aspect of search failure is the impact that it can have on future searches. In a recent study funded by the U.S. Department of Homeland Security (DHS) and reported in *LiveScience* in January 2010, researchers found that subjects' expectations of finding something had a direct effect on their success rates for finding the items in question.

In the study, subjects looked at X-ray scans of checked baggage and tried to identify the presence of guns and knives. In the first trial, a gun or knife was present in 50 percent of the bags, and subjects missed the weapons only seven percent of the time. In the second trial, the guns and knives were in only two percent of the bags, and the subjects missed the weapons 30 percent of the time. In short, when something is harder to find, our accuracy in identifying it drops significantly.

This is a trick our brain plays on us as it becomes bored when we do not find what we are looking for. Essentially, it stops paying attention, meaning we then miss things when they do appear.

While the implications for airline security are obvious and somewhat chilling, the implications for the enterprise are also worth examining. Applying the lessons learnt in the DHS study, we can assume that if a search query returns fewer correct results in relation to incorrect results, the knowledge worker's accuracy in picking out the relevant items will decline.

Conversely, just as in the DHS study, if the correct-to-incorrect ratio is better, meaning there is a higher number of correct results, then the knowledge worker is much more likely to find more of them.

For knowledge-based organizations, the lessons from this study are clear: Search tools must be improved to provide better ratios of relevant, useful results. Today's search tools focus on returning large sets of results in response to a search query. The correct information may very well lie somewhere within the results; however, the low signal-to-noise ratio virtually ensures low accuracy even if one were to comb through every last result.

Search results need to be highly contextual and limited in volume to ensure accuracy and provide a favorable ratio of correct to incorrect results. This keeps the knowledge worker engaged and not feeling that he is looking for a needle in a haystack; this, in turn, increases the probability of identifying the needed content.

Lack of Authoritative Content

Today, anyone can publish information on the Internet and make it look professional. Not only does this add to the mass of information available, but it makes it harder and harder for people to find authoritative content. As comedian Jon Stewart famously said, "The Internet is just a world passing around notes in a classroom."

As a result, the Internet has become a breeding ground for spurious information. Millions of Web pages, many of which may appear authoritative, contain biased information, blatant errors, misinformation, and disinformation.

Traditionally, authoritative content has been (and continues to be) information published in leading business, health, and science magazines and trade journals, not to mention academic and medical journals. (This is not to say that every bit of content published in such publications is absent of any errors, however.) Indeed, much of this content is not available for free on the Web, although leading services such as Dow Jones and LexisNexis aggregate such content and make it available by subscription. While most newspapers do not charge for access, a few (most prominently, the *Financial Times, New York Times,* and *Wall Street Journal*) do.

Authoritative content must pass a variety of tests including accuracy, authentication, authority, objectivity, and currency. Much content on the Internet will not pass even one of those tests, let alone multiple tests.

Many workers are simply not sophisticated enough to recognize authoritative content versus other content, however; to them, a Web page is a Web page is a Web page. These users also don't know to look elsewhere, corroborate information, and assess the accuracy of what they find. They consider Wikipedia to be on the same level as a reputable business journal and don't stop to consider that anyone can edit and update Wikipedia's entries, making the content somewhat suspect. While many Wikipedia entries are on a par with those in a bound encyclopedia (and far more likely to be up-to-date), the fact that changes can be made by anyone from one day to the next makes this source a potential minefield although it is also surprisingly accurate thanks to frequent updating by subject matter experts.

Knowledge workers need to become familiar with content sources for their industry and may also need training, perhaps from a corporate librarian or researcher, in how to choose sources and corroborate findings.

Persistent Reinvention of the Wheel

When time is spent recreating information that couldn't be found or when colleagues are unaware of similar research being conducted in a different part of an organization, the party or parties involved may be said to have been reinventing the wheel.

Companies organized into product divisions are prone to duplications of effort that cost untold millions every year. This slows projects down and adds layers of unnecessary complexity. In addition, there is a substantial opportunity cost because those who are duplicating efforts unnecessarily could have been directing their efforts elsewhere.

Reinventing the wheel also occurs when a knowledge worker does not seek out information about what has been done in the past before commencing a task. He may be unknowingly replicating work already performed, but he is also prone to making the same errors that his colleagues previously made and corrected in their work, as well as new errors. The ramifications and costs of this are truly boundless.

The challenge is to ensure that knowledge workers have access to information and systems that would allow them to learn when they or colleagues are undertaking projects that may overlap. Individual knowledge workers can take steps to make colleagues aware but, without enterprise knowledge-sharing systems in place, it is difficult to broadcast information on a group or enterprise-wide basis.

Poor Decision Making

Bad decisions frequently are made because there was too little or too much information or because the best information couldn't be found.

Acquiring information first can translate into a substantial competitive advantage for an organization and allows decisions to be made before competitors.

With information in the form of e-mail, instant messages, phone calls, voicemails, text messages, and social networks, all moving all the time and at twenty-first-century speed, it's a wonder we can keep up at all. In addition, even if we can keep up with the torrent of information, taking a step back and seeing the connections among contacts, companies, and bits of information is next to impossible for the knowledge worker who is literally surrounded by data and inputs vying for attention.

Making sound decisions in this environment is extremely difficult; so much information is available to use, but key data, such as knowing that a contact worked with a coworker at another company or that an executive started a new job, often is obscured by the sheer quantity of information.

Lost Opportunities

Someone, probably in an early Western, said "There's gold in them thar hills." This statement is equally applicable to the knowledge worker's inbox and content feeds but today, much of that gold goes undetected.

It is impossible to divine the contents of an e-mail message before opening it (where is Carnac the Magnificent when his presence is required by millions of knowledge workers?), but many e-mail messages do indeed go unopened, either by design (too many to process at a given moment and the knowledge worker guesses which should be opened) or by accident (too many e-mails period and an important one goes unnoticed).

The statement applies equally regarding the search for information. Do a search today for virtually any topic, and you'll probably get 564,768 results – if not more. The correct answer is frequently overlooked due to having to sift through too much information. Information Overload leaves the knowledge worker looking for a needle in a haystack, and it is unrealistic to expect them to catch every important action item, e-mail, or nugget of useful information that they are presented with.

Obtaining key information is not the problem; instead, the problem is whether it can be pulled out of the pile of extraneous information with which it is often delivered. What really is needed often is obscured by the sheer volume of background noise that bombards the knowledge worker when searching for key information. When the best and freshest information cannot be isolated and utilized to make critical decisions, key opportunities are missed.

The Need to Scan

Knowledge workers frequently are under great pressure to absorb vast amounts of information in short periods of time. As a result, much information is scanned, leading to missed information as well as poor retention of information. A 2008 Basex survey found that a majority of knowledge workers complain that their colleagues read only the first few lines of an e-mail (assuming it is indeed opened) and therefore missed key information.

Several times a week I receive a reply to an e-mail with a question about something that is clearly covered in paragraph two, three, or four of my original missive. In some cases, I now write a brief preface at the beginning of a new e-mail message, along the lines of "This message covers three items, namely A, B, and C."

When he composes a new e-mail message, Colonel Peter Marksteiner, former CIO of the Air Force Judge Advocate General's Corps, divides it into two sections to avoid this problem. The first section, BLUF, stands for Bottom Line Up Front, and serves a purpose similar to my preamble. The second section, Details, is more or less the main body of the e-mail message.

An example of the BLUF section of an e-mail from Marksteiner (to me) illustrates this quite well:

> BLUF: providing a response to your questions – (1) how to refer to me; (2) comments about BLUF; (3) additional background info/quotes/references, should you need them.

In the 2000–2001 time frame, serving as a midlevel staff officer in the Pentagon, Marksteiner typically received anywhere from 75 to 100 e-mail messages per day. He told me that "some [were] short and almost completely undecipherable because of all the acronyms and such, others [were] rambling and disorganized. The rare gem was the e-mail that clearly articulated, right at the outset, what the sender wanted, needed, or intended to communicate."

Marksteiner picked up the BLUF habit from an e-mail message he received. "I distinctly remember being grateful to that sender for putting some precious time back into my day by using e-mail to clearly communicate a focused message," he told me.

He contrasts this approach with what he calls "ego-send-trism," where a sender writes "a stream of consciousness that he expected me – and his other dozen or so addressees – to figure out for ourselves."

He not only uses the BLUF technique himself but insists that members of his staff use it as well. "It would be difficult to quantify the positive impact my insistence on using the BLUF technique has had on the information handling practices in those organizations I've had the authority to influence, but I'm certain it's profound," he commented. Others, the recipients of his missives, think it's great too. "I've consistently gotten great feedback about the utility of the technique over the last decade from peers and supervisors, many of whom adopted it in their organizations" was his parting thought to me on the topic.

Many knowledge workers find it almost impossible to know whether they are reading the most important or urgent e-mails or attending to the most critical tasks. Even experts in the field find it difficult to keep up. Amy Wohl confessed to me that she is overwhelmed by the amount of incoming e-mail she receives. "I have to figure out how much of it [e-mail messages] I'm actually going to look at. I'm convinced that I never get to look at the right things. I'm just making guesses, educated guesses, poking around in the pile, and deciding what to look at and what to pitch."

As a result of the pressure to keep abreast of multiple e-mail threads, instant message conversations, blog postings, meeting arrangements, and other demands, the knowledge worker's attention is spread a mile wide and an inch deep, significantly degrading his ability to focus deeply on one topic and fully apply himself. By attempting to accomplish a large number of activities at the same time, the knowledge worker ends up engaging in time slicing, the act of rapidly switching between tasks. This catches up with the knowledge worker when he finds that all of his projects and tasks have become a blur and he struggles to keep track of multiple trains of thought.

Information Overload–Related Maladies

We know that knowledge workers can sustain serious and long-lasting health problems in the course of general knowledge work.

According to Basex survey data from 2008, 35 percent of knowledge workers were already reporting such work-related health issues. Information Overload may very well be a contributing factor to some of these ailments.

The most common complaints were eyestrain, with 17 percent of knowledge workers reporting problems, and back pain, with 16 percent. Other problems include carpal tunnel syndrome, headaches, poor circulation, and assorted stress-related issues.

For many in the health field, sitting is the new smoking. Medical journal articles with titles such as "Your Chair: Comfortable But Deadly" are appearing more frequently, and excessive sitting, a condition directly tied to knowledge work, has been linked by physicians and researchers to diabetes, heart disease, obesity, and even increased mortality among workers who sit for long periods of time.

Today, some knowledge workers complain of attention-deficit/hyperactivity disorder (ADHD) as a result of their work. Now, diagnosing a complicated condition such as this is well beyond the scope of this chapter, but the underlying sentiment is clear: These knowledge workers feel that they can't focus on one thing and constantly flit back and forth between tasks. Whether this is due to ADHD or just the crushing weight of an overflowing inbox and multiple demands on one's attention, Information Overload exacerbates this feeling.

Perhaps most telling, when presented with a list of work-related health issues in the 2008 Basex survey, one respondent wrote: "Why is MENTAL health not listed here?"

Information Overload is not necessarily the root cause of these health issues (many of these ailments are endemic to working in front of a computer for hours on end), but there is no doubt that being overloaded by information can significantly exacerbate Information Age–related maladies. Information Overload without a doubt raises stress levels, encourages the spillover of work into personal time, and makes it difficult for the knowledge worker to take breaks that are needed to avoid health issues in the first place.

Because Information Overload – almost by definition – requires knowledge workers to spend more time in front of a computer display or smartphone, workers need to be aware of what they can do to minimize the aches, pains, and illnesses of the Information Age. Simple steps, such as using adjustable chairs, desks, and monitors; taking frequent breaks to both stand up and look away from the display; and not holding devices in awkward positions (this ranges from cradling a phone on your shoulder, thereby causing neck strain, to leaning over a smartphone or netbook, causing back strain), are all it takes.

Information Overload–Related Stress

Information Overload stress begets more stress and, not surprisingly, more Information Overload. As the pile of information grows, the stress rises at the same time that the ability to take action to reduce the pressure decreases.

The stress of Information Overload causes a host of problems, some of which manifest as physical ailments and others that simply impact our ability to perform at our best. In Basex surveys from 2008, knowledge workers reported stress leading to anxiety, chronic insomnia, gastrointestinal problems, and asthma. This was in addition to the other health issues previously detailed.

An overflowing inbox creates stress in a multitude of ways; there is anxiety over when the next e-mail will come, whether the response was timely enough, and what e-mail messages are piling up when the knowledge worker is not at work. One knowledge worker told me of an extreme, but perhaps not uncommon, situation, where employees at a small company were constantly checking their inboxes because their boss expected a 10- to 15-minute turn-around on e-mails and would respond aggressively (by calling up and shouting) if a reply was not forthcoming. Instead of focusing on their tasks, these workers were constantly worrying about what was happening in their inboxes, which ratcheted up their stress levels and reduced their job effectiveness.

While this example may sound a bit extreme, many knowledge workers report that they feel they must respond quickly and that they might not have responded fast enough to meet expectations. Indeed, the institutionalization of such a feeling led Intel to experiment with a "service-level agreement" to discourage the notion that an e-mail must be replied to within minutes instead of hours or days. (See Chapter 17 for more details.)

Other knowledge workers have reported feelings of hopelessness and an inability to take their minds off work during off hours because of the fear that more e-mail messages are accumulating.

Internet addiction is another very real problem that is exacerbated by Information Overload. An addiction to the Internet, and technology in general, is marked by excessive use, feelings of withdrawal (when not connected), an increased tolerance in our technology use (i.e., the ability to deal with larger e-mail loads than even five years ago), and negative repercussions (i.e., health issues, decimated work–life balance, and lack of social interactions). All of these symptoms should be familiar to knowledge workers. Information Overload functions as an enabler for Internet addiction, which increases stress levels.

Matt Brezina, co-founder of Xobni, a company that designs tools to lower e-mail overload, told me "if I don't check it [e-mail and news], I almost feel as if something is missing in my life. . . . I kinda feel lonely."

Stress is not limited to the workplace; just as work spills over into personal time, so does the stress that accompanies Information Overload. Knowledge workers are confronted with masses of information and demands on their time coupled with the inability to take their minds off work because of a constant stream of information that, thanks to mobile devices, extends the workspace to virtually anywhere.

According to Jerald J. Block, writing in the March 2008 issue of the *American Journal of Psychiatry,* those of us who constantly check our inboxes, refresh Web sites for new headlines, or spend hours on Twitter or Facebook may actually be suffering from a compulsive-impulse spectrum disorder or, in other words, Internet addiction. The idea that we crave the very thing that is crushing us may seem counterintuitive. However, as with any other addiction, both the Internet and technology cast a strange spell over us.

Dr. Block identifies four components of Internet addiction that are worth examining.

First, and most obvious, is excessive use. Trying to determine what is deemed excessive is problematic, but the established criteria are a loss of sense of time or the neglect of basic drives. So if you missed dinner because you were buried in work and lost track of time and didn't realize that you were hungry, then it might be time to take a break.

The second trait is withdrawal. A knowledge worker who has found it next to impossible to go all weekend without checking e-mail or using the Internet will be familiar with the feeling of being disconnected and somewhat frustrated. In Information Overload terms, we know that the pile of information is getting bigger and bigger the longer we stay away, and it appears as if we prefer to chip away at it a little bit at a time as opposed to in large chunks.

The third and somewhat more subtle component is tolerance. This explains why we always think our Internet connection is too slow, that if we just had one more piece of software things would really start moving along, and why the shift from using a computer only for a specific task (often turning it on and off to do one thing) to being constantly online seems so natural to us. We have built up a huge tolerance to the Internet and technology in general. This is why we believe we are able to deal with hundreds of e-mail messages a day, when only 10 years ago, we struggled with perhaps as few as 50.

The fourth and perhaps most important aspect of Internet addiction is marked by negative repercussions. For knowledge workers, this is where maintaining a healthy work–life balance comes into play. When Internet and technology use leads to arguments, lying, isolation, or fatigue, then it is time to reexamine one's work–life balance. This is increasingly difficult in today's interconnected and wired world, but it does need to be a priority.

What do these four aspects of Internet addiction mean to the knowledge worker? They are the indicators, the red flags that we need to be aware of, not just for ourselves but for each other. Managing knowledge work and knowledge workers effectively means that one must understand the importance of encouraging responsible and healthy use of technology as well as the value of unplugging and disconnecting from time to time.

Decimated Work–Life Balance

Seventy percent of knowledge workers surveyed report that they work during times that traditionally have been thought of as "personal time," such as during or after the dinner hour. The sheer mass of information that the knowledge worker has to manage all but guarantees that some of the excess will end up at home.

Our tools, although intended to improve our efficiency and productivity, contribute to this erosion of personal space and time. The urge to check our e-mail inboxes when not at work was bad enough before the advent of smartphones. Today, with BlackBerrys, iPhones, and other Internet-enabled mobile devices, the idea of being completely off the grid and separated from our work lives seems naïve and farfetched. In Basex surveys in 2008, when asked how they maintained a healthy work–life balance, many respondents commented along the lines of "what work–life balance?" and "I don't."

Information Overload forces us to work longer hours by driving down our productivity and efficiency; the end result is the spill-over of work into our personal time, which can have a negative effect on our health, social lives, and relationships. Only three percent of those surveyed indicated that they never find that work intrudes on their personal time.

For some, the breakdown in work–life balance is well established. Edward Hallowell, a psychiatrist who has studied the problem, said in a 2006 *Time* magazine article on Information Overload that a patient once asked him "whether I thought it was abnormal that her husband brings the BlackBerry to bed and lays it next to them while they make love."

A sales engineer at a technology company, responding to a survey question, commented that he is "not very good" at maintaining any semblance of a work–life balance. "But I like knowing that I'm caught up on work even when away from my computer. It gives me a sense of calm knowing exactly what's in my inbox even if I can't do anything about at the time."

The Compatibility Conundrum

While we are worried about the amount of information we currently have to deal with, we also need to focus on how and if our information will be accessible to future generations. Today we generate so much content that it is simply not possible to archive it and manage it properly.

Newspapers and photographs from the 1800s not only survive today but are viewable and readable by the naked eye. Documents and photographs created using computers and electronic cameras from the 1970s, 1980s, and 1990s aren't that lucky.

A picture taken in 1988 with a Canon RC-760, one of the first still-video cameras on the market, may be irretrievably lost unless the photographer has a paper print of the photo – or the original camera and a working player for the proprietary floppy disk, which is unlikely as only a handful of these devices still exist. The paper print is likely to have deteriorated significantly, given the poor quality of early still-video camera printing technologies.

More significantly, many of the images taken by National Aeronautics and Space Administration (NASA) space expeditions haven't been accessible in years, although there are some exceptions. In one case, 2,000 images from five Lunar Orbiter missions from the 1960s were rescued by Nancy Evans, a Jet Propulsion Lab archivist who had the foresight in the 1970s to warehouse a truckload of two-inch tapes, without any plans for their future.

She also stored three Ampex FR-900 tape drives, which originally cost $300,000 and were being discarded by Elgin Air Force Base in the 1980s, in the garage of her house.

It took until the year 2007, when she put together the resources to repair the FR-900 tape drives, that the images finally saw the light of day.

Contrast this with the discovery of an ancient basalt slab by a French engineering officer stationed at a fort near the Egyptian city of Rosetta. Etched into the stone was a priestly decree from ca. 196 BCE, using Egyptian hieroglyphics, demotic characters, and Greek. The Rosetta Stone, which serves as a key to previously undecipherable hieroglyphics, is notable as well for its longevity.

In addition, books, pamphlets, and broadsides printed hundreds of years ago are accessible without any special equipment.

Today, billions of files on older hard drives, 8-, 5¼-, and 3.5-inch floppy diskettes, obsolete tape cartridges, and computers that no longer turn on have been rendered, for all essential purposes, lost. Digital file standards come and go. Try opening up a WordStar or early WordPerfect file on your laptop today. The physical limitations of not having the correct drive notwithstanding, today's software programs may not be able to interpret the files correctly either. Of equal if not greater importance, there is no guarantee that the standards that we take for granted today (including .jpg for images and .doc for documents) will exist in decades to come.

In the course of writing this book, I spoke with corporate archivists at such companies as IBM, Western Union, and Xerox. They all expressed similar sentiments, namely a fear that the knowledge and information that was being created today might not be anywhere close to fully accessible in the not-too-distant future.

They also told me they strongly believed in paper. One archivist said she maintains at least 20 percent of her archive on paper in addition to digital files. She would do more but there simply isn't any room to store it. She is 100 percent confident that the paper archives will be accessible in 100 years but had serious doubts as to whether some of the digital files will be accessible in 10.

In addition to information contained in documents, more information in the form of images is being created as well. Simply put, people are taking more photographs than ever before, thanks to the fact that photography, sans film and processing costs, has become almost free. But this, too, comes at a price: While the earliest photographs (the word "photograph" means "light drawing") such as Daguerreotypes and ambrotypes are still visible to the naked eye today, many photographs taken within the past 25 years since the advent of electronic photography are no longer accessible.

The move from paper to digital images means that people no longer keep shoe boxes full of photos. These shoe boxes from earlier times have, until now, proven quite valuable to historians as a record of a particular place and time. Today, as we become more and more dependent on technology to access records, we are at the same time setting ourselves up to lose very large amounts of information.

One might presume that the technology deployed during the Information Revolution of the late twentieth century had increased our ability to preserve our history and cultural artifacts. In actuality, the opposite is the case.

THE TWO FREDS

Urgent Necessity prompts many to do things.
—Miguel de Cervantes

Fred Rogers, an American children's television show host, educator, and ordained Presbyterian minister, was born in 1928 in Latrobe, Pennsylvania, a small town near Pittsburgh. Rogers received a degree in music from Rollins College and started his career at NBC in New York working on music for television.

Rogers created the popular children's television show *Mister Rogers' Neighborhood* in 1968. The program ran for 895 episodes and, after *Sesame Street*, was the second-longest running program on the PBS network. The program, which used music composed largely by Rogers, took children through a variety of topics, from friendship, to war, to the death of a goldfish.

Fred Smith, an executive and innovator in the document and package delivery field, was born in Marks, Mississippi, in 1944. As an undergraduate student at Yale University in the 1960s, Smith wrote a paper for an economics class in which he outlined a new concept, an overnight delivery service, which eventually became FedEx.

Smith launched Federal Express operations in April 1973. By 1976, the company had become profitable and delivered about

19,000 overnight packages each business day. In 1979, Federal Express became the first company to use a computer system, which it named COSMOS (Customers, Operations and Services Master Online System), to manage packages. The following year the company deployed DADS (Digitally Assisted Dispatch System), which allowed it to offer same-day pickups from customers.

The work of these two Freds has created an imprint on multiple generations that will be hard to erase.

Rogers imparted a message to generations of children that they were "special" simply for being themselves. He meant well, but his message obfuscated the fact that being special came from achievements and hard work.

A question posed on the Yahoo Answers Web site puts it this way:

> Fred "Mr. Rogers" Rogers spent years telling little creeps that he liked them just the way they were. He should have been telling them there was a lot of room for improvement. Now we have millions of young adults with unwarranted self esteem who really can't do anything useful. Nice as he was, and as good as his intentions may have been, I think he did a disservice to the U.S. What do you think?

Smith ushered in an era of instant gratification, one where people are no longer content to wait – for anything. With the launch of 14 small aircraft, based at Memphis International Airport, with which the company delivered 186 packages to 25 U.S. cities, a shot was fired that was heard around the world: Documents and products could be reliably in another person's hands the following day.

But what does all this mean?

Today, our need for instant gratification causes us to interrupt others when we don't get an immediate answer. Because we are special, we operate with the (mistaken) belief that everything we are doing is both urgent and important. This in turn lends a false sense of importance to our mission, and that too causes us to interrupt others too much.

Patrick Riley, then a Ph.D. candidate at the School of Information, University of California at Berkeley, explained his feelings about this to me. "My generation," he said, "needs constant reinforcement from our friends and colleagues about how awesome we are and how we are doing such a great job at whatever it is we are doing."

As if to amplify Patrick's statement, Vishal Singh, a 17-year-old quoted in "Growing Up Digital, Wired for Distraction" on November 21, 2010, in the *New York Times,* can't make it through a book. "On YouTube, 'you can get a whole story in six minutes,' he explains. 'A book takes so long. I prefer the immediate gratification.'"

My own generation was on the cusp. The era I grew up in marked the end of a time of wishful anticipation, ushering in instant gratification in its place.

Not so long ago, if I wanted to order something that wasn't available in a local store, I would mail or telephone an order and I would have a feeling of anticipation, knowing that a parcel service would, within a week, be bringing my purchase.

My father's company, Spiratone, sold innovative photographic accessories by mail. Founded in the 1940s, the company relied on the mail to receive most of its orders, although toll-free phone ordering started to displace some mail-bound orders starting in the 1970s.

How it worked was simple and fairly typical of mail-order companies of the time. A customer filled out a catalog order form and sent that, along with a check or credit card information, in an envelope. It typically took two to three days for the order to arrive and, given the various steps in ordering process – even with computerization – it took an average of 3 days for an order to get entered, packed, and sent on its way to the customer. Adding in an average of 3 days for shipping, the entire process took 10 to 14 days.

Today, a television commercial for Zappos.com shows a customer expressing complete astonishment that a package ordered yesterday arrived so quickly: "I have a little problem. I ordered a dress yesterday afternoon and it showed up this morning. I'm not really emotionally ready for it yet."

As a result, she wants to return it. The customer service representative offers to accept the dress as a return and is shown on camera checking off "emotionally unprepared" on a form (the other choices were "too big" and "too small").

Indeed, the movement that started in 1973 today translates into this: People are no longer content to wait days and weeks for something to arrive, be it a document, camera lens, or a reply to an e-mail. By 1980, the advent of less expensive telecopiers and sinking telecommunications costs supported the expectation that information requests could – and should – be fulfilled on demand. The arrival of internal e-mail systems (prior to intercompany Internet-based e-mail) further heightened expectations.

Today, if I need to order something, whether it is food, a book, or even a camera lens, as long as I place my order by, typically, 4 P.M., I can have the item(s) the next day. In fact, many people incessantly track their packages' whereabouts, and delivery companies fuel our need for this information. Did the package leave the local station? Get a text or e-mail on that. Is it on the truck? Get a text or e-mail for that too. Was it just delivered? Another text or e-mail arrives.

Thanks to the two Freds, today we have a worker population that requires instant gratification in whatever they are doing. We send e-mail and then call the recipient two minutes later not only to ensure that the message was received but to underscore the sender's importance and presumed urgency.

Throughout the day, we mindlessly stream out "important" content to hundreds of people who have their own urgent and important matters to attend to.

Marsha Egan, author of *Inbox Detox and the Habit of E-mail Excellence*, told me that, when she was in the corporate world, people would come to her office with their urgent issue – but it wasn't her urgent issue. It didn't happen that often, but it was an interruption. Today, with e-mail, it happens all the time.

The two Freds need not shoulder that blame alone. Today we almost continuously invent new tools and technologies (see the timeline in Great Moments and Milestones in Information Overload History), examples of which include smartphones (some indistinguishable from tiny full-fledged computers) and social software such as Twitter, which can work together to alert tens of thousands of people that lunch is over and it consisted of a tuna fish sandwich.

We have created a monster in the very tools, such as mobile phones, smartphones, personal digital assistants (PDAs), e-mail, text messaging, and social networking that were supposed to make us more efficient and effective.

Today people expect results and responses faster and faster. An executive at a prominent luxury hotel recently told me of guests from certain regions of the world who call a manager within minutes of clicking the send button on an e-mail message, demanding to know why no response has been forthcoming.

Entitlement

In 1986, California enacted legislation to promote self-esteem ("The State Task Force to Promote Self-Esteem and Personal and Social Responsibility"). Soon teachers and coaches everywhere were rewarding and complimenting students and athletes on getting a C- on a test or coming in last in a sports competition.

The newest generations coming into the workforce bring this attitude of entitlement with them.

"Don't give me your tired old enterprise apps," whined a young editorial assistant in the November 2007 issue of *CIO* magazine, bemoaning the lack of cutting-edge collaboration tools available for the enterprise. "I want the new stuff because it's better. If you don't give me the tools I need, I'll leave you flat and find someone who will. If you can't understand that, I don't want to work for you because you just don't get it and chances are you never will."

Employees who feel entitled exhibit a variety of characteristics. Some resist change and drag their feet. Others come in seeking to reinvent their job and the company on day one. Many such employees act as if they are not accountable for their actions.

This attitude constantly frustrates business leaders and managers.

The combination of the need for instant gratification with entitlement is a deadly one, at least in terms of how it impacts the workplace. As a result of this, some workers have no compunction whatsoever in interrupting a colleague or more senior manager because, after all, what that person is doing could never be as urgent and as important as what they are doing.

What companies need is a culture of nonentitlement, where employees are fully responsible for their own actions and not constantly in need of positive reinforcement. Indeed, the idea culture is one where employees are proactive and take pride in themselves and the organization.

Mad about Information

Today we have a very clear vision of what work looks like, how we do it, and whom we do it with. A typical office will have desks with high-tech, ergonomic chairs, indirect lighting, flat-screen monitors and/or laptop docks on the desks, and desk phones with push-button dialing and information displays.

Beverages ranging from a latte to an energy drink – not to mention plastic bottles of water – are common, as are healthy snacks such as apples and bananas.

While this is how we view work, it's not how work has always been.

Indeed, one of the many, many pleasures of watching the television series *Mad Men*, a drama set on Madison Avenue in the 1950s and, more recently, in the 1960s, is the opportunity to see how work, the workplace, and the concept of work–life balance have all changed in the ensuing years.

In the world of *Mad Men* of 1965, the creation of FedEx is still eight years away; computers are behind glass walls, carefully watched over by scientists in white lab coats; telephones have cords (and multiline phones have thick cords); and the letter "e" would not be affixed to the word "mail" for some time.

In the offices of Sterling Cooper, the mythical ad agency where most of the key characters work, there are no computers, but IBM's influence is felt everywhere as IBM Selectric typewriters grace the desks of all of the secretaries.

A photocopier, namely the Xerox 914, is the highest form of technology that I have seen deployed at Sterling Cooper. Copies of memos are distributed (on paper and by hand), and most of the knowledge workers use a combination of paper and pen (or pencil) or typewriter. The use of a typewriter, in fact, was considered something that only women in the workforce, and almost all secretaries were women at the time, would use and men prided themselves on the fact that they don't type.

Work–Life Balance

Mad Men demonstrates, with a reasonable degree of accuracy (the show's producers are sticklers for this), that it was possible in the 1950s and 1960s to go to work, put in a day at the office, and enjoy oneself at the same time.

Indeed, based on 2010 conventions, the ad men at Sterling Cooper enjoy life a bit too much. They puff away at their desks. They drink (sometimes starting before breakfast). They flirt and have the occasional workplace romance. Some of the younger staff amuse themselves by drawing lewd cartoons of female workers or making racial or anti-gay jokes.

But they also seemingly enjoy far more of a work-life balance than their counterparts today.

Of course, one thing that is missing from the picture is e-mail. Also in the not-yet-invented category are the Internet, the Web, mobile phones, social networks, instant messaging, Twitter, FourSquare, and FedEx.

The characters in *Mad Men* don't follow the romantic notion expressed in 1950s sitcoms of always arriving home shortly after 5 P.M. to a wife who has slippers, a pipe, and a cocktail waiting. In fact, the ad men seem to go out for drinks, with clients or just with each other, quite a bit.

And they do not at all seem to be under the type of pressure that the typical knowledge worker of today enjoys.

Except for the occasional emergency phone call or surprise drop-in visit, workers were never on call or tethered to the office 24x7. The viewer is left with the impression that people 30 and 40 years ago were better able to spend time with their families and friends than we are today and it is likely this was the case.

Starting in the 1960s, more women began to join the workforce, and both husbands and wives worked longer and longer hours. (This resulted in so-called DINS marriages, "double income, no sex.") Indeed, researchers estimate that people today sleep between one and two fewer hours per day than their parents did a generation ago. (On the plus side, sleep aids, in part propelled by the real companies of Madison Avenue, are now a multibillion dollar market.)

The knowledge worker of the 1950s and 1960s had most of the information he needed at his fingertips and rarely was a victim of Information Overload. The lack of widely deployed computers, fax machines, and overnight deliveries kept the movement and creation of information to a reasonably comfortable level (after all, Telex machines could only transmit and receive at 60 word per minute), and the invention of tools that would feed the need for instant gratification was still decades away.

A FedEx television commercial from the 1990s points out the contrast nicely:

> In this fast moving, high pressure, get it done world, aren't you glad there's one company that can keep up with it all? Federal Express. When it absolutely, positively has to be there overnight.

BEEP. BEEP. BEEP.

I generally avoid temptation unless I can't resist it.

—Mae West

When I look around, I see temptation. Information. It's like crack. You get a little information and you immediately want more.

Three beeps indicate a text message. My friends and colleagues who want my attention send me text messages when they want an immediate reply. E-mail, despite being in real time, has become less so. The same goes for instant messages, which can be ignored as well.

I get so much e-mail that I turned off the various alerts (sound and screen) long ago. Had I left the e-mail chime on, it would be one continuous noise. For the same reason, my Lotus Sametime instant messaging software also no longer chimes.

Americans today spend a vast amount of the day consuming information. A 2009 report from the University of California at San Diego (UCSD) found that each person spends an average of 12 hours per day surfing the Web and watching TV, although the study counted one hour of watching TV and surfing the Web as two hours, so some hours were counted twice. While the typical individual watches TV for five hours, uses the computer for two, and spends one hour gaming, only 36 minutes are given to print media, representing a huge shift in how we consume information.

In a typical hour spent online, according to Nielsen data from 2010, the average user spends 13 minutes on social networking sites, five minutes on e-mail, and just over two minutes using instant messaging tools. Interestingly, when Nielsen looked at online activities on mobile devices, 26 minutes of every hour was spent on e-mail, compared to only six spent on social networking sites.

Our choices in media consumption and activity are not without consequence; the way in which we stimulate our brains as we consume information can have a very real impact on our cognitive abilities.

A study of 11 German schoolboys at the Deutsche Sporthochschule Köln (German Sports University Cologne), published in the November 2007 issue of *Pediatrics*, investigated "the effects of singular excessive television and computer game consumption on sleep patterns and memory performance of children." The research, led by Markus Dworak of the Institut für Bewegungs und Neurowissenschaft, which is part of the Deutsche Sporthochschule, involved having the boys play video games for one hour after doing their homework on alternate nights. The other nights, the boys would watch television or a movie. The researchers looked at the impact of different media on the boys' brainwave patterns while asleep and measured their ability to recollect information from homework assignments. Playing video games, as compared to watching television, led to a "significant decline" in the boys' ability to remember vocabulary assignments and also resulted in poorer sleep quality.

How Much Texting Is Too Much?

One area of particular interest – and a harbinger of things to come – is the increased use of text messaging, particularly in the teen and preteen age groups. Just as my colleagues and I tend to use instant messaging to communicate with someone sitting just a yard or two away, teens and preteens text. I can personally attest to situations where two or three children sitting in a car text to one another rather than have a verbal conversation. And it's not just teenagers. In fact, in order for me to make an appointment with my hair stylist, Michelle, I have to send a text – a phone call is simply not an option.

College freshmen, the Beloit College Mindset List for the Class of 2014 tells us, have no need for a wristwatch because their mobile phone tells them what time it is, and they use e-mail less frequently than those who are a few years older. The Beloit List was first published in 1998 by two professors at the university, and it is intended to give a glimpse into the experiences, attitudes, and mind-set of each incoming class. Instead of e-mail, this group is more likely to communicate through text or instant messaging or via a social network because they know their friends will respond more quickly.

According to Nielsen, in 2010, the average home in the United States has more television sets than people. The Kaiser Family Foundation found that as of January 2010, 61 percent of children between the ages of eight and 18 have a TV set in their own room and 29 percent own a laptop. Sixty-six percent of children today have their own mobile phone; in 2004, only 39 percent had one.

In 2010, the Pew Internet and American Life Project found that 93 percent of teenagers (ages 12 to 17) are active online, with 63 percent going online at least once a day. Among teenagers, according to Pew, 62 percent use instant messaging, with about one in four teens using it every day. These numbers have remained flat since 2006, reflecting the dominance of text messaging among teens. Seventy-one percent of teens report they prefer text messaging to other forms of communication including e-mail, instant messaging, social networking tools, and phone calls. Only 11 percent reported daily use of e-mail.

Text messaging is something that is taken for granted today, but it made its first appearance in 1992. By 1995, a mobile phone subscriber was sending on average 0.4 text messages per month. Text messaging, which is also known as SMS for "short message service," is the most widely used mobile data service, and 75 percent of the mobile phone user population today actively uses the service.

Today, the average user in the United States sends and receives 10 text messages per day, and an entire vocabulary not to mention dialect has evolved around texting. This texting subculture, which may not even qualify as a subculture given the percentage of the population using text messaging, involves acronyms (such as LOL for "laughing out loud"), abbreviations (such as "r u home"), and text-specific phraseology.

Sample Text Phraseology

Text phraseology has its origins in the shorthand used in online forums, chat rooms, and instant messaging sessions. Here are some examples:

1CE	once
.02	my (or your) two cents' worth
B9	boss is watching
CU	see you
CUL8R	see you later
Enuf	enough
G4C	going for coffee
GTG	got to go
IMHO	in my humble opinion
IWIAM	idiot wrapped in a moron
JFGI	just f – king Google it
KK	okay, okay
MOS	mother over shoulder
OIC	oh, I see
PTMYA	pleasure to make your acquaintance
ROFL	rolling on the floor, laughing

In the 12 months ending in June 2010, Americans sent 1.56 trillion text messages, according to the CTIA, a wireless industry trade association. If you think that's a lot, it is – the number was only two billion in 2003, the first year that the CTIA tracked this statistic, and 81 billion in 2005. Indeed, the average American spent 23 hours last year just on text messages alone.

According to research published by Nielsen in 2010, American teenagers send and receive a total of 3,339 text messages per month on average. Put differently, this represents 10 messages for every waking nonschool hour. For the 12-and-under set, the average is somewhat lower, a mere 1,146 per month.

Even these numbers don't tell the entire story. Matt Richtel, writing in the *New York Times* on November 21, 2010 ("Growing Up Digital, Wired for Distraction"), makes mention of Allison Miller, a 14-year-old who somehow sends and receives 27,000 text messages per month, "her fingers clicking at a blistering pace as she carries on as many as seven text conversations at a time." She blames multitasking for getting three Bs on her report card and admits that she frequently fails to return to her original task after a text message interrupts her. In the same article, Richtel quotes David Reilly, a school principal, who notes that the "unchecked use of digital devices can create a culture in which students are addicted to the virtual world and lost in it."

Texting is not a direct substitute for face-to-face conversations because such conversations have to occur in real time. Texting, however, allows one to have multiple conversations at the same time, and they appear to be in real time, although that may not always be the case.

The increasing popularity of text messaging portends a huge change in both the amount of information that younger people will exchange as well as the manner in which it is exchanged.

Compared to previous generations, those growing up today are being exposed to digital data earlier and more frequently.

In addition, because of the ease of communication that modern technology allows, younger people are growing up with a potentially wider social circle of friends, some of whom they have not met in person, with friendship no longer defined by geographic proximity.

In addition, technology such as texting and instant messaging – which costs relatively little compared to their parents' long-distance telephone bills a decade prior – has allowed younger people to be in almost constant contact with these friends.

Texting has had multiple changes on our information culture. For example, it has in many cases eliminated the need for telephone calls about small items, such as when to meet for a drink or what time a meeting is at. Additionally, it is also a cheap and effective communications medium with a low barrier to entry (no computer or Internet connection is needed).

Beyond one-on-one conversations, there are many use cases for text messaging including time-critical alerts, updates and reminders (ranging from flight information to a reminder to take one's medication), and content (such as news and weather). SMS platforms have also been used to great effect in areas of the developing world that lack Internet access to coordinate relief work, collect information, and determine resource allocation.

The Search for Whatever It Is We Are Looking For

Not only is information thrust upon us, but we spend a lot of time looking for it as well. A recent study by Nielsen found that there were 10 billion searches conducted in December 2009. The top search term for the year was "Facebook."

That Facebook was the top search term is not surprising in some respects. A separate study by Nielsen found that the average "global user" (its term, not mine) spent 5.5 hours in December 2009 on social networking sites. This was an 82 percent increase from December 2008.

People are large generators of information. A study conducted in 2007 at the Department of Psychology at the University of Arizona found that individuals speak an average of 16,000 words per day. A University of California at San Diego (UCSD) study found that, people notwithstanding, 45 percent of the information people get as words comes from television; other contributors are computers (26 percent), radio (11 percent), print media (9 percent), and phone conversations (5 percent).

When the researchers at the UCSD added up the total amount of data consumed in the United States in 2008, they found it to be 3.6×10^{21}, the equivalent of 100,500 words and 34 GB per day for each person.

Growing up, I would get my news from the morning newspaper, occasionally from a news radio station, and perhaps a bit more from the evening news.

In 25 years, much has changed in the news cycle. An excellent illustration of this is that, when Pope John Paul II died in 2005, CNN, the 24-hour news network, had never covered the election of a new pope before as it hadn't existed 26 years earlier, when the last papal election took place.

Today, the CNN model is considered somewhat outdated as first the Web and more recently Twitter and other social tools immediately push news out to millions of people as it is happening.

Information comes from many sources – people, computers, mobile phones, and radios and televisions – and they all want your attention.

CHAPTER

11

HEADING FOR A NERVOUS BREAKDOWN

Everybody gets so much common information all day long that they lose their common sense.

—Gertrude Stein

One of the more interesting aspects of my work comes from the many discussions I have with knowledge workers on the topic of Information Overload, how it impacts them, and what they are doing about it.

When I meet someone for the first time and explain my research in Information Overload, I usually brace myself. Everyone has an Information Overload story to tell. Some stories relate to coping and some to how the onslaught is simply overwhelming.

Nathan Zeldes, president of the Information Overload Research Group (IORG), a tech industry consortium, and Intel's former Information Overload czar, told me how he copes with too much information. He feels strongly about the value of such e-mail management strategies as checking e-mail only once a day, in his case after lunch, and setting up a folder system that separates messages into those that must be dealt with immediately, today, or can be followed up on later. Another point he stresses is that e-mail should not be used as a to-do list.

Zeldes also uses tools, such as a local search engine, to quickly find e-mail messages, and he offloads as much as possible to RSS feeds, which in turn can help to reduce the frustrations that arise from an overloaded and unwieldy inbox.

Shari Lawrence Pfleeger, a senior information scientist at the RAND Corporation, sees Information Overload as an impediment to getting her work done. She says:

> We are more connected than ever, but we must manage not only our connections but also the increasing volumes of information flowing over them. We continue to sort useful mail from junk mail, but we are additionally stressed by sorting useful phone calls from junk calls, useful e-mail from spam, and in general useful from useless (and even dangerous) information. To get really important work done, I find it helpful to take a holiday from my connections so that I can focus on the work at hand.

Thinking for a Living

Because Information Overload robs us of so much of our time, I felt it was important to understand more about what we as knowledge workers do in a day. What my colleagues and I found after surveying several hundred knowledge workers at the start of 2010 was striking, especially when compared to earlier research we published on the knowledge worker's day in 2008. Back then, when we found that the typical knowledge worker was able to devote only 12 percent of the day (approximately one hour of an eight-hour day) to thought and reflection, I expressed grave concern about how this meager amount of time was insufficient for most workers who essentially think for a living.

I spoke too soon.

We were, of course, very concerned about that 12 percent. So we decided to do more in-depth research, and we found out that knowledge workers don't devote 12 percent of the day to thought and reflection. Rather, they end up with only five percent of the day left for thinking and reflecting. (See Chapter 12 for more details on this.)

I spend a good part of my day exploring and searching, and I try to leave sufficient time for thought and reflection – after all, what we knowledge workers do is to *think* for a living. Five percent of the day is clearly not enough.

Stanley Hanks, the chief technology officer of Columbia Ventures, spends a "huge" part of his day sifting through "vast" amounts of information looking for "nuggets that might give us an advantage in our pursuits." Stanley does what I do: "I read, I pursue links, web search tidbits, e-mail for clarification, for hours on end."

Thought and reflection is not limited to one specific profession. A software test engineer at a medical device company noted that he is paid, in part, "to think about things and critically analyze them."

But, just as I have found, having all of this information at one's fingertips is both a blessing and a curse. As Stanley also told me, when he's working under a tight deadline, trying to finish a project or presentation, "it's an annoyance."

Some of the other key research findings include:

- 66 percent of knowledge workers feel they don't have enough time to get all of their work done.
- Over 50 percent of knowledge workers feel that the amount of information they are presented on a daily basis is detrimental to getting their work done.
- 94 percent of knowledge workers at some point have felt overwhelmed by information to the point of incapacity.
- 30 percent of knowledge workers have no time at all for thought and reflection during their day, and 58 percent had only between 15 and 30 minutes.

Bevrlee Lips, publisher of the magazine *Claims Advisor*, told me that her day is "a menagerie of interruptions from every possible angle."

Richard Solomon, CTO of Creative Technology, agrees. The day consists of "unnecessary emails, badly written, long messages, and misleading subject lines."

Josh Berry, a software developer, has found that instant messaging and e-mail "supply a constant stream of interruptions that disrupt my focus and prevent me from spending large, contiguous blocks of productive time on tasks at hand."

One person (who asked to remain anonymous) who took one of our surveys wrote that she struggles to manage the flow of information coming at her. "The only reason I'm doing this survey is to take a little break."

The Roundtable

In April 2010, I chaired a roundtable on personal Information Overload–fighting strategies as part of an IORG meeting. Instead of having formal presentations, I invited members to present their own strategies in this area. Maura Thomas, a principal at Burget Avenue Management Services, told the group that she uses Twitter as a search tool to find relevant information instead of browsing through headlines and RSS feeds. She said she reduces the amount of time she would have to spend looking for information that interests her by using Twitter to follow people who are focused on what is relevant to her and who are knowledgeable in the areas of her interests.

The use of Twitter to fight Information Overload sounds like a contradiction in terms, but Thomas stressed that Twitter is like any other tool and interrupts only if you let it. In this same vein, she noted that the key to managing Information Overload is to take control and go on the offensive – and to not allow yourself to be stuck in a defensive position where you are only reacting.

At the same meeting, Lesa Becker, director of organizational learning and development at Saint Alphonsus Regional Medical Center, and Paul Silverman, president of Integra Workshops, both advocated taking control of one's information flow through mindfulness. This means being aware of the present moment, not letting ourselves be distracted by stray thoughts, and being conscious of the impact of the choices we make. It includes carefully picking what technology, such as Twitter, to be involved in, based on the impact it has on you. For some, a service such as Twitter may be helpful; for others, it may be a torrent of extraneous and irrelevant information.

Another strategy for getting more done in a day was also brought up by Silverman, namely to do "the worst thing first." He explained that this strategy pays off because it allows the knowledge worker to take control of his day, get the most pressing and/or nagging task(s) done, and hopefully regain focus for the rest of the day by not having to spend time dreading that particularly unpleasant task. Silverman is right. I have adopted this strategy to some extent and find it works, perhaps by reducing the amount of time I spend dreading any relatively unpleasant tasks that might be on my plate.

One of my own personal strategies is the use of multiple computer monitors. In my case, I have two 22-inch displays, and this permits me to work with documents on the right display and write using the left display. It also significantly cut down on how much printing I now do – indeed, I used to print most documents I needed to work with, but now I rarely print anything anymore except for those rare letters that go via the U.S. Postal Service.

I have found, from time to time, that I must turn one of my monitors off so that my mind does not wander to what might be happening in the news or in an online forum. Doing so allows me to focus all of my concentration in one direction.

How the Other Half Lives

A lot of the people I talk to seem fairly well versed in examining and addressing the problem of Information Overload. But what about the prototypical knowledge worker who is simply trying to finish a day's work?

Respondents to Basex's New Workplace survey from 2006 fit this mold. What was perhaps most striking about the survey was not the statistics but the fact that hundreds of people took the time to provide fairly detailed answers to essay questions about how they cope.

What they said is not universally applicable, but it will resonate with more than a few here.

Meeting overload was a common theme: "I decline meetings to which I am not a primary decision maker."

Carving out time in the day for thought and reflection sometimes necessitates creativity. One survey taker said that "[o]nce I used my e-mail out-of-office message to notify folks that I was 'in a meeting' (with myself!) for a few hours."

Self-discipline is useful. "I basically ignore everything/everyone until [a project or task] is done," "I set goals for time use," and "I break down projects into discrete tasks (and complete them) to avoid boredom."

Many indicated the need to hide, and a few gave advice as to where one can best seclude oneself: "I hide from family [and] coworkers where I will not be found/disturbed (coffee shops, basement, someone else's office/desk work well)" and "I find a secluded spot . . . sometimes it's my car."

Setting the right environment for work is also key: "Usually I will (and don't laugh) get comfortable – this time of year – fuzzy slippers, loose sweatshirt etc., cup of hot chocolate, favorite tunes on the iPod!"

Finally, if all else fails, one person had an idea that might work in extreme situations: "Truthfully, I tend to turn grumpy to the point where no one will want to speak to me until I am finished."

The New Busy Is Heading for a Nervous Breakdown

The workplace today practically demands the constant consumption of information. Ads such as Microsoft's "The New Busy" treat such connectedness as a desirable treat. (See Chapter 20 for an in-depth discussion of this.) Unfortunately, the opposite seems to be true, and more and more people are coming to this realization.

Chris Trytten, director of product marketing at DigitalPersona, told me that there is "so much to process that keeping perspective is difficult. It's easy to get lost in minutiae."

Of course, knowledge workers for the most part spend their lives consuming information. Lee Liming is a technology analyst at the Argonne National Laboratory. His work requires him to do just that and make decisions based upon it. His approach is summarized by one comment he made:

> I can't do my job without information. I am reasonably disciplined about my sources of information, and at the same time not very rigid about it. (When I need something specific, I can get it quickly. The rest of the time, I selectively "surf" what's out there to find stuff that might be interesting. Serendipity is a part of my strategy for success.)

The biggest problem here is ultimately that there simply isn't enough time in the day to get everything done. So we have to pick and choose – when we can – or simply go with the flow and hope that whatever is leftover really wasn't that urgent or important.

Christine Hutcheson, director of marketing at Recommind, a company that makes search tools, hit the nail on the head: "I have no time to absorb and reflect on the information that is sent to me; neither do most people who receive the information I send them."

I'm an information addict – this has been the case since I was very young. My parents tell me I questioned everything, asking "why" repeatedly and never being satisfied with a simple explanation (sorry, Mom).

I'm not alone. Margaret McDonald, a colleague on the board of IORG, told me how her "biggest problem" is her "desire to know everything." This gets her into trouble the same way it has been getting me into trouble all of my life: "[It] leads me to follow links that aren't specifically helpful to the tasks I need to get done in the short term. In fact, even if I were to think of the information I'd uncovered and decide to find it again . . . I wouldn't know how to."

Finally, if you are wondering where all of this information comes from, I think I have found out. Pippa Smart, a consultant at PSP Consulting, inadvertently may be responsible for some of the overload we feel. Her work, Pippa told me, "mostly consists of finding information and using it to create more."

PART

II

WHERE WE ARE AND
WHAT WE CAN DO

Wenn du eine weise Antwort verlangst, mußt du vernünftig fragen.
(If you expect a wise answer, you must ask a sound question.)
—Johann Wolfgang von Goethe

echnology has enabled not only the faster communication of information, but it has allowed anyone and everyone to become an information publisher. While in earlier days, too much information was simply a nuisance, in the Information Age, too much information has become a significant impediment to business and progress.

CHAPTER 12

MANAGING WORK AND WORKERS IN THE TWENTY-FIRST CENTURY

Being busy does not always mean real work.

—Thomas A. Edison

To put the challenges of the knowledge economy in perspective, consider this: At the turn of the twentieth century, approximately 90 percent of the workforce in the United States was comprised of unskilled labor. Even as recently as 25 years ago, the majority of the workforce was made up of industrial workers. In today's workforce, knowledge workers form a plurality.

Indeed, today there are 78.6 million knowledge workers in the United States alone. These knowledge workers are found in all economic stations. An accounting clerk is a good example of an entry-level or rudimentary knowledge worker. An architect or engineer is an excellent example of a skilled knowledge worker, as is an airline pilot or physician. And a rocket scientist or Nobel Prize winner represents the highly skilled knowledge worker.

The Industrial Revolution changed the rules of commerce by making it practical for a merchant to travel relatively quickly to a distant town or city. However, few workers besides itinerant salespeople regularly worked far from home. Until recently, most workers performed their jobs in a building owned by their employer, and that workplace was typically no more than a 30-minute commute away. Today, distance has become irrelevant in commerce and increasingly in labor; where one lives with respect to one's workplace may be irrelevant as long as key utilities (power and Internet connectivity) are present.

In fact, we may be experiencing the end of an era that mandated this separation of home and work, a phenomenon that came about in the Industrial Age because workers had to perform their tasks at a factory in order to work efficiently. These days, many managers, especially those older and more traditional, assert that they cannot manage people whom they cannot see. Some workers will always require the structure of the traditional workplace, but this number will decrease as older workers retire.

Indeed, in earlier – that is, pre-industrial – epochs, there was little separation between work and home. The grocer and his family lived above the shop; the village blacksmith and the tailor performed their work at home as well. Because family members and neighbors were typically nearby, there was a fairly tight integration among work life, family life, and social life.

The model of the separate and distinct workplace that emerged in the Industrial Age became the template for the knowledge economy before technology made it possible to work virtually anywhere. Now it appears that the different aspects of life, namely work, family, and social, are once again coalescing.

Today the ability to remain permanently connected to work regardless of venue has given rise to a new kind of worker, one more nomadic than the oft-romanticized road warrior who flies from meeting to meeting, racking up platinum frequent flier status on the way. This new breed of worker is also different from the telecommuter, who would sit in a fixed home office day in and day out. The nomads may almost never set foot into a formal workplace, yet they might not perform terribly much of their work at home either.

The need to physically go to work has greatly diminished; work can take place at a nearby café with Wi-Fi, at a home office, at customer sites, or in an airplane (especially with the move towards the availability of in-flight Internet access on more and more flights). Additionally, few tools are required: While road warriors might lug 15 pounds of hardware including chargers and spare batteries, nomads use and require only a smartphone or tablet. Such flexibility has the potential to allow for a better work–life balance, although the risk of allowing work to intrude into personal time increases as well.

What one does at work has changed dramatically too. Compared with 1960, the number of jobs today that require high levels of abstract tasks and thinking has increased dramatically while those involving manual tasks have decreased significantly. The number of jobs involving routine tasks decreased noticeably from 1970 through the present as well.

In 2006, Basex surveyed Global 2000 companies and discovered that 80 percent of companies surveyed were not sufficiently prepared for the types of changes we are discussing. A major contributing factor to this problem is that we have yet to see a management science specific to the knowledge economy come about. For lack of anything better, managers have continued to employ the management science that developed out of the Industrial Age despite the great differences in our information-based economy.

It took over 150 years from the dawn of the Industrial Age until we started to see the development of a management science for that period. The turn of the twentieth century brought with it the thinking and experimentation of people such as Frederick Winslow Taylor, who published *The Principles of Scientific Management* in 1911, and Ransom E. Olds, who developed the first automotive assembly line in 1901. Using the Industrial Age's management science in the knowledge economy, as well thought out as it is, is akin to inserting a square peg into a round hole, given the significant changes in how work is performed, the location of the worker, and the nature of the finished product (e.g., physical widgets versus slightly more amorphous products like professional services and consulting).

It probably won't take 150 years from the dawn of the knowledge economy (we can assert that it started in 1982, when AT&T published "The Theory of the Information Age" in an attempt to describe the new era) to develop a canon of management science, but it won't be instantaneous either.

As a result of the chasm between management science and the reality of the knowledge economy, managers are not terribly well prepared to manage knowledge workers. When combined with the fact that over 40 percent of knowledge workers regularly work in nontraditional, non-Dilbertian environments (such as home offices, hotel rooms, and airplanes), where managers cannot directly observe and interact with them, it becomes obvious why we need a new management science sooner rather than later.

Further complicating matters, knowledge workers view their own work as being largely self-managed as well. When surveyed by Basex in 2006, 80 percent indicated that their work is largely autonomous. Only 19 percent agreed with the statement "The work I do is primarily defined through formal policies and procedures."

The lack of a new management science leads to many new problems ranging from Technology Sprawl (my phrase that describes a condition where the deployment of technologies is simply out of control, thereby creating a situation where companies have deployed multiple platforms that attempt to perform the same function), the decimation of work-life balance, and the rise of the problem of Information Overload.

To manage successfully in the knowledge economy, we must recognize key differences in how knowledge workers work. For all intents and purposes, they own the means of production and take it home with them every day, along with invaluable knowledge they acquire as they perform their tasks. Their work is generally not tied to a physical or specific location. They also have rather different expectations, often more demanding, about work and tools compared to the expectations of industrial workers.

Frequently, we fail to understand what knowledge workers do. Indeed, in some cases it may appear as if they are doing nothing. This confusion can appear in other lines of work as well, as illustrated in one episode of the *John Larroquette Show*, a situation comedy set in a bus depot. John Hemingway, the depot's manager (played by John Larroquette), fires someone at the beginning of the episode because he believes he doesn't really do anything. For the remainder of the episode, he tries to figure out exactly what this person's job had been. At the very end, a bus comes crashing through the wall of the depot. The driver exits the bus, turns to the manager, and asks what happened to the person who was supposed to hold up the stop sign as he backed in.

In the course of their jobs, knowledge workers perform tasks that can be grouped under a few overarching categories. The tasks include searching, creating content (sometimes re-creating), thought and reflection, sharing knowledge, and networking. All of these areas can be accomplished in a more traditional way, that is, through direct contact with people, or increasingly, as aided by technology.

A typical day in the life of the knowledge worker is comprised less of traditional work and more of a frenetic pace that intermingles people and technology interruptions with attempts to create content, find things, and attend meetings.

In early 2010, Basex conducted a survey asking knowledge workers to describe their workday. The questions included topics such as how long the typical workday was, how much time was devoted to various information sources, and how knowledge workers were impacted by Information Overload.

The pie graph illustrates the results of this survey.

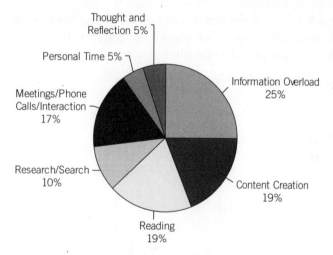

The Knowledge Worker's Day

For our purposes, we define content to include e-mail-related tasks, so e-mail time is essentially split between content creation and reading content. It is interesting to note as well that the vast majority of knowledge workers spend between 30 minutes and no time at all managing their inboxes.

Since the underpinnings of knowledge work are thought and reflection, it's ironic, to say the least, that these activities take up a mere five percent of the day, and Information Overload, the thing that holds the knowledge work back, occupies the greatest part of the day. In 2008, we had discovered that thought and reflection took up only 12 percent of the day, and had found that number worrying enough. The drop to five percent represents a serious problem.

In case you are wondering why allowing time for thought and reflection is important, one need only go as far as findings reported in the May 11, 2009, issue of the *Proceedings of the National Academy of Sciences of the United States* from a study by a team of researchers led by Kalina Christoff at the Department of Psychology, University of British Columbia, Vancouver. The researchers reported that imaging studies showed that the major cross-sections of the human brain become quite active in periods of rest and that they believe that such downtime allows the brain to perform a kind of housekeeping (e.g., synthesizing information that has been acquired or connecting the dots between ideas).

The solution is quite simple, of course: Bring back more time for thought and reflection if we want knowledge workers to be more productive, efficient, and effective.

COMPONENTS OF INFORMATION OVERLOAD

All of the books in the world contain no more information than is broadcast as video in a single large American city in a single year. Not all bits have equal value.

—Carl Sagan

Information Overload is not just one specific problem; it must be seen as an amalgam of multiple problems and issues. Indeed, its origins and manifestations are so varied that few knowledge workers will see the same root causes and impact on their work. One knowledge worker might see it as e-mail overload, another as a search issue, and yet another as a communications issue.

As a result, containing the problem (notice we don't say "eliminating the problem") is a huge logistical challenge. Understanding whence Information Overload comes is the first step toward understanding how to stem the tide.

E-mail Overload

Every knowledge worker has to process multiple low-value ("We are now storing paper clips in the supply closet on the north side of the second floor instead of near the reception area") or no-value (a reply to 300 colleagues saying "Thanks. Great.") e-mail messages each day.

Today e-mail is challenging the knowledge worker's ability to do his job as resources (mostly the time the knowledge worker can allocate to e-mail) are becoming increasingly constrained while millions of knowledge workers continue to pump more and more e-mail into the system, further exacerbating the problem. (See "Information Overload and the Tragedy of the Commons" in Chapter 6.) Making matters even worse is that the quality of e-mail messages is frequently poor when compared to more formal correspondence such as a memo or letter.

E-mail is often written in a rushed fashion, and not much thought is given to its organization. Much is definitely not written in a manner that conveys the most important messages to the recipient(s) in a clear and succinct manner.

A common mistake is to lump multiple issues and themes into one e-mail. The writer believes he is doing recipients a favor and saving them time. Interviews with hundreds of knowledge workers by Basex from 2005 through 2008 reveal that the overwhelming majority of e-mail messages are scanned, not read thoroughly. As a result, the first few sentences may be the only ones that are actually read and comprehended by the recipient(s). What happens to the other 20 paragraphs of the e-mail? That possibly important content disappears into the ether.

E-mail, at this point in time, is also the lingua franca and most important communications tool within the enterprise. It has clearly supplanted the telephone in recent years in terms of frequency of use. As a result, its importance as a communications medium should not be underestimated. Most knowledge workers incorrectly assume that their messages are being understood loud and clear and continue to bang away at the keyboard, sending incomprehensible missives. Given the importance of e-mail, however, knowledge workers need to dramatically change their e-mail habits so that the system itself does not implode.

A 2008 Basex survey revealed that the vast majority of knowledge workers, 84 percent, manage e-mail in their first working block of time; this is also the time when knowledge workers feel they are most productive. Anything that can be done to remove unnecessary e-mail can only improve their productivity.

Unnecessary Interruptions and Recovery Time

According to our research at Basex, the chances of your finishing this chapter without being interrupted several times are slim to none.

In fact, as I was writing this section, my mobile and desk phones rang, I received several instant messages from colleagues, another colleague came to my office in person to ask a question, and numerous e-mail messages arrived in my inbox. The arrival of the e-mail messages, despite their quantity, was the least intrusive of the interruptions because I had turned off my e-mail alert and chime years ago, when it became a continuous noise that never ended.

Nonetheless, these interruptions represent a significant problem in the workplace and are perhaps one of the most visible symptoms of Information Overload.

This is because, instead of multitasking, what we actually do is task switching, which is really a series of continuous interruptions. While we do this in the belief that we are being more efficient and getting more done, nothing could be further from the truth. Each interruption comes with a penalty.

In 2003 through 2005, Basex conducted research that led us to uncover the phenomenon of "recovery time," the time it takes an individual to return to a task after he has been interrupted. Recovery time is generally imperceptible because the individual is not aware – even if he returns to the task – that he is struggling to get back to the point at which he was before the interruption.

For example, a 30-second interruption can result in as much as 5 minutes of recovery time. In some cases, the knowledge worker never returns to the original task and, when and if it is restarted later, the penalty (i.e., recovery time) is far greater. Indeed, interruptions plus recovery time consume as much as 28 percent of the knowledge worker's day.

With a knowledge worker population of approximately 78.6 million, this means we are losing a minimum of 28 billion hours each year in the United States alone.

Each time an individual switches tasks and tries to return to the previous task, he has to go back in time and recollect his thoughts and recall exactly what he has done and what he has yet to do. Some repetitive work may be involved as well (e.g., redoing the last few steps). This of course assumes that the individual returns at all – in some instances, the task is forgotten altogether. The interruptions also increase the likelihood of errors being committed.

When this happens over and over again (which is the case for most people during the workday), the ability to devote thought and reflection to a particular task – the hallmark of the knowledge worker – becomes nearly impossible. The human brain is curious and always seeking new information. As a result, external stimuli – the beeps and bleats of technology indicating a new message or call – are like the siren Loreley, the beautiful Rhine maiden who lured passing sailors to their doom with her singing and long, golden hair.

Because of the increasing likelihood of interruptions, getting work done often requires finding a place without a phone or Internet connectivity of any kind. In the past, an airplane seat would do, but even this is changing. In a 2005 survey by Basex, multiple respondents reported taking drastic measures to work unmolested, such as going into conference rooms, drawing the shades, turning off the lights, and working undetected as well as going to cafés that were not near their office so no one would bother them.

In other words, regardless of where one is, the likelihood of being able to work uninterrupted is near nil.

Indeed, the problem of Information Overload isn't a new one, but it is one that has been exacerbated by the fact that 1.) we have countless new gadgets and tools that deliver an ever increasing amount of information and 2.) the rate of information creation has increased dramatically. As a result, in order to keep up, people attempt to multitask, something that our brains simply aren't capable of handling with any degree of efficiency.

There are certain things knowledge workers can do to control how people interrupt them, whether it is by setting the appropriate presence state on their instant messaging client (e.g., "away," "do not disturb," "available") or putting up a "do not disturb" sign on the door or the entrance to the cubicle. In 2009 a company named CubeGuard was formed to create physical barriers to reduce personal interruptions.

It is important to note that not all interruptions are created equal. With apologies to George Orwell, some interruptions are more equal than others.

An interruption for the interruptee is not necessarily an interruption for the interrupter. In addition, many people have difficulty determining whether a matter is important, urgent, both, or neither. A question may be important, but it could also wait. Someone might have a great sense of urgency to address a matter, but it might not be important.

Further, there are relative degrees of importance, such as personal, group, and organizational importance.

Technology has dramatically increased the problem of interruptions. Even as recently as 20 years ago, only two of the five typical distractions mentioned in the first paragraph of this section were technically feasible, and taking steps to counter them was easier (one could forward the phone to voicemail or set it on do not disturb, and one could close the door and post a do-not-disturb sign). Add to the mix RSS feeds, Twitter, BlackBerry Messenger, and Facebook, and you get the picture.

Over the past decade, the world has seen tremendous changes in the ways people work, and further change is expected. E-mail, closely followed by instant messaging in some circles, has become a staple of communication both internally and externally. By 2006, 40 percent of the knowledge worker population was working from nontraditional, non-Dilbertian environments, ranging from home offices to hotel rooms, and from airport lounges to customer sites, on a regular basis, meaning more than once each week. That figure will grow steadily over the next decade. Indeed, at IBM alone, 40 percent of its workforce works outside of IBM offices each and every day.

In addition, much more so than even five years ago, co-workers and colleagues can be located across time zones and national borders, not in the next cubicle. While companies struggle to integrate cultures with different languages and customs, knowledge workers know that the next interruption may come from 10 time zones away and outside the normal workday, upsetting the delicate work-life balance.

Need for Instant Gratification

Perhaps thanks to the advent of Federal Express in April 1973 (see Chapter 9, The Two Freds), which for the first time enabled next-day delivery, people today also increasingly seek instant gratification. They want everything "absolutely, positively" now. Even overnight isn't good enough anymore.

The expectation of instant gratification is even more acute among younger workers, Generation Y in particular. They have grown up with the expectation that they can instantly communicate via text message, e-mail, mobile phones, and social networks – and that a reply will be immediately forthcoming. As a result, these workers expect and agitate for ways to communicate quickly when they enter an enterprise setting.

This need for instant gratification tends to exacerbate the problem of Information Overload time and time again. Witness a typical instance, in which a coworker sends an e-mail and then immediately contacts the recipient through IM or by phone to ask if he has received the original message. By doing this, the sender not only may have interrupted the recipient with the first e-mail but, by redoubling the attack, interrupted the person a second time. He also wasted his own time by not simply letting the e-mail do its job, which is to serve as an asynchronous means of communication. If an immediate response had been absolutely necessary, which is unlikely, then e-mail was the wrong tool to use in the first place, and IM or a phone call would have been more suitable.

Everything Is Urgent – and Important

For a variety of reasons (some of which are covered in Chapter 9), we work with the presumption that everything we are sending or saying is both important and urgent at the same time. That consequently means that we believe that the tasks the recipient of our missives is undertaking are of lesser importance.

Many companies and, in turn, managers are frequently faulted for making everything a high-priority item – which means that, in actuality, nothing is really a priority.

An issue's importance can be accurately determined only by balancing the criteria laid out earlier – the personal, group, and institutional importance as well as the urgency of an issue.

Most people do not take the time or are not aware of the need to differentiate between the urgent and the important. The result is people thinking that everything that arises is both urgent and important. A question about the financial report that's due in six weeks is important, but it's probably not so urgent that it can't wait for a better time. The following is also true: Something that is not that important – even with a deadline – can wait until it's truly convenient for both parties. What then is a truly good interruption? For the interrupter, it would be an interruption that is both urgent and important to both parties, a confluence of interests.

CHAPTER 14

E-MAIL

Men have become the tools of their tools.

—Henry David Thoreau

ow many e-mail messages did you receive today? How many of these were either important, urgent, or both – to you? And how many e-mail messages did you receive three years ago? Five years ago? Ten years ago?

Unless you just returned from an extended Martian holiday, the answer is probably troubling. Depending on the job, a knowledge worker might be the recipient of several hundred e-mail messages, only a dozen of which, at the most, are both important and urgent for him. According to my research, the overall average number of e-mails received per day is 93 as of 2010. These figures are in addition to the other messaging tools he uses, ranging from desk and mobile phone, to social networks, to instant messaging (IM) and text messaging. According to Pingdom, an Internet monitoring service, 107 trillion e-mail messages were sent in 2010. This amounts to 294 billion e-mails per day.

A look at the actual numbers from large corporations in 2009 is revealing. An Intel employee receives 350 e-mail messages per week on average. Intel executives receive an average of 300 e-mail messages per day. Intel employees spend, on average, 20 hours per week managing e-mail.

At Morgan Stanley, the average employee receives 625 e-mail messages per week. However, the typical Morgan Stanley executive gets over 500 per day.

Three years ago, the same individual who today receives several hundred was likely to receive at most 100 e-mail messages, with a dozen important ones; five years ago, it was probably 50, with a dozen important ones. Ten years ago, those early adopters probably received a dozen – and they were all important and/or urgent.

Update one's status? Send an e-mail to a few hundred of one's closest colleagues.

Finish a report? Send another e-mail to a few hundred of one's closest colleagues.

The fact is that we use e-mail opportunistically rather than with an understanding as to what the impact of its use might be.

Sending that status report to those few hundred colleagues actually cost the organization approximately 24 hours in lost time when one calculates the few minutes each person spent opening the e-mail he didn't need to receive in the first place – plus the "recovery time," which is the time it takes to get back to where the person was in the task that was interrupted.

E-mail has become a form of currency. In this case, the currency is used either to 1.) show how important the writer is or what the writer is doing, by including everyone in the organization as a recipient, or 2.) acknowledge the importance of higher-level managers by making sure that they are carbon-copied on every single e-mail message.

Sorting through one's inbox, let alone reading any quantity of e-mail, can take hours. With an average of three minutes per message, reading 100 e-mails will occupy approximately five hours per day. Clearly, no one can afford to spend that much time reading e-mail. After all, that would leave only three or so hours left to compose new e-mail messages and replies!

Reading only the dozen urgent and important e-mails would only take 36 minutes.

I have often likened the e-mail inbox to a form of assembly line. A message comes in, the dreaded ding sounds, and the drone (me) quickly opens the e-mail message and takes appropriate action.

Until recently, it was assumed that ubiquitous e-mail within the enterprise has made knowledge workers more productive. That may no longer be the case. If e-mail continues in this manner, it has the potential to contravene productivity gains and actually slow down the works.

Action has to be taken. And one solution is for people to read and act only on urgent and important e-mail.

So how does the recipient know which messages are urgent or important? The truth is that he doesn't. An important message could come from an unknown correspondent as much as it could from someone who is familiar. But e-mail authors don't tend to help the recipients here. For example, many e-mails are sent with ambiguous or nonhelpful subject text. The subject field is an opportunity to sell the recipient on why this e-mail is important (to the recipient) and what to expect upon reading.

Contrast these two e-mail messages:

REPLY	FORWARD	DELETE	FOLDER	CHAT	FOLLOW-UP	TOOLS

From: Jason Black
To: Michael Smith
Subject: Accounting Dept.

REPLY	FORWARD	DELETE	FOLDER	CHAT	FOLLOW-UP	TOOLS

From: Jason Black
To: Michael Smith
Subject: New Hires in Accounting Dept./salary budget?

Clearly, the second subject line conveys far more information. Sometimes, if an e-mail thread continues, the subject of the e-mail does not – but it should. In such cases, this should be conveyed in this way:

REPLY	FORWARD	DELETE	FOLDER	CHAT	FOLLOW-UP	TOOLS

From: Jason Black
To: Michael Smith
Subject: June Departmental Review (was New Hires in . . .)

In addition, when replying to an e-mail, an author needs to be conscious of how a reply will be perceived. For example, not replying "with history" is not of much help.

REPLY   FORWARD   DELETE   FOLDER   CHAT   FOLLOW-UP   TOOLS

From: Michael Smith
To: Jason Black
Subject: Re: June Departmental Review
This is a great proposal and I will shepherd it to the right people.

Replying with history ensures that the correct message is delivered without ambiguity.

REPLY   FORWARD   DELETE   FOLDER   CHAT   FOLLOW-UP   TOOLS

From: Michael Smith
To: Jason Black
Subject: Re: June Departmental Review
This is a great proposal and I will shepherd it to the right people.

> **From:**   Jason Black
> **To:**   Michael Smith
> **Subject:** Re: June Departmental Review
> I suggest we use the attached as a template for this client.
> It has worked well for us in the past.

Luis Suarez, an IBM social computing evangelist, threw off the shackles of e-mail, reducing the volume of e-mail he receives by 80 percent, as reported in an article he penned for the *New York Times* in June 2008 entitled "I Freed Myself From E-Mail's Grip".

He wrote:

> I stopped using e-mail most of the time. I quickly realized that the more messages you answer, the more messages you generate in return. It becomes a vicious cycle. By trying hard to stop the cycle, I cut the number of e-mails that I receive by 80 percent in a single week.
>
> It's not that I stopped communicating; I just communicated in different and more productive ways. Instead of responding individually to messages that arrived in my inbox, I started to use more social networking tools, like instant messaging, blogs, and wikis, among many others. I also started to use the telephone much more than I did before, which has the added advantage of being a more personal form of interaction.

Eight E-mail Tips

1. **Use restraint in communications.** Don't cc the world, don't include more people than necessary in any communication, and avoid reply to all wherever possible.

2. **Write clearly.** Better yet, refrain from combining multiple themes and requests in a single e-mail. And make sure the subject is specific as opposed to general. (Writing "Help needed" without further details helps no one, especially the recipient.) These simple steps will add instant clarity with little effort.

3. **Read what you write – before you click send.** Unclear messages result in excessive and unnecessary back-and-forth communications that would have been unnecessary were the first missive unambiguous and to the point.

4. **Read what others write – before replying.** While it would be nice to believe that people will place the most important information at the very beginning, often the key facts are buried in the closing paragraphs. What you are about to ask may already have been covered.

5. **Don't send mixed messages.** E-mail messages should stick to one topic. Writing about the midyear accounting review and adding in a question about a dinner meeting at the end is not only inappropriate, but it is likely the question will be overlooked.

6. **Keep messages short and to the point.** My informal study of the matter has shown that many e-mail recipients don't read past the third sentence.

7. **Value your colleagues' time as if it were your own.** If a response to an e-mail is not immediately forthcoming, don't pick up the phone or send an instant message asking "Did you get my e-mail?"

8. **Avoid the temptation to chime in unnecessarily, with a one-word e-mail such as "Great!" or "Thanks!"** These messages only add to inbox clutter.

Suarez didn't go cold turkey. Because some discussions were "too private and confidential" for public consumption, he did not give up his IBM e-mail address.

He also substituted one technology for another in many cases so the 80 percent decrease in e-mail traffic is illusory to some extent. He used a lot of RSS feeds instead of e-mail subscriptions and relied heavily on Beehive, IBM's Facebook-like social internal networking site. He relied heavily on IM "because it allows real-time interaction."

But the story of Luis Suarez is a cautionary one. Yes, with careful planning and negotiation, you can rid yourself of e-mail.

It's important, however, not to throw the baby out with the bathwater here. There are a lot of good things about e-mail and how we use it (it's less intrusive, we don't have to respond in real time, we document what we are saying) – and there are some not-so-good things as well (we obsess over it, we feel compelled to respond in real time, we send too much of it, we cc and bcc too much, we just don't know when to stop replying).

E-mail has become a critical tool in the knowledge economy arsenal, yet it's also a subject of derision.

Why?

Because we simply don't know how to manage our own use of it and how to use it intelligently.

The research I've done at Basex shows that we lose a great deal to poorly thought out use of a variety of tools, including e-mail, telephone, IM, and so on.

We constantly use the various tools at our disposal to interrupt one another – incessantly. Send an e-mail? Better call or IM to make sure it got there. Received an advisory e-mail? Make sure to say "thanks" to the sender – and might as well reply to all so everyone can see how we're on top of things.

The Cost of Too Much E-mail

I send you an e-mail. You open it, read it, think about it. No big deal. It only takes you just a few minutes to get back to where you were.

But magnify that by the size of your team, maybe 20 people, your division, 2,000 people, your subsidiary, 20,000 people and so on.

And then consider the number of people whom you cc'd on your last note. It was 15, wasn't it? Or was it, as a recent e-mail I saw, more like 300? After all, e-mail is a great way to keep people informed – or is it?

It wasn't even the cc'ing of the 300. Only 10 people really needed to get that note, but the other 290 each lost maybe five minutes of their day. That was, until a colleague hit reply to all.

Let's just stop and recap for a moment. By including 290 people unnecessarily in the e-mail, the sender was responsible for the loss of a minimum of 24 hours of colleagues' time.

Now imagine that, in this 20,000-person organization, one percent of the population sends out e-mail like this once a day.

That's an immediate loss of 4,800 hours a day, or 200 person-days. Just in one day.

Now back to our friend about to hit reply to all, just to say "Great. Thanks." Three hundred people will see an e-mail and many will open it, let's say half. We just lost 12.5 person-hours.

Fortunately, not all 20,000 knowledge workers in the company send out such e-mail. (If they did, it would result in a loss of 20,000 person-days each time it happens.)

Most e-mail messages include far fewer recipients; the average number of people cc'd on e-mail I get is three. (I am not including e-mails with zero cc recipients in this tally.) Still, each time we create a new e-mail message, it has the potential to cost our colleagues quite a bit of time.

What can be done about this is quite simple. When you feel the urge to send an e-mail, choose your recipients carefully. Think of the cc field as a need-to-know field. If a person doesn't fall into the need-to-know category, don't include him. When you get an e-mail, even if you feel the need to be polite, try to restrain yourself and don't select reply to all and write "Great. Thanks."

E-mail and the Network Effect

E-mail usage is a very good example of the network effect (see a discussion of Metcalf's Law in Chapter 6), which describes the effect that one user of a good or service has on the value of that product to others. The network effect usually is thought to be a positive thing. For example, the telephone would be useless if only one or two people had such a device. The more people who own telephones, the more valuable each telephone is to its owner.

E-mail of course has benefited from the network effect. When e-mail was first invented, there was a limited number of users on the ARPANET who could send and receive messages. When MCI Mail and CompuServe's mail system were connected to the NSFNET in the late 1980s, this first commercial use of Internet-based e-mail expanded the base of users greatly, and the value of e-mail increased commensurately as well.

Just as networks become congested at some point after achieving critical mass (an excellent example was MCI's long-distance network in the 1980s, when the company sold the service to more customers than its nascent network could handle, leading to a high number of busy signals and incomplete calls), a negative network effect can ensue.

Today this is happening in e-mail as resources (mostly the time knowledge workers can allocate to e-mail) are becoming increasingly constrained while knowledge workers continue to pump more and more e-mail into the system, further exacerbating the problem. Making matters even worse is that the quality of e-mail messages is frequently lacking when compared to more formal correspondence such as a memo or letter.

Reply to All

One of the most overused and abused features of modern (ca. 2010) e-mail systems is the reply to all feature. The overuse of this function is, without question, a huge source of e-mail overload in almost every organization. But there are still many instances where its use is not only warranted but helpful, including e-mail messages where only a few people are copied and a reply to all is warranted.

In January 2009, amid much fanfare, Nielsen, a global concern whose businesses range from television and other media measurement to business publications, announced that the company would eliminate reply to all functionality in the company's e-mail client. When I first read of this, I had to check my calendar to make sure it was not on or about April 1 and then make sure I was not reading *The Onion*. Needless to say, I was somewhat skeptical. I spoke with Gary Holmes, the company's chief press officer, who confirmed that this was in fact the new policy.

A 2009 memo from the company's CIO, Andrew Cawood, which sounds more as if it were taken from either the comic strip *Dilbert* or the hit television show *The Office* (a documentary-style situation comedy set in the offices of a paper merchant), went like this:

From: Nielsen Communications
Sent: Tue 1/27/2009 10:16 AM
To: All Nielsen People – Worldwide
Subject: 'Reply to All' Function to be Disabled

A Message from Andrew Cawood

In December, the Nielsen Executive Council (NEC) held an Act Now! event to review suggestions from across the business that would eliminate bureaucracy and inefficiency. Beginning Thursday, January 29, we will implement one of the approved recommendations: removing the "Reply to All" functionality from Microsoft Outlook.

We have noticed that the "Reply to All" functionality results in unnecessary inbox clutter. Beginning Thursday we will eliminate this function, allowing you to reply only to the sender. Responders who want to copy all can do so by selecting the names or using a distribution list.

Eliminating the "Reply to All" function will

- Require us to copy only those who need to be involved in an e-mail conversation.

- Reduce non-essential messages in mailboxes, freeing up our time as well as server space.

This is one of the many changes being implemented as a result of the NEC Act Now! initiative. If you have any suggestions on how we can continue to improve the way we work, please send your comments to Nielsen Communications.

Andrew Cawood
Chief Information Officer

The irony of this is only partially revealed by reading the memo. It appears that Nielsen did not actually disable reply to all functionality but merely removed the button that triggers it. According to reports published online, many employees now use the more cumbersome keystroke "shortcut" or simply added the reply to all button back by customizing the toolbar. Much of the online discussion was at Techcrunch, where an article on the topic also appeared. Posts there by people who said they were Nielsen employees indicated that they were largely ignoring the policy through workarounds.

In case it's not apparent to the reader, I do not agree with this approach to solving the reply to all problem. It's not that reply to all abuse doesn't significantly contribute to Information Overload – it does. Rather, it's this sort of knee-jerk reaction to the problem that results, if anything, in more Information Overload rather than less, as the move not only generated countless e-mail messages discussing it but required employees to spend time and effort figuring out workarounds.

Knowledge workers click on reply to all for several reasons, including the fact that it's typically next to the reply button (the one that would generate just a reply e-mail message to the sender). Indeed, instead of eliminating the button, Nathan Zeldes, president of the Information Overload Research Group (IORG) and the individual responsible for Information Overload reduction strategies at Intel at the time, had a far more prosaic suggestion: Move the position of reply to all on the toolbar away from reply, making people less likely to click it.

My advice to Nielsen and others is along similar lines: I would have recommended that Nielsen modify the e-mail client to notify the sender if he were about to send to more than five people and ask if he wished to continue.

As to how the change is working for them, Holmes, in the course of a conversation a few months after the announcement, declined to comment.

On the other extreme, Google Labs provides a Gmail add-on that makes reply to all the default reply setting.

In September 2008, Darick Tong, a Gmail engineer, posted this on the official Google blog:

> When we're working on features for Gmail, the email etiquette on the team is to reply all so everyone involved is kept in the loop. Mark was an intern here this past summer who got frustrated when he'd reply to an email only to realize that he forgot to reply all and had to resend the message. Thus, this Labs feature, which makes reply all your default selection.

The reaction online was swift and not favorable. Four members of the LifeHacker discussion forum had the most insightful comments. To wit:

> Oh god, I hope people at my office don't find out about the reply-all default preference. I already get so, so many unnecessarily "reply-all"-ed e-mails it's not even funny.

* * *

> I have always hated reply-all, and now it can be a default? *I feel cold.*

* * *

> Reply All . . . that brings back some fun memories from my days in Cubeland. I always enjoyed the 4 pages of quoted conversation, preceded by "Me too."

* * *

> Setting Reply to All as the default should come with a big warning dialog advising the user that replying to all too many times can result serious injury or death, or at the very least, the recipients wishing these things upon you. Or maybe you should have to pass an e-mail etiquette test before being able to change the setting.

In case, after all this, you are not convinced that reply to all can be a problem, I will leave you with two scenarios.

The first I found in a comment posted to an April 2008 article citing my advice on this topic. The article was written by Toni Bowers at TechRepublic.

A knowledge worker employed in a fairly large call center reported that someone sent an all-hands e-mail (to 2,000+ people) to see if someone would work her shift for one day in the coming week. The questionable wisdom of this notwithstanding, the real problem began when colleagues began to reply to all, at first saying they couldn't work the shift. This was followed by other reply to all e-mails, admonishing various senders "Please don't send to everyone next time" and "Yeah and don't reply all."

Things got a bit worse after a while, and the conversation degraded: "Well, you reply all too so you're no better" and "You're all stupid, we're trying to work here" are representative of the banter.

This avalanche eventually overloaded the e-mail server, and the IT department had to shut it down.

The second was related to me by Colonel Peter Marksteiner, who told me about what he referred to as a "data smog outbreak" during the Air Force Cyber Symposium at Maxwell Air Force Base in Alabama in July 2008. Several hundred experts from the military were present to "identify strengths, weaknesses, opportunities and threats to the Air Force in the cyberspace domain," according to the meeting's Web site. The very same week, Marksteiner reminded me, was the inaugural meeting of the Information Overload Research Group in New York City.

In what was a truly powerful demonstration of the need to manage e-mail as much as other threats, a somewhat unsophisticated e-mail user forwarded what the sender referred to as "the funnest (*sic*) card/dice game" to multiple respondents. The message ended up being sent to two fairly large e-mail group lists, and the ensuing barrage of "take me off your list" replies – with many users hitting reply to all – shut down the e-mail server supporting two bases, including the one that was hosting the cyberconference. Ironically, while the brass were contemplating the threat hackers and terrorists in far-off lands such as China and Russia might pose, a single user within the base managed to render thousands of military e-mail accounts inaccessible.

Profanity in E-mail (Expletive Deleted)

The term "expletive deleted" entered the lexicon in the early 1970s when President Richard Nixon provided edited transcripts of internal White House discussions to the public with profane words and phrases indicated in that manner.

Although most knowledge workers wouldn't need this type of redacting, the problem of profanity in e-mail at Goldman Sachs has apparently reached critical mass, and, in 2010, the firm announced that it will enforce a strict policy of no dirty words in electronic messages. This action is notable because a June 2007 e-mail from a Goldman executive was extensively quoted at Senate hearings in April 2010, including the phrase "that . . . was one s--t deal." The firm's policy covers instant and text messages in addition to e-mail messages.

Knowledge workers have long complained that there is simply too much e-mail, but, until recently, profanity in e-mail was not a huge concern. However, the use of naughty words in some organizations has reached epic proportions. The news about Goldman and e-mail has been making headlines in the business press, and one comment posted on the *Wall Street Journal* Web site was telling. Arun Nisargand wrote:

> I am amazed at the lack of professionalism on the Wall Street and the investment banking community. In the engineering community and large Fortune 500 corporation where I work, profanity has never been a issue. It is not used or tolerated. In verbal, written, or e-mail communication. There is no written policy or directive. We just know how to behave.

While cleaning up one's language may indeed be an admirable pursuit, the emphasis on dirty words (think George Carlin) obfuscates the real problem, which is that we send too much e-mail period.

Perhaps, however, some good will come out of this, namely that the 34,000 people will, as a result of the new policy, end up sending fewer e-mail messages each day, and that the practice will spread beyond Wall Street.

Expletive deleted, maybe eliminating obscene e-mail is the silver bullet we've been waiting for.

A Day Without E-mail

While I came up with the idea of Information Overload Awareness Day (see page 223) in 2009 to draw attention to the problem, others have also found ways of achieving the same goal.

In November 2009, Belgium celebrated a day without e-mail, where people were encouraged to send as few e-mail messages as possible, according to the government minister who organized the event. This minister even cited my research on the cost of Information Overload as part of the justification for the occasion.

While turning off the spigot (or the computer) may sound like an admirable pursuit, it is inherently misguided. In the mid-2000s, hundreds of companies, including Deloitte & Touche, Intel, and U.S. Cellular, experimented with no e-mail Fridays or similar concepts. The goal was to halt the flow of noncritical internal e-mail (e-mailing customers or responding to urgent matters would be permissible under such codes, however). Violators were made to wear funny hats or shirts and/or pay a token fine.

The problem with these experiments is that many knowledge workers ignored the rule, and those who didn't were faced with twice as much e-mail (both to send and receive) as normal after the e-mail holiday.

While the goal may have been to increase face-to-face and telephone contact, the result was business as usual. Workers stockpiled e-mail messages as drafts, abiding by the letter of the law and not sending them, and sent them en masse after the holiday.

What managers should have been doing was to find new and more efficient means of communications for workers so that fewer e-mail messages overall would be sent – every day, not just on a no-e-mail day.

The reason this is not happening very quickly is that e-mail has become what I call the path of least resistance. It's frequently used when another – more suitable – tool should be used. Examples of this range from word processing (writing long documents in e-mail) to instant messaging (asking whether I want Russian dressing on my sandwich is more appropriate via instant messaging than e-mail for a variety of reasons).

In October 2009, a *Wall Street Journal* writer, Jessica Vascellaro, proclaimed that e-mail's reign as "king of communications" was over. Her rationale for this stance is that as we increasingly are connected 24/7 through mobile devices, the near-real-time nature of communication via services such as Twitter and instant messaging leave the slower pace of e-mail in the dust.

Meanwhile, more and more e-mail messages are sent every day. New tools such as Twitter and Facebook have not supplanted e-mail but instead often contribute to more and more e-mails being sent, as many users do not turn off e-mail notifications. Indeed, the normal daily quotient of e-mail continues to rise.

While Vascellaro raised some valid points, the e-mail-ingrained culture of the business world has not yet been threatened. Changing the way that we use e-mail is a daunting task.

Today, e-mail serves as a common medium that supports rapid and near-real-time information exchange for hundreds of millions of people. Making changes in a small organization can be difficult;

just imagine what it would take to change *all* of those people's ways of working.

Finally, while e-mail may seem to be an unending challenge for the knowledge worker, it's really just the tip of the iceberg. Information Overload is far more complex than too much e-mail. It's too much content, poor search tools . . . the list goes on and on.

It will take a lot more thought and reflection in terms of studying how millions of people communicate and interact through e-mail before we can really begin to effect positive change. But that day will surely come.

What to Do With 2.5 Billion E-mail Messages

In December 1, 2006, amended Rules of Civil Procedure concerning electronically stored information (ESI) took effect in all federal courts. This change impacted a large number of constituencies, ranging from CIOs to records managers, to lawyers and judges.

These rules came about because 95 percent of records are created and stored electronically, and, as a result, all discovery is now e-discovery. It will be no surprise to learn that the volume of ESI is exponentially greater than the volume of stored paper records (which we will refrain from calling SPRs). E-mail is unquestionably the main culprit. A single knowledge worker can easily generate 25,000 pieces of e-mail per year; a company with 100,000 employees could find itself with 2.5 billion e-mails in its archives.

The mass of e-mail is one of several reasons for the new rules. Another is that electronic information is dynamic; a lot of it changes without operator intervention. In addition, ESI is much more difficult to destroy than are stored paper records.

Perhaps of greater significance is that ESI may need to be retrieved or restored – and this may not always be possible. (See Chapter 8.)

But there's more. (Disclaimer: I am only going to be able to scratch the surface here – an in-depth analysis of the new rules and their impact on knowledge economy companies would require a separate book.)

New Rule 26(f) requires parties in proceedings to discuss "any issues relating to preserving discoverable information." The need to preserve evidence has to be balanced, according to an Advisory Committee Note, with the need to continue routine activities because halting the operation of a computer system could put a company out of business today.

Rule 34 adds ESI as a separate category of information, stipulating that the rule covers all types of information, regardless of how or where it is stored. The Advisory Note makes it clear that this is not meant to create a "routine right of direct access to a party's electronic information system, although this might be justified in some circumstances."

But for me the most interesting part is found in Rule 26(b)(2) (B), covering inaccessible data. What we create today may not be accessible at some point in the future. The rule addresses ESI that is considered inaccessible, given the undue burden and expense of retrieving it if this is even possible. A party is not required to provide discovery of ESI from sources that it identifies as not reasonably accessible (due to the undue burden and cost that would be incurred) unless the requesting party can demonstrate "good cause."

Unfortunately, the rule does not define the term "inaccessible," which may turn out to be a good thing. (It also fails to identify sources, which we can infer to be a place where data [or information] is stored.) What is "inaccessible" today might – with a change in technology – very well become accessible tomorrow; moreover, what *is* indeed accessible today might not be accessible tomorrow. Sources that might be considered inaccessible at a given point might include backup media and deleted data. One thing is clear: If a document or data point is regularly accessible in the normal course of business, a party may not make it "inaccessible" to avoid producing it.

I'll conclude this section with a look at the safe harbor provision for ESI loss. New Rule 37(f) prohibits a court from imposing sanctions for failing to provide ESI lost as a result of normal system operations. This means that, since IT systems may routinely modify, overwrite, and delete information, companies need not worry about such lost ESI. The only time a company must intervene is if litigation is reasonably anticipated, at which time a litigation hold would serve notice to all records custodians that the normal operation of the system must be suspended. Keep in mind that, in the knowledge economy, everyone is his own records custodian.

Deleting E-mail, Deleting Knowledge

Many litigation lawyers, among others, maintain that a corporate-wide program of e-mail deletion, say on a 30-day or similar basis, would be a good risk management policy for many corporations so that "sensitive" e-mail messages might be deleted but not in a manner that would be illegal. However, it would be completely illegal to learn of a Justice Department investigation and start hitting the delete key. Unfortunately, companies pursuing such general e-mail deletion policies are deleting the history and experience contained in those e-mail messages as well.

There is probably little that goes on within an organization that is not, in some manner, shape, or form documented in an e-mail message. In fact, e-mail systems have become a very important aspect of a company's institutional memory, holding the sum of what has been perceived, discovered, and learnt by numerous employees with various points of view and differing expertise.

In the past two decades, e-mail messages to external parties have replaced written correspondence, both the kind prepared on an IBM Selectric typewriter with carbon paper and, more recently, the kind stored in word processing files. To the best of my knowledge, no one has suggested deleting older Word files on a monthly basis.

The genesis of e-mail deletion policies has much more to do with the cost of online storage; in the pioneering days of corporate e-mail, when network server space was regularly measured in megabytes and then hundreds of megabytes, pruning e-mail file size made sense – it was practical only to preserve the most recent e-mail messages. Although today IT managers still worry about managing storage, it is not because space is scarce.

Granted, managing knowledge is a far more ambitious task than even trying to catalog all that is known. Success here is dependent on the development of a culture and mechanisms that foster ideas and thoughts, in addition to having a system that is all-knowing about people, places, and things.

However, I cannot imagine flushing out a major component of a firm's knowledge every 30 or even 60 days. Simply from personal experience, I regularly find valuable information in my own e-mail files; sometimes the knowledge is contained in e-mails written or received three or four years ago, sometimes it is found in e-mail messages that are 10 years old. Magnify my experience by a corps of millions, and it is mind-boggling to think how much valuable knowledge might be destroyed by misguided managers every month.

CHAPTER **15**

THE GOOGLIFICATION OF SEARCH

Knowledge is of two kinds; we know a subject ourselves, or we know where we can find information upon it.

—Samuel Johnson

As they exist today, Information Overload and search are at loggerheads, at opposite ends of the spectrum. One would assume that a search tool would provide correct information, such as answers or relevant documents, when used. This is less likely to be the case as time goes on and more information is created.

One reason for search's poor showing is what I call the "Googlification" of search.

Today, the Internet (largely in the guise of the World Wide Web) is the starting point for knowledge workers in search of answers. Many of their questions, however, will go unanswered. According to comScore, a market research firm, over 2.2 million searches are executed across the globe on the Web every minute. Not surprisingly, many of these queries will be unsuccessful.

The search tool of choice today is Google. Google is the latest in a series of search engines on the Internet that started with Archie in 1990. Google is notable for its minimalist user interface (in contrast to its competitors, which built Web portals around their search engines) as well as its PageRank technology, which ranks Web pages based on the number and PageRank of other Web sites and pages that link to them, predicated on the premise that pages that other sites link to more are worthy of a higher ranking in search results.

Google's clean home page and simple search box makes it appear deceptively simple to sort through information. Indeed, using Google just may be too easy.

While there are two types of search, keyword and category (or taxonomy), Google only uses the former. Users type a few words into the search box, and that is supposed to generate satisfactory results. Unfortunately, the reality is that over 50 percent of all searches fail where the failures are immediately apparent. This is a figure that has been cited by numerous researchers.

What these researchers failed to recognize was that not all search failures were apparent and obvious. After studying the matter further, I found out that 50 percent of the searches a user believes to have succeeded failed in some way although the user was unaware of this failure. (See the "Failed Searches" section in Chapter 8 for a more in-depth look at this phenomenon.)

These failures happen because keyword search isn't always the best approach. It is possible to get incredibly precise search results with keyword search. Indeed, there is no question that keyword search is a powerful search function. Being able to enter any word, term, or phrase allows for great precision in some situations – but it can also result in an inability to find useful information in many others.

However, the use of a taxonomy, or categories, in search allows knowledge workers to follow a path that will both provide guidance and limit the number of extraneous search results returned. Using a taxonomy can improve search recall and precision due to four factors:

1. In keyword search, users simply do not construct their search terms to garner the best results.
2. Users also do not use enough keywords to narrow down the search.
3. Google's search results reflect Google's view of the importance of a Web page as determined by the company's PageRank technology, which looks at the number of high-quality Web sites that link to a particular page. This doesn't necessarily mean that the first pages in the search results have the best content but only that they are the most popular.

4. Web site owners can manipulate Google and other search engine results through search engine optimization (SEO). There is an entire industry built around this service, and the use of SEO can dramatically impact the positioning of a Web site on the results page.

Unfortunately, in part thanks to Google's ubiquity as well as its perceived ease of use, the concept of search to most people seems to equal keyword search. As more and more Web sites and publications (the *New York Times* being one prominent example) move to a Google search platform, the ability to find relevant information may be compromised.

In the case of the *Times*, much of the search functionality previously available disappeared when it deployed Google Custom Search. Only those visitors who know enough to use the *Times*' "advanced search" option are able to specify a date range and whether they want to search by relevancy, newest first, or oldest first. Although the *Times* has been working to improve it, the "advanced search" experience is still lacking compared to the newspaper's earlier system.

Thanks to the Googlification of search, however, most visitors access only the search box, and their ability to find the answers they are seeking is hobbled by that system's limitations.

Search and the Quest for the Perfect Dishwasher

Even if a knowledge worker were to enter a perfectly-formed query into Google's search box, there is still a high degree of probability that he would not find what he was looking for. While, in the past, providing the best, most accurate search results and winnowing the wheat from the chaff had more to do with not providing out-of-date and/or non-relevant information than anything else, today that is no longer the case.

In the Web's earliest days, once marketers figured out how to game the search engines of the time with keywords that had nothing to do with the content on the associated Web page, search had become fairly useless. Indeed, it was the broad acceptance of Google in the early 2000s that made Web search useful again. Search engines including Google continue to be overwhelmed by various forms of Webspam; as soon as Google and others vanquish one form of spam, however, another rears its ugly head.

Paul Kedrosky, founder of GrokSoup (now defunct), one of the first hosted blog platforms, an analyst on CNBC, and publisher of a financial blog, tried to use Google to help him select a new dishwasher in December of 2009. His conclusion (which was dispatched as a tweet): "To a first approximation, the entire web is spam when it comes to appliance reviews."

In "Dishwashers, and How Google Eats Its Own Tail," an article that was published in *Infectious Greed* on December 13, 2009, Kedrosky explains how Google "has become a snake that too readily consumes its own keyword tail" as marketers exploit Google's technology to rise to the top of the search results page, regardless of whether they deserve to be there or not.

As a result of this attack of sorts, Web search's usefulness is once again in question as low-quality, unreliable, and frequently plagiarized content continues to supplant legitimate entries in search results.

It appears that getting the right answer or response from Google has never been harder, and even Google is taking notice of the problem. On January 21, 2011, writing in the *Official Google Blog*, Matt Cutts, the head of Google's Webspam team, wrote that there had been "a spate of stories" [examples including "On the Increasing Uselessness of Google," "Why We Desperately Need a New (and Better) Google," and "Content Farms: Why Media, Blogs & Google Should Be Worried"] concerning Google's less than stellar search quality.

Google is fighting the war on Webspam on three fronts, namely 1.) individual Web pages with repetitive spammy words and phrases, 2.) hacked Web sites, and 3.) content farms (sites that either produce shallow content of their own or copy other sites' content). The topic of Webspam could fill a book unto itself but it is worthy of this brief mention because it brings Information Overload to a whole new level in terms of making it harder for knowledge workers to find what they are looking for.

If we were to repeat our study of the failure rate for searches, Webspam would most likely result in an increase in the number of searches that actually failed but were not recognized as a failure by the searcher. This is a dangerous trend if it continues unabated.

The problem has even given rise to a new type of search engine. Blekko, "a better way to search the web," uses slashtags to cut out spam sites and my tests of the search engine show that it provides significantly less spam in its results.

Google has heard "the feedback from the web loud and clear" and believes that the company "can and should do better." In January 2011, it announced changes that combat all three types of Webspam. This includes changes to its algorithm and enables users to provide "explicit feedback" on spammy sites.

The Search Experience

Many search firms, including Google, are trying to improve the search experience, and there are a few encouraging signs of progress.

In 2010, Google introduced a new search interface, Google Instant, which shows constantly evolving search results based on the individual letters and words that are typed into the search box. This is a dramatic change from the original clean Google page.

Indeed, compared to the traditional Google interface, Google Instant can almost be termed somewhat glitzy. The question that needs to be asked, however, is whether the new functionality actually makes for a better search tool.

Google thinks that Google Instant is a crucial step forward. Speaking at the launch of Google Instant in September 2010, Google cofounder Sergey Brin commented, without a trace of irony, that "we want to make Google the third half of your brain." Marissa Mayer, the company's vice president for search products and user experience, noted that "there's even a psychic element to it."

What Google Instant does is start to show search results as one types the search query. In some respects, Google Instant appears to know what to type before one types it. (This in itself is not a brand-new feature; Google has had a "type ahead" suggestion option for some time.)

With Google Instant, as one starts to type, results appear. For example, in one test, I used the search query "BMW 335d review." When I typed the letter "b," "bank of america" and "best buy" appeared as choices, and search results for Bank of America appeared. Once I added the letter "m," the system correctly guessed that I was going to type "bmw" and results for BMW appeared.

In some cases, the correct or best answer or content appears before one finishes typing. Indeed, by the time I had finished typing "bmw 335d," the word "review" appeared in gray and the appropriate results were immediately below the search bar, including reviews in *The Diesel Driver* and *Automobile* magazines.

The order of word entry in a multiword search query does not seem to influence the final result, but the interim results displayed as the entry is formulated will vary, of course.

My tests of Google Instant do indicate that the new feature improves the user experience to a small extent. Unfortunately, while it may make searching faster, Google Instant does little if anything to provide better search results. What it does do is provide search-before-you-type functionality by conducting searches and displaying results based on the most likely word combinations, determined as one types. This improves one's ability to refine a search without hitting enter, so one can see if a mistake in wording occurred or if one needs to add terms to narrow the search parameters.

As mentioned, Google has had the "type ahead" feature that completes the search query for quite a while now, and the basic mechanics that dictate suggested words appear unchanged. The interface has been tweaked, so instead of simply having the suggestions appear below the query in a drop-down menu, the most likely one appears in light gray text, completing the query. Users can select that text if it fits their search or use the arrow keys to select the suggestions from the drop-down list that changes as the word is being typed.

The real change to the user interface is the display of instant search results that appear under the search box. These suggested responses can serve to guide the knowledge worker into making a more precise search query (i.e., formulate the search query better) and zero in on the exact result that is sought. But this is all dependent on the knowledge worker inputting a properly formulated search query in the first place.

According to Google, the average search query takes nine seconds to type, and Google Instant can cut that down by two to five seconds. Put differently, for the 78.6 million knowledge workers in the United States, if each uses Google 20 times per day for a search, each knowledge worker would save 70 seconds. That would add up to 1,263,889 man-hours per day that Google Instant would be saving.

Despite the potential time savings, Google Instant does not really address the main problems with search. One of the fundamental problems with search is that a query returns results, not answers. Indeed, in many cases, the results page only contributes to the problem of Information Overload as the knowledge worker still has to sift through the results to find what may or may not be the "right" answer.

Although a user can use the instant results to narrow down a search more quickly by not having to hit enter and refresh the results manually, the underlying search process has not changed. Thus, my concerns with the overall Google search experience remain the same: The very way in which search tools function today exacerbates the problem of Information Overload and does little to alleviate the problem.

Does the King of the Watusis Drive an Automobile?

Today, a search results set may include images, videos, blogs, news, Twitter posts ("tweets"), book content, discussion forums, and more, thanks to the information explosion we are experiencing and our need for faster and better information.

In the 1957 movie *Desk Set*, Katharine Hepburn played Bunny Watson, a corporate librarian at the research department at a television network whose department answered questions much in the way we use search engines today. (A memorable quote from the movie: "Oh yes, we've looked that up for you, and there are certain poisons which leave no trace, but it's network policy not to mention them on our programs.")

Spencer Tracy plays a computer salesman whose company is installing a mainframe computer at the network that would ostensibly replace the organization's research department among other functions.

The librarians, of course, are shocked at the concept of a machine replacing them.

To demonstrate that Bunny and her colleagues can better respond to inquiries than the new computer system, they devise a challenge. The question that fuels the competition is: "Does the king of the Watusis drive an automobile?"

Of course the researchers provide a far better answer ("He drives a specially built Pontiac") than the computer was capable of.

Oddly enough, or perhaps not, a computer still can't replace corporate librarians and still can't tell us what kind of car the king of the Watusis drives. At this point, Google (and other search engines) are capable of answering very simple (simply phrased) questions and not much more.

But they are getting better.

Today, when I go to Google and type in "weather" – actually just the letter "w" suffices – I get an option to view weather for a particular location (and Google will remember my location), as opposed to the traditional collection of links that cover the gamut in meteorology.

When I type in "restaurants in New York," a map appears showing me seven prominently featured possibilities with a legend on the side, with links to restaurant reviews for each. I'm not sure how Google arrived at this particular list, which range from the Russian Tea Room, to Fraunces Tavern (where George Washington made his farewell speech to his troops), to Joe's Shanghai.

Google executives have told me they have brought together some of the world's top linguists, psychologists, and computer scientists to make this search response happen and that they study how users actually use Google to learn what they want.

As the sheer mass of information continues to grow, what users want and expect has changed. Not surprisingly, Google executives tell me that users want answers. Google admittedly has done more to provide answers than earlier experiments in natural language query such as Ask Jeeves, a late 1990s experiment in such search that unfortunately couldn't answer the vast majority of the questions posed to it.

Today Google can in fact tell me a lot, if I know how to ask. For example, if I want to know what 33°C is in Fahrenheit, all I have to do is type in "33 degrees Celsius in Fahrenheit," and Google immediately tells me that the Fahrenheit equivalent is 91.4 degrees. If I want to know how much 50 euros is worth today, I type "50 euros" and Google tells me that it's "67.9900 US dollars." I don't even have to tell the system I am looking for the dollar equivalent; it makes that assumption and provides the information.

In 2010, the year I am writing this book, Google is, without a doubt, the world's most popular search tool, but this wasn't always the case. Indeed, the likelihood is that a Google successor (it might even be Blekko) may be just around the corner, and that title will belong to someone who comes up with a way of providing even better answers.

Improving Search

To increase the odds that you will find what you are looking for, we've prepared five simple search tips that should result in better and more accurate results, regardless of where you are searching.

1. **Boolean logic.** Search engines typically use a form with a search box into which one types the search query. To control the search results, use Boolean logic by typing AND or OR. Many search engines including Google default to AND when processing search queries with two or more words. To exclude words, use NOT (java NOT coffee, java coffee). For increased relevance, use NEAR (restaurants NEAR midtown Manhattan).

2. **Options.** Most search engines include options. (On Google, these are found by clicking on Advanced Search). Use options to narrow down the field you are searching. Examples include file format (.ppt,.doc,.pdf, etc.) or Web site (basex.com).

3. **Search tools.** When it comes to search, one size does not fit all. Use a variety of search tools beyond Google. Try search visualization tools such as Cluuz and KartOO on the Web and KVisu for behind the firewall.

4. **Meta search engines.** A meta search engine runs several searches simultaneously. Tools that may be helpful include Clusty and Dogpile.

5. **Archived (out-of-date) materials or nonexistent Web sites.** The Wayback Machine on the Internet Archive is useful for both older versions of Web pages and sites that have disappeared over time.

CHAPTER 16

SINGLETASKING

In order to improve the mind, we ought less to learn, than to contemplate.

—René Descartes

When computers were able to perform only one task at a time, life was much simpler – especially when viewed with respect to Information Overload. (Of course, when most people's desks didn't even have computers, life was even simpler as it was unlikely that a file or folio would jump up on the desk demanding attention while the worker was focused on something else.)

Computers were first introduced into the office at large via video display terminals (VDTs), "dumb" terminals that had no processing power and served only to connect the user to a mini or mainframe computer. (Earlier users connected via electromechanical teletypewriters, but these were not widely deployed.) These VDTs were capable of supporting one task at a time, be it word processing or data entry.

Unlike today, where every desk is likely to have a computer, most jobs prior to the early 1990s did not require constant computer access; many required no computer access at all. Workers frequently shared computer terminals, either via a separate work-station dedicated to computer access or a terminal placed in between two desks so that it could be shared by two workers.

The earliest personal computers, which started to arrive en masse in offices in the mid-1980s, were also limited to one task at a time, although they were "smart" as opposed to dumb because the computer power and storage were local.

These early machines ran on MS-DOS, short for Microsoft Disk Operating System, the operating system that dominated the IBM PC-compatible marketplace from the introduction of the first IBM PC in 1981 until around 1995, when Windows (which was partially DOS based) started to supplant it.

With minor exceptions (software that provided multitasking-like functionality), in a pre-Windows world, a user could run one program at a time and therefore perform one task at a time. This meant that other computer programs were not able to interrupt the worker's focus, for example, on a document or spreadsheet. It was not only inconceivable but technically impossible for an alert for an instant message (which really didn't exist then anyway) or a new e-mail message to pop up in the middle of the knowledge worker's work.

Multitasking, however, which is the ability for a computer to execute more than one task or program simultaneously, was the much sought objective for computer systems designers.

In their view, multitasking would allow knowledge workers to become more efficient. Users could accomplish more if computers could do more.

By enabling technology-assisted multitasking, those early pro-grammers unknowingly started a chain reaction that has led to the crushing Information Overload we see today.

Not only are today's computers capable of multitasking and provide larger displays so more programs can appear at the same time, but some users use multiple displays to have even more resources available to them simultaneously. Interestingly, research shows that the most important thing to consider when selecting a monitor setup is not the number of monitors but pixels, with the optimum being around 2560 ×1440 on a 26- to 30-inch screen.

Computers today provide so many useful and appealing options to do that a knowledge worker can procrastinate for hours, checking personal e-mail, chatting with friends, visiting social networking sites, reading news – before performing actual work.

"We Have Met the Enemy and He Is Us" was the title I gave a report on Information Overload back in 2007. At that point, I had studied a large enough sampling of knowledge workers to see a pattern emerge: A large portion of the interruptions and lost productivity that knowledge workers deal with is self-created.

It turns out that most people have very little self-control. Indeed, they devote what Linda Stone, a former executive at both Apple and IBM who studies such things, called continuous partial attention to work. Steven Johnson, an American science writer, describes continuous partial attention this way in his 2005 book, *Everything Bad Is Good for You*: "It usually involves skimming the surface of the incoming data, picking out the relevant details, and moving on to the next stream. You're paying attention, but only partially. That lets you cast a wider net, but it also runs the risk of keeping you from really studying the fish."

In 2008, Linda Stone wrote in *Business Week* that continuous partial attention is not multitasking, although I think she is engaging in a case of Talmudic *pilpul*, or hairsplitting, by taking on that argument. On her Web site, around the same time, she commented:

> Continuous partial attention describes how many of us use our attention today. It is different from multitasking. The two are differentiated by the impulse that motivates them. When we multitask, we are motivated by a desire to be more productive and more efficient. We're often doing things that are automatic, that require very little cognitive processing. We give the same priority to much of what we do when we multitask – we file and copy papers, talk on the phone, eat lunch – we get as many things done at one time as we possibly can in order to make more time for ourselves and in order to be more efficient and more productive. To pay continuous partial attention is to pay partial attention – CONTINUOUSLY. It is motivated by a desire to be a LIVE node on the network. Another way of saying this is that we want to connect and be connected. We want to effectively scan for opportunity and optimize for the best opportunities, activities, and contacts, in any given moment. To be busy, to be connected, is to be alive, to be recognized, and to matter.

We pay continuous partial attention in an effort TO NOT MISS ANYTHING. It is an always-on, anywhere, anytime, any place behavior that involves an artificial sense of constant crisis. We are always on high alert when we pay continuous partial attention. This artificial sense of constant crisis is more typical of continuous partial attention than it is of multitasking.

In other words, continuous partial attention is a state of being, while multitasking is an activity. Obviously, they feed into each other; our desire to maintain what has also been called "ambient awareness" by being constantly in the loop leads to multitasking as an attempt to stay up-to-date with events as they unfold.

Attempts to multitask unfortunately do not do us much good; researchers appear to have demonstrated that human beings can perform only one task at a time. Allowing one's self to exist in a state of continuous partial attention leads to inevitable multitasking, and our brains simply aren't capable of handling this with any degree of efficiency.

In a 2007 interview with *American Way* magazine, I put it this way: "You only think you are more productive, [but] you're really drinking the Kool-Aid of productivity." Over time the relentless intrusions that fuel frenetic multitasking can really add up.

When I spoke to Doug Heintzmann, director of strategy at IBM Lotus Software, he noted the "penalty that you pay to do the context switching between all the various different pieces of information coming in is frankly quite debilitating." The only way he can survive is by "finding some time, a number of hours to concentrate on the key, most important project that I have to tackle, [and getting] heads down, and in the zone."

Instead of multitasking, what we do is continuously switch among tasks, which is really a series of continuous interruptions. We do this in the belief that we are being more efficient and effective in our work, but each time we task switch it is actually a tiny interruption, and it comes with the same penalty as a larger interruption. (See "Unnecessary Interruptions and Recovery Time" in Chapter 13.)

The negative impact of multitasking is supported by studies conducted by Decio Coviello, Andrea Ichino, and Nicola Persico and presented in their working paper "Don't Spread Yourself Too Thin: The Impact of Task Juggling on Workers' Speed of Job

Completion." Through studies of the case loads of Italian judges, they found that judges who had multiple tasks to complete at once were slower to complete those tasks then those who had tasks assigned to them sequentially to complete one after another. They conclude that each new task assigned pulls focus and energy away from already existing tasks, slowing the entire process.

Multitasking is not limited to knowledge work; nor is it limited to the relatively safe realm of the office or cubicle.

A 2010 study at Ohio State University showed that the number of pedestrians who have had to visit an emergency room because they became distracted and injured themselves doubled to 1,000 in 2008 from those that occurred in 2007, a figure that itself was nearly double the 2006 figure. Everyone no doubt has stopped at a traffic light and watched someone cross the road in front of them while texting; it is easy to understand how these statistics are rising exponentially.

Drivers are not immune either. Nationwide Mutual Insurance conducted surveys in 2008 that show that 72 percent of drivers say they engage in multitasking (i.e., doing other things while driving), such as making phone calls, eating, or drinking. Other activities drivers engage in behind the wheel include shaving, applying makeup, turning around to deal with recalcitrant children in the back, and adjusting the radio or iPod. It would appear that the older one gets, the more one seems to believe one can multitask while driving: 16- and 17-year-olds multitask to a lesser degree (60 percent) while drivers in the 18- to 44-year bracket multitask much more frequently (80 percent).

In 2006, the National Highway Traffic Safety Administration (NHTSA) reported that driver inattention and distraction is a factor in 80 percent of automobile accidents, and research continues to prove that attempts at multitasking while driving are dangerous. Just like in the office, however, drivers apparently believe that they are capable of doing more than one thing at a time and that accidents caused by driver inattention must happen to someone else.

While deaths attributed to distracted driving fell by six percent in 2009 from the previous year (as part of an overall decline in traffic fatalities), crashes related to distracted driving claimed 5,474 lives and injured 448,000 people in the United States in 2009, according to a report released by the U.S. Department of Transportation in September 2010. Sixteen percent of fatal crashes in 2008 and 2009 involved reports of distracted driving, up from 10 percent in 2005. However, the overall number of traffic accidents in the United States declined in 2009.

Sixteen percent of all drivers younger than 20 (the age group with the highest proportion of distracted drivers) involved in fatal crashes were reported to have been distracted while driving. However, drivers between 30 and 39 were most likely to be involved in a fatal crash while distracted by a mobile phone.

"We are not talking about numbers, but about lives being broken and people being killed in crashes that were 100 percent preventable," Ray LaHood, the secretary of transportation, posted in his blog. In a formal statement accompanying the report he stated: "These numbers show that distracted driving remains an epidemic in America, and they are just the tip of the iceberg."

"We're hooked on our devices and we can't put them down, even when it means jeopardizing our own safety and the safety of others," LaHood added in his blog. "And we have young people texting habitually long before they learn to drive who then can't even imagine turning off their devices when they climb behind the wheel."

"You see it every day: Drivers swerving in their lanes, stopping at green lights, running red ones or narrowly missing a pedestrian because they have their eyes and minds on their phones, not on the road," wrote LaHood in an op-ed piece in the *Orlando Sentinel.* "Yet people consistently assume that they can drive and text or talk at the same time. The results are preventable accidents."

The problem has gotten to the point where mobile operators and phone manufacturers have come up with a solution that has the potential to limit distractions behind the wheel by essentially disabling a mobile phone in a car that is in motion. In January of 2011, T-Mobile unveiled just such a service, DriveSmart, although it cannot distinguish between a driver's phone and a passenger's. In an emergency, the driver can override the DriveSmart system and place a call.

Sometimes a person's inattentiveness can have fatal results outside of a vehicle. In the last few years, multiple lives have been lost at pools where the lifeguard on duty was texting instead of watching the pool. Lifeguards are trained to scan their areas in 10-second cycles because a swimmer can drown in a mere 20 seconds.

Paul Atchley, associate professor of psychology at the University of Kansas, has studied issues relating to attention and told me that teenagers need to be texting to feel connected. Despite knowing that texting and driving is unsafe, they persist in the behavior. And when they do, it changes how safe they perceive road conditions to be. Atchley shared the following thoughts with me:

> Some of our latest work shows that when younger drivers choose to text, they perceive the driving conditions to be safer than they actually are. In our research, drivers who initiate a text think freeway driving is equal to driving on a calm street, while drivers simply reading a text think freeway driving is attentionally demanding, such as driving in intense weather conditions. Choosing to send a text changes one's attitudes about the safety of the behavior and it may be one reason the behavior is so difficult to change.

Attention

In 1890, William James, in his textbook *Principles of Psychology*, provided what has become the classic definition of attention:

> Everyone knows what attention is. It is the taking possession by the mind, in clear and vivid form, of one out of what seem several simultaneously possible objects or trains of thought. Focalization, concentration, of consciousness are of its essence. It implies withdrawal from some things in order to deal effectively with others, and is a condition which has a real opposite in the confused, dazed, scatterbrained state which in French is called distraction, and Zerstreutheit in German.

James' definition helps us understand what attention is. More recently, scientists have made great strides in understanding how attention works. Their research has led them to consider attention to be an organ system, which is defined as "differentiated structures in animals and plants made up of various cells and tissues and adapted for the performance of some specific function and grouped with other structures into a system."

We also know that attention has its own circuitry in the brain and that specialized networks carry out various functions, namely achieving and maintaining alertness, the control of thoughts and feelings, and orienting to sensory events.

Three Types of Attention

There are three types of attention. The first is orienting. Without this, we could not orient to new stimuli. Indeed our bodies send out rewards in the form of adrenaline when we react to something new. The problem is that there is so much that is new in the world that it's tempting to react more to new stimuli than to focus on existing ones. If we constantly react, however, we will never complete ongoing tasks.

The second type of attention is a range of response states from sleepiness to total alertness.

The third is executive attention, a term whose use has come into vogue recently. Executive attention looks at an individual's ability to plan and judge – as well as to resolve conflicting information.

Executive attention, based in the frontal cortex, uses the anterior cingulate, the part of the brain that is the control center of our higher-order skills that result in coherent behavior. Without executive attention, we could never plan, analyze, or move forward.

The act of paying attention is itself a taxing task, and by no means an easy one.

Maggie Jackson, author of *Distracted: The Erosion of Attention and the Coming Dark Age*, notes in her book that we are in danger of becoming an increasingly shallow society if we continue to let our attention be negatively impacted by distractions.

Being a productive modern knowledge worker is to be constantly restraining oneself from the temptation to fracture our attention. The allure of Facebook, the Internet, and real-time communication with friends and colleagues via Twitter, instant messaging (IM), and text messaging is strong and ever present in the knowledge worker's environment. Indeed, those temptations have been incorporated into work itself, so the distraction that IM creates cannot simply be dismissed as socializing; it is now a critical part of work.

Exercising self-control is critical to being a productive worker. Schedules must be kept, nonwork activities must be kept to a minimum, and distractions must be filtered out. Unfortunately, self-control is also finite. Studies in both humans and animals have shown that resisting temptation depletes glucose levels, which in turn reduces the ability to focus on challenging tasks.

In one study, human volunteers were divided into two groups. One group was told they may eat the provided chocolate chip cookies while the other group was told to not touch the cookies but instead to snack on some radishes. Needless to say, the group eating the cookies was not exercising self-control by resisting the charms of the radishes, but the radish-eating group had to resist the appeal of the tasty cookies.

Both groups were then asked to complete an impossible puzzle, and the length of time they would commit before giving up was measured. The cookie group lasted an average of 19 minutes before giving up, faring much better than the radish group, who on average gave up after just 8 minutes.

The study was repeated with dogs, where one group did nothing and the other was asked to sit still for 10 minutes (a mentally exhausting task for a dog) and then attempt to remove treats from a chew toy that had been altered to make it impossible. The results were the same: The dogs that had already exerted self-control had far less patience for the new task. The study was repeated a third time, with half of the dogs from the self-control group being given a sugary glucose drink and half being given a sweet-tasting placebo. The dogs that were given the glucose drink performed just as well as the dogs that had not had to exercise self-control, while the placebo group performed poorly.

The studies show us two things: 1.) Our ability to exert self-control is tied to glucose levels (so eat more snacks), and 2.) the act of restraining ourselves is mentally and physically taxing.

There are ways to cut back on multitasking and interruptions, shaping your own environment and work style so that you better use your attentional networks. If you have a difficult problem or a conundrum to solve, you need to think about where you work best. Right now, people hope they'll be able to think or create or problem-solve in the midst of a noisy, cluttered environment. Quiet is a starting point.

The other important thing is to discuss interruption as an environmental question and collective social issue. In the United States, stillness and reflection are not especially valued in the workplace. The image of success is the frenetic multitasker who doesn't have time and is constantly interrupted. By striving toward this model of inattention, we're doing ourselves a tremendous injustice.

Automaticity

The ability to do one thing on autopilot, so to speak, while doing something else is known as automaticity. Novice drivers, those first learning to handle a car, need to devote their full attention to driving. That's why they turn off the radio, ask passengers not to talk to them, and don't text or make phone calls.

As drivers gain more experience, driving becomes automatic. The brain is rewired to make driving less of a conscious effort. As a result, experienced drivers can listen to music and, if a car brakes suddenly in front of them, they will immediately and subconsciously apply the brake.

But automaticity does not mean that distractions while driving do not have their effect. Having an involved conversation on a mobile phone (or even with a passenger in the car) can easily go beyond the limits of a driver's capability to drive on autopilot. This is because driving does involve a lot of brainpower, whether it's processing vast amounts of visual information or predicting what random drivers ahead or behind of us might do next and allowing for multiple outcomes.

Brain scans by neuroscientists studying this issue have shown that the brain has difficulty paying attention to sights and sounds at the same time. If the brain is focused on a visual task, its ability to handle an auditory task decreases markedly, and vice versa.

In 2008, John Hamilton of National Public Radio conducted a series of experiments with pianist Jacob Frasch, in an attempt to determine the extent to which an individual loses focus when attempting to multitask. To confirm the results, I attempted to duplicate the experiment on myself.

Playing the piano involves a similar amount of hand-to-eye coordination as driving does, as well as coordination between our hands and feet (for pedals, in both cases). Playing the piano also has a similar amount of automaticity to it, similar to driving. I have played the piano since I was five years old and I have been driving since the age of 16. Even when I am out of practice, I can still sit down and play many of the Beethoven Sonatas I memorized for performances years earlier.

In the NPR experiment, Frasch spent approximately one hour playing a variety of works by major composers including Bach and Brahms. He had no trouble talking about his childhood while playing a Bach minuet, although when I listen carefully to the interview it is evident to me that a few notes were slightly delayed as he formed his sentences. To the casual listener, however, this would not be apparent.

Where the difficulty in multitasking while playing the piano became apparent was when Hamilton asked Frasch to do something that required more brainpower, namely an arithmetic problem. As Hamilton asked Frasch to calculate 73 minus 21, Frasch responded that it "might take me a while." It is clear when listening to the recording that Frasch had to stop playing for a moment in order to calculate the answer to what ordinarily would have been a fairly simple problem.

When I replicated the experiment, I played the Moonlight (Mondschein) Sonata by Ludwig van Beethoven, a piece I have played since I was 14. A friend started a casual conversation by asking me questions about the weather. (Frasch was asked about his childhood.)

I had no problem playing the first movement of the sonata while commenting on the rainstorm we had just had.

As I played the second movement, my friend asked me about my childhood, and I noticed that I had a slight hesitation in both answering the questions and playing the piece, but this was imperceptible to my friend.

Toward the end of the second movement, he asked me to perform a simple subtraction problem (80 minus 24). It was clear to both of us that I stopped playing, thought about the answer, returned the answer, and then continued to play.

As I began the third movement, which requires far more concentration than the first two, he asked me the same question again. This time it threw me off track, even though it was the same question. I played several wrong notes, and my tempo was completely off as I attempted to play the intricate arpeggios and do simple arithmetic simultaneously.

After reflecting both on my test and my work habits (e.g., my inability to work listening to music with clear audible words as well as loud distracting commercials), I have no doubt of the accuracy of the 2006 NHTSA survey that revealed that driver inattention and distraction are a factor in the majority of automobile accidents. I believe that this is the case both on the road and in the office (although accidents in the office hopefully do not place the knowledge worker in any physical danger.)

Switching modes (or gears) takes time, and each interruption, as we know, not only takes up a specific amount of time but carries with it the penalty of recovery time. In the office, the danger is less that we will collide with someone than that we will miss critical information or a deadline. On the road, it could result in a major accident.

The Supertaskers Among Us

Effective multitasking is not completely impossible, as there are a few select individuals whose performance when juggling multiple tasks actually improves. These are the supertaskers, and they comprise approximately 2.5 percent of the population.

We know this thanks to a 2009 study conducted by psychologists at the University of Utah designed to examine to what extent subjects could talk on a mobile phone and drive at the same time.

The 200 subjects participated in a driving simulation that mimicked ordinary traffic conditions, with occasional instances where they would have to slow down to avoid hitting something in front of them. As a baseline, each participant drove with no other stimulus and then drove while engaging in a conversation via a hands-free mobile phone. The researchers read sets of two to five words, with simple math problems that had to be identified as true or false interspersed between the word sets. The subject was then asked to recall words in the order that they were presented.

The study found that 97.5 percent of the subjects' driving was significantly impaired while on the phone in that they took an average of 20 percent longer to hit the brakes when necessary. Word recall dropped 11 percent, and math accuracy dropped 3 percent.

However, the study also revealed that 2.5 percent of the subjects drove and multitasked the same or actually better while on the phone. For that group, brake response times remained the same, math accuracy was unchanged, and word recall accuracy actually rose three percent.

Statistically, you have about a one in 40 probability of being a supertasker. It's not completely out of the question that you are a supertasker; however, people who are very good at things tend to underestimate their abilities, while those who are not as good tend to overestimate. This finding is backed up by research from Stanford that shows that those who frequently multitask are actually worse at it than those that avoid multitasking. So ironically, the supertaskers among us are likely to be the ones who seldom try.

For the majority of knowledge workers, while they may believe that they are faster and more efficient by multitasking, multitasking actually slows down the flow of work and can introduce errors and mistakes. You are unlikely actually to be a supertasker, and thus you are hurting your own productivity when you try.

C H A P T E R

INTEL'S WAR

No man's knowledge here can go beyond his experience.

—John Locke

Since its founding in 1968 by Bob Noyce and Gordon Moore, Intel has been a leader in the silicon revolution, having developed the microprocessors that formed the foundation of the PC Revolution (the Intel 8088 chip was selected by IBM as the CPU of its first personal computer) and the Internet revolution.

Today, the company is the world's largest semiconductor chip maker, employing approximately 79,800 people, with 55 percent of those employees in the United States. The company's net revenue in 2009 was $35 billion.

Intel also has a history of developing programs and practices to deal with Information Overload issues for well over a decade. The company's efforts were led by Nathan Zeldes, who, in 1995, as an IT staff member for Intel in Israel, started developing what he refers to as "first-generation solutions" to deal with the problem of e-mail overload. Zeldes traces his work on Information Overload issues to the introduction of IBM PCs to the workplace. The presence and use of the computers quickly created multiple new and unforeseen problems, including that of Information Overload.

Intel's internal research indicated that each knowledge worker lost approximately eight hours per week due to Information Overload, which for a company its size resulted in a cost of $1 billion per year.

Recent Information Overload Initiatives

By 2006, Zeldes had discovered, through internal Intel surveys, that the typical Intel employee was receiving 50 to 100 e-mail messages daily and spending 20 hours per week handling e-mail, of which 30 percent of the messages were unnecessary. Top executives reported receiving up to 300 messages per day. Intel as a company received on average three million e-mail messages a day. These numbers are unquestionably higher today.

Recognizing the cost of the problem, Intel launched a series of seven-month-long pilot initiatives aimed at combating Information Overload from a different angle.

The three pilot programs were:

1. **Quiet Time.** This program was a weekly four-hour block of uninterrupted time with minimal distractions for knowledge workers. The time was to be used as they saw fit, as a break from the constant stream of interruptions that Zeldes felt were compromising efficiency and productivity.
2. **No E-mail Day (NED).** This program called for one day during which members of a group would revert whenever possible to higher levels of verbal communication instead of e-mail. The intent was to combat unnecessary e-mail use, such as cubicle-to-cubicle e-mailing within the same office.
3. **E-mail Service Level Agreement (SLA).** The E-mail SLA was a policy agreement that extended the acceptable time frame for replying to e-mail to 24 hours, instead of the ingrained expectation of an almost instantaneous response that required constant monitoring of inboxes.

Zeldes solicited and received support from senior management for the programs, and the manager of a group of engineers volunteered her team for the pilot program. The majority of the group was based in Austin, Texas, with the remainder working out of Chandler, Arizona. There were a total of 300 engineers in the program, including a subgroup of 150 working on a special project. In both locations, team members would work with members in the other location, and there were no geographic distinctions in tasks, working styles, or environments. For the most part, members of the pilot program communicated within their own team, so the effects of communicating with people outside the pilot program (who were not adhering to the rules) were not considered to be significant.

Quiet Time: A Time for Thought and Reflection

The Quiet Time pilot was designed to provide knowledge workers with a window of time that would be relatively free of interruption and allow for greater thought and reflection. During this time, which ran from 8 A.M. to noon on Tuesday mornings, workers would use their own discretion as to what to work on.

Participants were to set their e-mail client to be offline so they could compose and read e-mail but not receive new messages. Instant messenger presence status was to be set to do not disturb, calendars were blocked so meetings could not be scheduled, phones were to be forwarded to voice mail, and do-not-disturb signs were displayed on office doors.

In surveys conducted regarding the Quiet Time pilot, significant gaps were revealed between how managers and engineers experienced the program.

The Quiet Time program was moderately successful, with 71 percent recommending that the pilot be applied to other groups, although many supplied caveats or suggested that changes be made first.

After the pilot concluded, 42 percent of those surveyed said it was at least somewhat effective. Managers in particular had a largely positive reaction to the pilot, and while it wasn't as popular with engineers, the pilot still received moderate support from them.

Changes suggested by program participants included clearly communicating and enforcing the expectations of the program, particularly at a managerial level, and communicating to outside groups that they needed to respect the program. Additionally, participants indicated that clear rules were needed to define what a legitimate interruption was and that the program could not succeed as a one-size-fits-all solution; it needed to be tailored to different roles. Many also said that the basic premise, a specified time for thought and reflection, was flawed and that the type of work they were doing, coupled with the reality of a globally distributed company, made a mandated quiet time unrealistic.

One worker put everything into perspective: "We should have at least four hours *per day* [emphasis added] of uninterrupted time to work, and it shouldn't have to be a mandated program. People need to be more disciplined in not scheduling and in declining unnecessary meetings. That said, Quiet Time is a step in the right direction."

When asked about specific areas of their work and the effect that the Quiet Time pilot had, only one area, "collaborate with coworkers," received more negative feedback than positive. Even in this case, only 18 percent of those surveyed felt that the pilot had a negative impact. Also worth noting, 45 percent of those surveyed found the program had a positive impact on their ability to do work requiring concentration, which was its goal.

While Quiet Time was not generally viewed negatively, most engineers felt the pilot had little impact. Managers, however, felt the pilot gave them an opportunity to complete work in a timely fashion, find more time to innovate and create value, and concentrate on tasks.

Interestingly, according to surveys during and after the pilot, the number of engineers who felt that their coworkers respected their quiet time actually dropped as the pilot progressed. There was a nine-point drop in the number who felt their quiet time was respected (40 to 31 percent) and an eight-point rise in the number who felt it was not respected (19 to 27 percent), suggesting that the rules of Quiet Time were quickly forgotten as the pilot program went on.

An unexpected issue that arose was that team members were taking the rules too literally. "About two months in when we did our mid survey, we found that people interpreted the prohibition against interruptions too strictly," Zeldes said, "so if they had a question at 8:30 that prevented them from doing their job they would sit and fume until noon." In response, the commonsense aspect of the program was reiterated: An urgent question could, of course, be asked if necessary, largely solving that problem.

The practice of Quiet Time was extended after the pilot's completion and is being evaluated for use in other groups at Intel.

No E-mail Day

No E-mail Day (NED) took place on Fridays, within a group of 150 people. E-mail sent to those outside of the group was allowed, as was critical internal e-mail.

The title of this pilot program, "No E-mail Day," was not entirely accurate, as e-mail was still permitted, but workers were encouraged instead to move around the office and initiate face-to-face contact with co-workers. This was both to reduce e-mail loads and to encourage verbal social contact between workers to improve the quality of intra-office communications.

Different types of knowledge workers use the same tools differently, so it was not surprising that the prepilot survey revealed that managers and engineers perceived e-mail differently, with higher numbers of managers than engineers viewing e-mail as a significant problem.

E-mail habits also differed somewhat when comparing managers and engineers. Sixty-nine percent of engineers read e-mail as soon as they noticed it, compared to only 53 percent of managers, indicating weak time management habits on the part of the engineers and only slightly better inbox discipline among managers.

The pilot also presented logistical challenges in that members of neither group were at their desks sufficiently long enough to make face-to-face encounters a regular occurrence. In many cases they were left with e-mail as the only means of communication, which made it impossible for them to follow the pilot's directive and thereby limited the possibility of any positive outcome. Managers in particular, who spend a large portion of their working time in meetings, found it extremely difficult to communicate without using e-mail. If the program had been run in a more cubicle-based group, the pilot might have had more of an impact and generated more enthusiasm.

Only 29 percent of those surveyed after the pilot ended said the program was at least somewhat effective. Managers especially did not like NED; only 11 percent felt that it was even somewhat effective, and not one of them thought that continuing the program was a good idea.

Changes suggested in the postpilot survey concerned enforcement of the rules of the pilot; however, most simply felt the pilot's concept was flawed and unrealistic, particularly during busy periods of work. One employee wrote, "The basic premise is flawed. Teach people which method of contact is most appropriate instead of applying a blanket rule with no consideration of the communication in question."

Both managers and engineers were asked if the pilot had a positive, negative, or simply no impact on specific areas of their work. Engineers had higher numbers of positive responses than managers in every area, although in general the majority of both groups said that NED had no impact. Engineers, who as a group were less dependent on e-mail than managers, who were frequently away from their desks, saw the greatest benefit in NED.

The program's ultimate impact on e-mail overload was small but not insignificant; 45 percent said that the number of e-mail messages they sent on No E-mail Day was lower than on other workdays, and 29 percent said that the pilot had a positive effect on lessening their e-mail overload.

E-mail Service Level Agreement

The E-mail Service Level Agreement was a top-down SLA regarding response times for e-mail. The term "service level agreement" was chosen because it describes an agreement to a level of service that often includes deadline and response times.

The program was implemented across the entire group of 300 and, according to Zeldes, "failed miserably at creating any change [in e-mail habits]." Zeldes attributes the ineffectiveness of the pilot to a "culture of urgency" regarding e-mail that is deeply entrenched and resistant to change.

Group members were told that they could take up to 24 hours to respond to e-mail. The intended goal was to reduce time spent managing inboxes and to allow workers to check in two or three times a day instead of constantly monitoring their inboxes for fear of missing an e-mail to which the sender expected an immediate response.

Managers and engineers had markedly different understanding of the terms of the E-mail SLA. When asked before the pilot what the current expectation, either expressed or implied, was for responding to e-mail, 23 percent of engineers said they did not know. By contrast, 100 percent of management at least had some form of understanding (although this varied by individual) as to what was expected. Even after the pilot, only four percent of

engineers, compared to 33 percent of managers, correctly identified 24 hours as the official E-mail SLA.

Clearly, there were significant failures in communicating and
following through with the E-mail SLA. For example, during the
pilot, when asked if having an explicit SLA helped to reduce
the frequency with which they checked e-mail, only 28 percent of
respondents agreed. By the end of the pilot, that number had fallen
to 18 percent.

After the pilot ended, 53 percent of managers said the E-mail
SLA had helped them reduce the number of times they checked
their inboxes, compared to only 12 percent of engineers.

This discrepancy suggested very poor communication of the
E-mail SLA to engineers and showed that engineers felt that managers' expectations had not changed with regard to the need for
quick responses to e-mail messages, despite the official 24-hour
response time allowed.

The E-mail SLA worked for the people who set the expectations, in this case the managers, but did not work for those to
whom the expectations applied. For an E-mail SLA to be effective,
management would have to lead by example and strongly support
it with actions, not just lip service. Nonmanagers would have to feel
confident that they can avoid responding instantly to e-mail without
repercussion, or they will just ignore the SLA.

While the e-mail centric culture of Intel contributed to the
failure of the E-mail SLA, what is more striking is the gap between
managers and engineers. For this sort of initiative to take root, it
is not enough to officially change the explicit expectations; the
implied ones must be changed as well.

There are numerous lessons one can derive from the pilot programs, but six points stand out:

1. Quiet Time appears to have been at least moderately effective during the time when it was run, but the long-term effect
   is not yet clear. However, the amount of time that knowledge
   workers have for thought and reflection is continuing to
   decline (see Chapter 12), and 34 percent of knowledge workers feel that they simply do not have enough time in the day
   to get everything done.
2. No E-mail Day and the E-mail SLA pilot programs failed to
   gain traction and never became effective. Both of these

programs, however, did shine light on the need to make changes in the overall information diet of knowledge workers and that such changes will indeed have a positive impact on increasing knowledge worker efficiency and effectiveness.

3. Programs must be tailored to groups in ways that reduce friction and increase participation. The failure of NED was in part a result of not taking into account the work habits of the group's members; they were far too e-mail-centric and spent too much time away from their desks for the program to succeed.

4. Total withdrawal from a habitual activity or behavior pattern for a mandated period of time does not result in long-term behavioral adjustment. Attempts to modify behavior must target all communications tools with an eye toward friction-free adoption and permanence.

5. Knowledge workers have a tendency to react negatively to one-size-fits-all mandated rules for communication that do not take into account the varying work styles of individuals and groups.

6. Attempts to institute programs to tackle Information Overload must be applied universally to management and employees. The failure of the E-mail SLA demonstrates the vastly different experiences that occur when management and non-management fail to communicate and a perceived unequal application of the rules of the program exists.

As one participant in the pilot wrote in the postpilot survey, "[D]on't legislate communication, teach proper usage of different mediums of communication." Although some legislation may be necessary to enforce proper usage of communication tools, education about their proper usage is ultimately the path that will reduce Information Overload while allowing flexibility based on conditions such as deadlines and work styles.

CHAPTER 18

GOVERNMENT INFORMATION OVERLOAD

If a little knowledge is dangerous – where is the man who has so much as to be out of danger?

—Thomas Huxley

There were 23,911,691 government employees in the United States (including uniformed military, federal, state, and local governments) as of 2010. Of this number, almost 12 million are knowledge workers, making government knowledge workers the largest single such contingent in the United States, which has a total of 78.6 million knowledge workers.

In many respects, these government knowledge workers are no different from their peers in the private sector. They receive an average of 93 e-mail messages per day, lose around 25 percent of their day to Information Overload, and spend only five percent of their time in thought and reflection.

A survey of government and education workers conducted by Xerox and Harris Interactive found that 58 percent of those surveyed reported spending nearly half of their average workday filing, deleting, or sorting paper or digital information. Analysis by Basex found the cost to taxpayers of spending over half the day managing information is approximately $31 billion in the aggregate.

The same survey also found that 38 percent of government and education workers said that they had to redo reports or other work as a result of not finding the correct information. Twenty-four percent said they later discovered they had used the wrong information in preparing their work, and 37 percent agreed that their organizations are drowning in paper (yes, paper: 50 percent of the processes of those surveyed are still paper based).

These numbers serve to illustrate that government knowledge workers face the same problems as their private sector counterparts with respect to technology sprawl, failed searches, and overflowing inbox.

However, the problem of Information Overload in government is separate and distinct from the problem in the private sector in two ways, namely the cost (which is footed by the taxpayer) and the potential for Information Overload to adversely impact military, counterterrorism, and law enforcement operations, which in turn can result in the loss of life and the erosion of national security.

The Government's Information Problem

Governments, like businesses, have strict information retention policies. However, the situation becomes more complicated when dealing with divisive political issues, changes of administrations, and security clearances.

Consider what happened in 2009, when an outgoing presidential administration began to work its way through the housekeeping and administrative tasks required of it by law. As the United States prepared for the transition from the Bush administration to the Obama administration, the National Archives, charged with preserving and indexing presidential records, had to launch an emergency plan to deal with the looming deluge of electronic records. The incoming data comprised around 100 terabytes of content, which is 50 times the amount the Clinton administration left behind.

Much of the Bush administration's content was in the form of e-mail, the use of which has exploded over the past decade, and it comprised as much as 40 terabytes of the records. This number can only be expected to grow in the current and future administrations. There is no doubt that Obama and his team, given his admitted addiction to his BlackBerry smartphone, will generate even more data that will have to be archived and indexed.

The effort to incorporate the records was complicated by foot dragging by the Bush administration; its members were reluctant to provide details about the size and format of the records that they eventually turned over as well as details about the records management system that had been used to index the text-based records. The format issue is particularly relevant because many of the records were in unfamiliar formats, including large quantities of digital photographs. Without preparation and prior knowledge of what formats to expect, the National Archives would have struggled to process them.

In addition to the size of the records, there were concerns that the proprietary format of the records would become obsolete. This has already occurred at the National Aeronautics and Space Administration (NASA). Today there are millions of files on 8″ and 5 1/4″ floppy diskettes and on various obsolete tape cartridges, some of which include NASA's earliest photographs of earth. Most of this information is inaccessible with today's technology.

Despite a new $144 million computer system, there were concerns about the ability of the National Archives to absorb the content and make it accessible to future generations. In the words of Paul Brachfeld, the archives' inspector general, "Just because you ingest the data does not mean that people can locate, identify, recover, and use the records they need."

With the growth of social media usage by both politicians and government agencies, an additional problem is determining what records the National Archives are mandated to keep. In October 2010, a directive was issued by the National Archives that specified the criteria for identifying and storing records. The uniqueness and availability of the information in other places, evidence of agency polices contained in the information, and the tool used (including whether the tool was officially sanctioned) were identified as key aspects to consider when dealing with information.

The archivist of the United States (known as AOTUS), David Ferriero, summed up the problem rather succinctly when he wrote on his blog in November 2010, that the casual and informal tone of social media should not "be confused with insignificance."

While only a fraction of the information turned over to the National Archives will be of any interest to researchers and the public, by law it must all be archived. However, without proper indexing and storage, the data is next to useless.

Information Overload Turns Deadly

The U.S. military and security agencies also generate massive amounts of information in operations that have become increasingly high tech and produce immense quantities of data.

In 2007 alone, the Air Force collected what amounted to approximately 24 years' worth of continuous video from Predator and Reaper unmanned drones in the skies over Afghanistan and Iraq, a fact first reported by the *New York Times* in January 2010. All video collected by drones is watched live by a team of intelligence analysts; so this translates into approximately 24 years of analyst team time being used in one year.

The amount of data (and the amount of time spent watching the videos) will only grow as more advanced drones are deployed that can record video in 10 (with future plans for up to 65) directions at once instead of the one direction that is currently supported.

The use of unmanned aerial vehicles (UAVs) is an expanding phenomenon not only in the military but also domestically. On September 1, 2010, the U.S. Customs and Border Protection agency began operating unmanned Predator B drones out of Corpus Christi, Texas, expanding drone coverage over the entire 2,000-mile southern U.S. border. Previous coverage had extended from California to west Texas.

The advantages of UAV use are clear: Pilots are not in danger, intelligence-gathering capabilities are improved, and the ability to conduct strikes in remote areas is enhanced.

There are of course myriad issues that the use of UAVs for military operations present, ranging from humanitarian arguments that drone missile strikes are more likely to result in civilian casualties, to political considerations about where they can operate, as seen in recent disagreements with Pakistani authorities.

Complicating and contributing to these issues is the huge problem of how do deal with the flood of information that drones are returning to the analysts.

Mistakes such as falsely identifying threats can lead to unnecessary and potentially tragic civilian casualties, which inflame international public opinion and impair the military's ability to operate effectively. Likewise, missing a real threat because of Information Overload could also lead to fatalities.

The use of these unmanned and increasingly sophisticated data collection tools will only increase, making it critical that we develop systems to organize, parse, tag, and act upon the data that is collected in an effective manner. The Air Force in particular is working on this problem, even resorting to tapping into the knowledge base and best practices of sports broadcasting professionals, who are used to dealing with multiple data feeds and the challenges of producing live broadcasts. But the military will have to move quickly to stay ahead of the mountain of incoming data.

A stark example of the deadly consequences of Information Overload-caused errors in a military setting was reported by the *New York Times* on January 16, 2011. In February 2010, an incident in Afghanistan occurred that resulted in significant loss of life. Because drone operators and analysts were in a state of overload, critical information about a makeup of a group of Afghan villagers who were assembling into a convoy in a village was not relayed accurately to ground troops. In the heat of the moment and faced with a flood of incoming data coupled with a multitude of urgent requests for information via instant messenger and radio, the drone team overlooked information reporting that there were children in the crowd. As a result, the team erroneously designated the convoy a threat, which then led to an airstrike that killed 23 Afghan civilians. An unnamed senior military officer told the *Times* that it was "an accurate description" to attribute the tragedy to Information Overload, adding that the deaths could have been avoided "if we had just slowed things down and thought deliberately."

The problem of Information Overload is not limited to isolated incidents in the military. Art Kramer, a neuroscientist and director of the Beckman Institute research lab at the University of Illinois, told the *Times* that "[T]here is information overload at every level of the military – from the general to the soldier on the ground."

A Culture of Secrecy

Government agencies are comparable to rival divisions within a company; they compete for resources, mindshare, and prestige. Unfortunately, infighting and overlapping responsibilities can result in poor information and knowledge sharing, redundancy or neglect around key areas, and, ultimately, deadly real-world consequences.

Trouble exists on structural and cultural levels as well. Intelligence and law enforcement agencies depend on knowledge sharing to spot threats and create actionable intelligence, yet the ability for the various agencies to share that knowledge is hamstrung by outdated and somewhat nonsensical classification systems, incompatible tools, and a culture that promotes extreme siloing of information. This stovepipe mentality, where information moves up or down in a hierarchal manner, not horizontally to where it is needed, fails to match the innovative, network-based threats that we face in the form of nonstate actors, terrorism, and organized crime.

Additionally, the sheer volume of content has increased significantly as the intelligence community rightly begins to shift away from a culture of secrecy, where classified information is deemed to have more value simply by virtue of its classification, to a more open model that leverages open source intelligence assets (anything legally available, including newspaper articles, social content, and conference proceedings). In 2005, following the recommendation of the 9/11 Commission and the Weapons of Mass Destruction Commission, the Office of the Director of National Intelligence created the Open Source Center to collect, analyze, and disseminate open source intelligence as well as train analysts to take full advantage of these resources.

There have been a few bright spots in government information sharing, such as Intellipedia, a Wikipedia-style information resource developed for the U.S. intelligence community in 2005, and the Center for Army Lessons Learned, a resource for military personnel to share best practices and local knowledge. Sadly, the overall effort of the military and intelligence community to address information issues has not yet caught up with efforts that are being made in the private sector.

The most extreme example is the failure of knowledge sharing that led to the September 11, 2001, terrorist attacks. In that instance, multiple agencies had small pieces of the puzzle that could have led to the arrest of the hijackers but, because of outdated systems, a lack of intra-agency communication, and what even then was a dizzying amount of information to filter and sort, the terrorists were able to successfully slip through cracks in the system and commit those heinous acts.

To say we have learnt our lesson from that experience would not be entirely accurate. We did indeed learn some lessons, but at this point they seem to have resulted in the creation of more information, more agencies, and more bureaucracy, and, thus, more Information Overload.

The National Counterterrorism Center (NCTC), created in 2004 (following recommendations of the 9/11 Commission), has a mission to break "the older mold of national government organizations" and serve as a center for joint operational planning and joint intelligence. In other words, the various intelligence agencies were instructed by the 9/11 Commission to put aside decades-long rivalries and share what they know and whom they suspect. Unfortunately, while this sounds good in theory, in practice this mission may not yet be close to be being fully carried out.

In addition to the fact that old habits die hard (such as a disdain for inter-agency information sharing), it appears that the folks at the NCTC have failed to grasp basic tenets of knowledge sharing, namely that search, in order to be effective, needs to be federated and contextual, that is to say it needs to simultaneously search multiple data stores and present results in a coherent manner.

Discrete searches in separate databases will yield far different results compared to a federated search that spans multiple databases. All reports indicate that intelligence agencies are still looking at discrete pieces of information from separate and distinct databases and that the agencies themselves are not sharing all that they know.

In July 2010, the *Washington Post* released a series of reports entitled "Top Secret America," which outlined the massive post-9/11 expansion of the intelligence and security sectors of the U.S. government and private contractors. In the first report, "A Hidden World, Growing beyond Control," reporters Dana Priest and William M. Arkin detailed the explosive post-9/11 growth in the security sector.

The report noted that there are approximately 1,271 government agencies and 1,931 private companies, with an estimated 854,000 individuals holding top-secret security clearances working on intelligence, homeland security, and counterterrorism at 10,000 locations in the United States. The exact number of people employed, programs in operation, and money that is being spent is unknown even to those who are involved in and oversee the programs.

Redundancy in the intelligence community is commonplace, with multiple agencies having overlapping missions. For example, there are 51 federal organizations and military commands that track the flow of money to and from terrorist networks.

The sheer volume of incoming information received by security agencies is staggering. According to the report, the National Security Agency (NSA) intercepts 1.7 billion e-mail messages, phone calls, and other types of communications every day, of which only a small percentage is sorted into 70 separate databases for analysis. Presumably, the rest is discarded or languishes in storage, unusable and useless. And that is just one agency.

The mass quantities of incoming information are matched by the outgoing information that is produced at the NSA; intelligence analysts who deal with intercepted domestic and foreign conversations publish approximately 50,000 reports per year, or 136 a day.

The deluge of information that intelligence and security agencies must deal with creates the potential for a repetition of the mistakes that contributed to 9/11, where critical information was not shared and connections were missed.

The Consequences of Not Connecting the Dots

For intelligence agencies, keeping up with the deluge of incoming information is not unlike sandbagging to protect against a flood. All points of the levee must be monitored because if one spot breaks, the rest of the levee is at risk as the water flowing through the gap keeps enlarging the breach.

For instance, misuse of e-mail can be deadly to government agencies. In early January 2009, a cascading series of reply to all e-mail messages in the State Department snowballed and nearly shut down the e-mail system in what amounted to a self-administered denial of service attack. The matter was not taken lightly: a warning was sent to all State Department employees promising unspecified "disciplinary actions" for using the reply to all function on e-mail with large distribution lists.

On December 25, 2009, the high-stakes game of sandbagging that intelligence agencies conduct to protect against the crushing information load they must filter through took a dangerous turn. The man who would be dubbed the "Underwear Bomber" – named for his unorthodox (and unsuccessful) method of attempting to set off explosive chemicals that were sewn into his underwear – boarded a Detroit-bound flight in London.

In this case, multiple agencies had information about Umar Farouk Abdulmutallab, the Nigerian man accused of trying to blow up Northwest Flight 253. In May 2009, Britain had put him on a watch list and refused to renew his visa. However, the visa denial was due to immigration fraud and not any terrorist activity, and thus was not shared with American agencies.

In August, analysts at the NSA overheard al Qaeda leaders in Yemen discussing a plot involving a Nigerian man, presumably Abdulmutallab. In November, British intelligence officials sent word to their U.S. counterparts that U.S.-born Yemeni radical Anwar al-Awlaki, a prominent al Qaeda recruiter and cleric, had been in contact with a man named Umar Farouk. The last name, Abdulmutallab, was omitted for reasons unknown, contributing to the failure to connect this piece of the puzzle to other information that U.S. officials had and would obtain.

One week later, also in November, the accused's father, a prominent Nigerian banker, warned the American embassy (and a CIA official) in Abuja, Nigeria, that his son was a potential threat. As a result, Abdulmutallab's name was entered into the 550,000-name Terrorist Identities Datamart Environment (TIDE), a database of the U.S. National Counterterrorism Center. However, because there was "insufficient derogatory information" available, his name was not added to the FBI's 400,000-name Terrorist Screening Database. The Terrorist Screening Database is the watch list that feeds into the 14,000-name Secondary Screening Selectee database and the 4,000-name No Fly List.

Additionally, despite his presence in the TIDE database, Abdulmutallab was able to keep his U.S visitor's visa, which had been issued in June 2008. Overruling State Department objections, his visa was not revoked at the request of U.S. Intelligence officials, who believed that revoking it could compromise active investigations of al Qaeda.

While intelligence agencies sorted lists and passed around cables, Abdulmutallab bought his plane ticket to Detroit with cash and boarded the flight with no luggage.

Despite the trail of activity and multiple potential red flags, almost unbelievably, no one saw a pattern emerge.

The puzzle pieces over seven months included these:

- Signal intercepts in Yemen that reference a plot involving a Nigerian man.
- The United Kingdom notifies the United States of a connection between radical Yemeni cleric Anwar al-Awlaki and Umar Farouk.

- Umar Farouk Abdulmutallab's father, a prominent Nigerian banker, warns U.S. of his son's radicalism.
- Abdulmutallab is placed in the TIDE database.
- The State Department attempts to revoke Abdulmutallab's U.S. tourist visa.
- Abdulmutallab buys a plane ticket in cash and boards with no luggage.

The failure to connect these pieces of information (and we can safely assume there were other tidbits, considering the fact that U.S. intelligence officials actively prevented the State Department from revoking Abdulmutallab's visa to prevent the compromising of other investigations) is a clear failure of knowledge management and a chilling example of Information Overload at work.

Shouldn't a system somewhere have put the pieces of this puzzle together and spit out the following warning:

> Plot involving Nigerian discussed in Yemen +
> Anwar al-Awlaki + Umar Farouk +
> Umar Farouk Abdulmutallab + visa +
> cash ticket purchase + no luggage =
> DANGER!?

Given the vast amount of intelligence that the government receives every day on suspected terrorists and plots, it is clear that analysts were overwhelmed and did not notice the underlying pattern.

The failure to identify the potential threat occurred despite, or perhaps because of, the massive buildup in government information production around terrorist security threats. The lesson here is that quantity does not trump quality; it is critical for intelligence agencies to develop vastly improved ways to share information and to make connections between pieces of intelligence.

CHAPTER 19

THE FINANCIAL CRISIS AND INFORMATION OVERLOAD

A library of wistom . . . is more precious than all wealth.
—Richard de Bury

The recent breakdown of the nation's financial sector and the recent events in financial markets worldwide beg a discussion of the role of Information Overload in the context of finance and the economy.

Headlines have made it painfully clear that in the sub-prime mortgage crisis that began in 2006, institutions were unsure of their assets and liabilities. Usually, this would be attributed to an inadequacy of available information, but that's far from the case here.

Beyond the already outlined losses to productivity that Information Overload causes to our economy, it also has the ability to adversely affect the complex systems that our economy increasingly relies on.

Despite advances in technology, we have yet to create financial systems that are immune to Information Overload. If anything, we have built complex systems for finance, real estate, and banking that have evolved and surpassed our ability to understand them.

This was the case with the recent financial crisis that began in mid-2006, where the new products that had been developed by the financial industry became so complicated that calculating the risks proved impossible for regulatory authorities and consumers. Risks were not transparent for investors, who were not able to see the larger picture and understand what investments were contained in the financial products that were being purchased.

A major aspect of the growth of new financial products was the derivatives market, where simple mortgages were packaged into financial products such as mortgage-backed securities, asset-backed securities (ABS), collateralized mortgage obligations, and collateralized debt obligations. In many cases, the complexity was the result of the expansion of ABS, which involves the bundling of assets with predictable and similar cash flows into single managed packages, to include subprime mortgage loans that are inherently more risky and often include loans to individuals with poor credit.

As a result of the expanding real estate market and market perception that encouraged buyers to purchase homes with the expectation that property values would continue to rise, subprime mortgage lenders were able to pass on their risky debt to Wall Street. The debt was then packaged with other loans and sold to investors. Because originating mortgages is a very lucrative business, the risks in lending to individuals with poor credit and in some cases without even proof of income or down payments were ignored.

The resulting packaged debt contained significant risks for investors, but these were downplayed and obscured by the process that created the financial product.

The complex financial products that were created with the bundled debt were simply too complicated for investors to understand. Investors were not the only ones misled; credit ranking agencies, banks, and brokerage firms all failed to comprehend the risks and, as a result, were negatively impacted when the housing market collapsed.

When the crisis reached a tipping point in 2007, it prompted mortgage lenders to declare bankruptcy, let loose a global credit crunch, and resulted in the collapse of the once-thought-untouchable real estate market. As a result, the number of foreclosures doubled in 2006–2007.

The collapse occurred when new home sales stalled and prices for homes stagnated. Interest rates then began to rise with fears of inflation driving them higher. The complex financial products began to look much more risky to investors, particularly since, by this point, the debt had been repackaged so many times that determining the subprime exposure in the product became next to impossible for the average investor.

No Information Overload in 1907?

The Panic of 1907, a financial crisis in the United States during which the stock market fell almost 50 percent, was accompanied by a recession and numerous runs on banks. Bank panics were not unusual at the time; this panic was the fourth to occur in 34 years. At the onset of the Great Depression, there were thousands of bank failures as well.

In recent decades, however, bank failures were rare so the 14 in 2007 made headlines. Banks are also in a completely different operating environment compared to the banks of even a few decades ago, which were smaller. Today's banks have far more customers and accounts than did those much smaller banks. As of 2010, three banks, namely Bank of America, JPMorgan Chase, and Citibank, each had more that $2 trillion in assets.

Today's bankers cannot give clear and comprehensible explanations of their assets because their instruments are so complex that they themselves do not understand them fully. These bankers are markedly different from those who visited the home of J. P. Morgan in 1907, which had become a revolving door for New York City bank and trust company presidents as he attempted to stave off a complete collapse of financial markets. Those bankers from a previous era were able to present everything about their banks' financial conditions on simple balance sheets that did not require pages of footnotes.

The financial markets have become far more sophisticated in the past decade; ever notice just how many screens a typical trader works with? In 2008, L. Gordon Crovitz, the *Wall Street Journal*'s former publisher, pointed out that better and more complete information was available in 1907; the workflow device for traders then was a "simple pencil and scrap paper," but that's all they needed.

The point is simple enough: Rather than too little, we have far too much information today, and that impedes our decision-making abilities and throttles our ability to resolve crises. While Information

Overload is certainly not a direct cause of the recent travails, it nonetheless is playing a key supporting role.

Information Overload in the Market

Thus far, we have focused on Information Overload as the unintended result of advances in technology, misguided enthusiasm for new communications tools, and, in this chapter, the creation of overly complex financial products.

However, it is not just the financial products that have evolved and become more complex; the way in which trading is conducted has dramatically changed with advances in technology and increased automation.

In financial markets, it estimated that approximately 70 percent of U.S. equity trades are triggered by algorithms in automated high-frequency trading (HFT). The increasingly sophisticated algorithms are capable of making trades in fractions of a second (650 microseconds to be precise) as they scan multiple markets and vast amounts of historical data looking for opportunities. The algorithms can even detect other algorithms' activity and adjust strategies accordingly.

Traders are using software tools that analyze the massive amount of online unstructured data to extract sentiment around companies, analyze it, and then trade on it, often without human assistance. The software analyzes words, sentence structure, and emoticons from blogs, company Web sites, editorials, news articles, and social software tools such as Twitter. If the software detects anything that reflects positively or negatively on a company or a section of the market, then it can trigger automated trading.

According to the Aite Group, a financial services consulting firm, around 36 percent of quantitative trading firms are currently exploring the use of unstructured data in automated trading. The trend is not likely to stop there, given the competitive advantage that even a few seconds can give a firm in high-frequency trading.

Due to use of these new tools, between 2005 and 2009, the average daily share volume on the New York Stock Exchange went up 181 percent. The sheer volume and speed of this kind of automated trading created obvious problems as humans are rendered relatively obsolete (we are just too slow). The HFT systems are moving so fast that differences in broadband speed have emerged as a critical competitive advantage. To gain the upper hand, special HFT-only fiber optic cables are planned to link Chicago and New York City (decreasing transaction speeds by 3 milliseconds) as well as a new undersea cable to link New York City and London.

The fiber optic cables are not for the general public, but instead will be used by HFT firms, which will pay a premium to gain advantage over rivals by exploiting minute differences in prices over incredibly short time frames. Take, for example, a stock that is $10.53 in New York and $10.54 in London but in a tenth of a second jumps to $11 and then back down to $10.54. The HFT system with the fastest connection is at a distinct advantage over its competitors running over slower broadband and is able to buy the stock in New York and sell it in London faster than a human would even register that an opportunity even existed.

The vast increase in information that is being dealt with in the financial markets, as well as the automated manner in which deals are being made, exposes the markets to problems related to Information Overload, some of which are severe and have the potential to cripple markets.

In May 2010, the Dow Jones Industrial Average tumbled more than 900 points in a matter of minutes, in part because of the actions of automated trading systems. When examining what became known as the Flash Crash, Jeffrey Donovan, a software engineer at Nanex, a data services firm, uncovered the activity of trading bots in electronic stock exchanges that send thousands of orders a second. The orders had buy and sell prices that are not near to market prices, meaning they would not ever be part of a real trade. The activities of these bots were not noticeable unless viewed on an extremely small time scale, in this case just milliseconds.

When Donovan noticed the strange activity, he began plotting the actions of the trading bots and found that distinct patterns emerged. The patterns showed that the bots were (and still are) making extremely quick and nonserious orders (meaning with no intention of buying or selling anything) at almost all times.

Donovan's theory, although not universally supported, is that rival trading companies could use bots to introduce noise into the market and use the delay caused by the noise to gain a millisecond advantage in trading, which in high-frequency trading would be significant.

There are other theories to explain the activity, including that the bots are actually real trading algorithms being tested, that they are a sort of financial radar that is probing the market, and even that they are an emergent artificial intelligence of sorts. Ultimately, no one really seems to know what the bots are doing or to whom they belong.

It is possible that the introduction of these orders on a time scale small enough to avoid detection may have played a part in the May 2010 crash and may play a role in future crashes. However, although Donovan believes that this kind of bot activity may have been a factor, he also stresses that there were many other variables, which makes assigning blame next to impossible.

In financial markets that are increasingly driven by HFT systems, cutting through the Information Overload to be the first to act on an opportunity has become the number-one priority for traders. This race to be the fastest has led to automated algorithms, mysterious trading bots, and competition so fierce that the speed of light (in the fiber optic cables) has literally become the limiting factor in how fast trades can be made.

Regulatory authorities are aware of the issues posed by the adoption of increasingly complex technologies. In September 2009, the Securities and Exchange Commission (SEC) created the Division of Risk, Strategy, and Financial Innovation, which as part of its mission will monitor new technologies. The new division is the first to be created by the SEC in 37 years and combines the former Office of Economic Analysis and Office of Risk Assessment, with the addition of new duties that cover the development of new financial technology and products. In January 2010, the New York Stock Exchange penalized Credit Suisse for "failing to adequately supervise the development, deployment, and operation of a proprietary algorithm" and fined the company $150,000.

20

THE TECH INDUSTRY AND INFORMATION OVERLOAD

Automation applied to an inefficient operation will magnify the inefficiency.

—Bill Gates

J ohn Burroughs, the essayist and naturalist, is quoted as having said "A man can fail many times, but he isn't a failure until he begins to blame somebody else."

While it's clear that technology has been an enabler for Information Overload, it may be overreaching to blame the technology industry for the entire problem.

With every significant development, from Gutenberg's printing press, to Carlson's photocopier, to IBM's personal computer, mankind found itself able to create and distribute more and more information. The rapid advances made in information and communication technology in the past two decades have further exacerbated the situation, although one can also view the Internet as the latest in a centuries-long effort to democratize access to information.

Unfortunately, these developments brought with them neither the tools to better filter the information that was generated nor the knowledge of how to use the tools in the most responsive manner. As a result, the technology industry needs to take some responsibility in addressing the problem.

The first time, from what I can tell, that the tech industry acknowledged the issue publicly was in the mid-1990s, when Reuters, a business information provider, decided to exploit the problem in the guise of Information Fatigue Syndrome. (See Chapter 6 for a more detailed discussion of IFS). After receiving a considerable amount of coverage, however, Reuters moved on to the next campaign and forgot all about IFS.

The tech industry (which, given their dependency on information, somewhat ironically refers to its customers as "users") not only should shoulder some of the blame, but it should also contribute to the development of a long-term solution. There is an entire ecosystem built around information, with millions of consultants and information producers, which serves to prove that the knowledge economy is in full swing and that the genie is out of the bottle and won't return anytime soon.

The Industry Comes Together?

In January 2007, at the invitation of Intel and Microsoft Research, I joined approximately two dozen executives and researchers on Microsoft's campus for a two-day discussion about the problem of Information Overload. The workshop was organized by Mary Czerwinski of Microsoft Research, Sheizaf Rafaeli of the University of Haifa, and Nathan Zeldes of Intel. Attendees were invited based on their "proven track record" in studying and combating the problem.

Our group didn't really have an agenda other than to discuss Information Overload. In fact, if anything, this meeting resembled an unconference. We created the agenda as we went along, and about half of the attendees (including me) made informal presentations on how we saw the problem. We also formed small discussion groups to zoom in on topics such as "Information Overload in the Enterprise."

The entire workshop was devoted to what was extraordinarily productive interaction thereby fulfilling Zeldes' promises of keeping face-to-face time "relentlessly productive." It was comprised of plenary group discussions and smaller round table sessions rather than formal presentations (there were none, actually, and no slide presentations either for that matter).

To reduce Information Overload during the event itself, the conference organizers created a wiki through which a lot of preliminaries were handled, including personal statements about the issue and backgrounds from those who were to attend. That allowed us to roll up our sleeves (metaphorically, since the Seattle area was in the midst of an ice storm and big chill) and get to work right away.

Attendees ranged from Gloria Mark, an associate professor at the University of California at Irvine, who studies how information technology impacts human behavior; Max Christoff, Executive Director, Head of Mobile Computing for Morgan Stanley, who focuses on knowledge worker productivity issues; to Deva Hazarika, who founded a company, ClearContext, which builds products that help knowledge workers use e-mail more effectively. Others at the meeting came from a wide range of backgrounds (and countries) including academia, the financial industry, and major software companies, such as Google, IBM, Intel, and Microsoft. It is important to note that, despite the presence of representatives of these large corporations, this really was a grassroots effort, and this meeting and what was to follow were largely individual efforts, not corporate ones.

Over the course of two bitterly cold days in Redmond, we shared our thoughts, research, and findings, but we also recognized that what we had covered was merely the tip of the iceberg that the corporate world was careening towards. At that point we formed what we called a steering committee to figure out next steps.

I volunteered to be on this committee, and Zeldes of Intel was the chairman. Other original members included Bill Boyd of Outsource Marketing (now at Group Health Cooperative); Deva Hazarika; Yoram Kalman, at the time a Ph.D. candidate at the University of Haifa (and currently a faculty member at the Open University of Israel); and David Sward of Intel (now at Symantec).

Eighteen months later, in June 2008, the Information Overload Research Group (IORG) was born in a very public debut that included a front-page story in the *New York Times*. The *Times* cast the group's opening conference as the technology industry's realization that it not only created the tools that allowed Information Overload to flourish but that the onus was on it to do something to counteract the problem.

The *Times* headline dutifully reported "Lost in E-Mail, Tech Firms Face Self-Made Beast." Unfortunately, what Matt Richtel wrote in the article about companies "banding together" couldn't have been further from the reality of IORG, which had, up until then, no corporate support aside from a contribution from Intel. Instead of the world's tech firms coming together, the group was made up of a handful of managers from a few large companies (notably, Intel and Xerox), multiple small businesses (with a heavy concentration of software companies that were offering solutions to the problem of Information Overload), and a few academics.

The article was, however, spot on in terms of the extent of the problem and what the tech industry was thinking:

> "Companies are also realizing that there is money to be made in helping people reduce their digital gluttony. Major corporations around the world are searching for ways to keep software tools from becoming distractions," said John Tang, a researcher at IBM, who is a member of the new group. "There's a competitive advantage of figuring out how to address this problem," He also said that there was "a certain amount of irony" in the fact that the solutions are coming from the very companies that built the digital systems in the first place.

The organization is still in start-up mode and is striving to achieve sufficient momentum so it can truly have an impact and achieve its mission, namely to raise awareness and push for solutions that address Information Overload.

Today, while the problem continues to worsen, key industry players continue to pay lip service to the problem.

Information Overload does appear from time to time in industry messages. Smartphones, of course, are emblematic of the problem of Information Overload, something Microsoft appears to recognize. The October 2010 "Season of the Witch" commercial shows a person (presumably a Microsoft Windows Phone 7 user) walking through a sea of smartphone users who are so engrossed and engaged in their (presumably non-Microsoft) devices that they have fallen off bicycles and bumped into things yet are still fixated on their screens.

"It's time for a phone that saves us from our phones," the commercial concludes. Microsoft's November 2010 news release for the new Windows Phones says they are "designed to get users in, out and back to life."

Another commercial with the same tagline shows (among other things) a man totally engrossed in his smartphone at a urinal. As he is using it, he drops the phone (presumably in the urinal), picks it up, and appears to continue using it. A man at an adjacent urinal looks at the first man and says "Really?" in amazement.

Yet Microsoft may not have communicated the anti-Information Overload message across divisions. "The New Busy" marketing campaign, launched in May 2010 for Microsoft's Hotmail e-mail service, is a bit tone deaf concerning Information Overload. What the ads seem to get across best is that wasting time is, indeed, the new busy.

> The new busy aren't like the old busy. Let the old busy have their stress balls, their antacids, and their crazy eyes. We're the new busy. We're redefining busy. Because we know that having a full calendar means having a full life. Take a look around, explore the world of the new busy, and check out how Hotmail can help you to it all.

One of the problems is that we live in a society that encourages information consumption and multitasking. Microsoft's "The New Busy" campaign for its Hotmail e-mail service promotes 24 × 7 connectedness as a desirable trait, something that makes one productive. "The New Busy is doing three things at once," it tells us. It fails to mention that we become less productive and less able to accomplish a task as we add more to our plate.

Tom Farmer, a partner at Solid State Information Design, a corporate communications firm, noticed this as well. "The New Busy is heading for a nervous breakdown," he told me. Indeed, the "cascade of unmanaged, nonhierarchical information that is fired at you constantly, without time or geographic boundaries, is ultimately disorienting."

Information Overload Awareness Day

By mid-2009, I was somewhat frustrated by the slow industry acceptance of IORG and its mission and decided to take action on my own to bring more awareness to the problem of Information Overload.

I have found that the most effective means of reducing Information Overload is by calling attention to it so, in late 2008, my colleagues and I at Basex had decided to name Information Overload as our Problem of the Year. We had set a precedent for this back in 2003, when we named spam e-mail as the Basex "Product of the Year" and, somewhat akin to the way *Time* magazine editors must have felt about naming Adolf Hitler and Saddam Hussein as Man of the Year, believed our action would lead to greater recognition of the problem in the world at large. This brought a lot of media attention to the problem, and hundreds of newspapers and magazines wrote about what we had done.

To maintain this momentum, I decided to do something rather dramatic in terms: namely give Information Overload its own holiday, so to speak. So, on August 12, 2009, 350 knowledge workers representing 30 countries gathered online for several hours in observance of Information Overload Awareness Day. The online event was not the only one to take place that day. Information Overload Awareness Day had gotten significant advance publicity, and there were several in-person gatherings around the globe as well.

For 2010, we moved the observance from August to October, given the high number of people on vacation in August. Our goal of calling attention to the problem of Information Overload was resounding success. The morning of October 20, CNN ran a "Happy Information Overload Day!" piece, countless TV and radio stations wished their listeners a happy Information Overload day, news and talk shows ran special segments on Information Overload, and there were hundreds of discussions and posts in the blogosphere.

In conjunction with the observance of Information Overload Awareness Day, Basex and IORG issued a joint challenge to knowledge workers everywhere: starting October 20, send 10 percent fewer e-mail messages.

The average knowledge worker receives 93 e-mail messages per day, and many are unnecessary. If every knowledge worker in the United States were to send 10 percent fewer messages, the cost of Information Overload could be reduced by as much as $180 billion per year.

Our keynote speaker for the first year was Nathan Zeldes from Intel, who addressed the cost of the problem to large organizations and key factors in driving solutions for it. Intel's own research indicated that its knowledge workers were losing approximately eight hours per week due to Information Overload, a fact that led Zeldes to devise and apply a number of solutions starting in 1995. (See Chapter 17 for complete details on what Intel did.) Zeldes noted that, while most activity remains centered around personal solutions, "what the world needs are organization-wide solutions."

Maggie Jackson, author of *Distracted: The Erosion of Attention and the Coming Dark Age* and one of the first journalists to interview me on the topic of Information Overload, writes for the *Boston Globe* on the topic of work–life balance. She was a featured speaker that day and discussed the erosion of attention to work, to information, even to eating and leisure activities. If we continue to squander how we use attention, Jackson pointed out, we may descend into an era where emptiness rather than fulfillment rules, where one never goes sufficiently in depth in any one area because a virtual clock is ticking guaranteeing that something will intrude three minutes hence.

Another speaker was Ed Stern from the Occupational Safety and Health Administration (OSHA), part of the U.S. Department of Labor, who talked about Information Overload in government. I consider Stern's solution to the problem, namely the use of artificial intelligence technology to allow ordinary citizens to wade their way through mountains of OSHA rules and regulations and actually come out with the answers they need, to be pioneering. Indeed, what Stern has been doing at OSHA may very well be one of the great – and largely unheralded – fights against Information Overload in government.

At the suggestion of Henry Feintuch, president of Feintuch Communications, who has served as public relations counsel to Basex for over two decades, we offered a 50 percent discount to those knowledge workers who would promise not to multitask during the event. Incredibly enough, a few folks paid the full $50, presumably because they felt they couldn't control themselves.

What Software Companies Are Doing

The first time I realized that there were dozens of start-ups that were attempting to create various solutions that address Information Overload was in 2008, when I spoke at a Churchill Club event focusing on the topic and was accosted by half a dozen people, including a Stanford professor, who were doing exactly that.

Since then, I've come across some really interesting solutions so I thought I would mention a few.

One trend has been self-imposed isolation software. A number of software packages have been brought to market in recent years, designed to force the user to focus on a specific task or set of tasks and block out extraneous noise (such as private e-mail, social networking, Twitter, blogs, hobby sites, etc.). In other words, they attempt to improve on the signal-to-noise ratio by removing as much noise as possible. The way they work is somewhat akin to parental-control systems that allow parents to prevent their children from accessing inappropriate Web sites and content. In this case, it's the adults who are imposing these control systems on themselves.

It's similar to *MAD* magazine's Spy vs. Spy in some respects as users use the power of one piece of software to defend their turf from foreign invaders, namely Facebook, Twitter, e-mail, and more.

These programs have various names, such as RescueTime, Freedom, Isolator, and LeechBlock. Their goal is to block tempting distractions and allow the knowledge worker to focus more on work.

Freedom works by asking how long the user wishes to disable Internet access (anywhere from one minute to eight hours). LeechBlock provides more selective blocking, something that may be a necessity in an age where more and more work tools, from word processing to even our telephone extensions, are accessed via the Net.

Another approach is the fill-the-screen method. Provided your computer only has one display, using a program such as WriteRoom or Scrivener that completely fills the screen and gives the user the equivalent of a blank sheet of paper in a typewriter à la the original WordPerfect word processing software. It does this by turning off unnecessary menus.

Software such as Isolator hides or blurs other programs to force the knowledge worker to focus on the task at hand.

A Freedom user I spoke with, who asked to remain anonymous, is a big fan of the program. "It helps me get everything done with fewer distractions," he told me. "Without it, I would constantly be checking my friends' Facebook status instead of working on [my] research project."

A software crutch such as a distraction blocker may sound like a good idea, but it does little to change one's behavior in the long term. It's also limited to the computer the worker is using and doesn't block interruptions such as text messages from smartphones and other devices. My anonymous Freedom user later reported that the purchase of a new smartphone had tripped him up since Freedom only provides its nanny function on the computer he is using. I reminded him, as Jim Balsillie, co-CEO of BlackBerry maker Research In Motion, pointedly reminded me, that these devices do have an off button. Knowledge workers need to develop good work habits that are innate and not subject to the arbitrary whim of a piece of software.

A third approach is a variety of tools that address the e-mail inbox, including ClearContext, Gist, and Xobni. Microsoft has added anti-Information Overload functionality such as MailTips in its Outlook mail client, and IBM's Almaden Research Center has developed Mail Triage, which allows users to triage e-mail on a smartphone before returning to their desks. Tungle is a quasi member of this category because its software reduces e-mail by improving the scheduling process.

Many knowledge workers employ these tools because they believe they are more productive as a result of their use. They may very well be a good first step in developing better information hygiene, but, ultimately, the onus is on knowledge workers to take responsibility for reducing the impact of Information Overload by using tools more intelligently and taking responsibility for the consequences of their actions.

CHAPTER 21

WHAT WORKS BETTER WHEN

Everything is self-evident.

—René Descartes

Workers today are faced with an unending stream of messages and a plethora of communications tools with which to communicate and collaborate. But which tools are appropriate for a given circumstance? Over the past decade, we at Basex have interviewed hundreds of knowledge workers about their usage habits with respect to various real-time and near–real-time tools, with the goal of uncovering what works better under which circumstances.

Today, choices include desk phones and mobile phones, instant messaging (IM) and text messaging, and e-mail, not to mention messages that can be sent to one or more persons via Facebook, Twitter, or other social tools.

It was not too long ago that a telephone system outage would have been a major disruption at my (or at any) office. Today, while some businesses would certainly feel a major impact, many knowledge workers might remain unaware of such a failure because the office phone is used so rarely. Indeed, 76 percent of knowledge workers surveyed by Basex reported using the telephone for 30 minutes or less in a typical workday. According to Nielsen, mobile phone usage is dropping in all areas of measurement. In 2010, the average length of a mobile phone call fell to 3.8 minutes, down from 4 minutes in 2009. The number of calls made fell as well, to 188 a month, down 25 percent in the last three years. For 18- to 20-year-olds, there was also decline in average monthly mobile phone talk time, which fell by 17 percent in 2010 compared to 2009.

Until recently, many knowledge workers still thought of the telephone first and foremost when it comes to real-time communications. Increasingly however, as reflected by the decreased time spent on the phone, it seems that communication patterns are shifting toward other mediums. Texting and IM are rising as the preferred means of communication, not just among young people but in other age groups as well.

Although IM has made great headway in the past half decade in particular, there are some people who still use such tools sparingly, or incorrectly. The uninitiated might ask, "Why couldn't you just pick up the phone instead of sending an IM?" In actuality, the phone call is likely to be far more disruptive.

Even with tools such as IM, the potential for misuse exists. IM conversations can go back and forth for far longer than necessary, negating any efficiency gains. I have found that the use of the code "NNTR" (no need to reply) in my IM conversations can stop what should be a simple exchange from escalating into a drawn-out and unnecessary exchange.

Today, members of Generation Y who are just entering the workforce are far more likely to text a friend than to call. As mentioned in Chapter 10, the average teenager sends and receives 3,339 text messages per month, or more than 100 per day, according to data from Nielsen.

They also send far fewer e-mail messages, which they consider to be more formal. Some consider a phone call so formal that they text asking if it's okay to call prior to placing the call.

E-mail, seen by many as the ultimate business communications tool, has problems of its own. E-mail has become the path of least resistance for knowledge workers, and has clearly supplanted the telephone in recent years in terms of frequency of use. It has reached this status due to its unprecedented ease of use, asynchronous nature, and ubiquity in both the consumer and business worlds. However, none of these factors implies that e-mail is the best tool for the job at hand; rather, it is simply the easiest and most familiar. In reality, it is extraordinarily ill-suited for many tasks, including managing unstructured tasks, such as tracking the progress of a project or communicating project goals and relevant information on a group level.

E-mail's problems are rooted in its use for tasks that it is inherently unsuited for. For example, in structured processes such as customer resource management, enterprise resource management, and business process management, exceptions that cannot be handled by the formal process structure often find their way into e-mail, where visibility and tracking are lost. The move into e-mail leads to a loss of current information on the status of the exception, and those who are not in the e-mail chain are cut out of the loop. This creates a blind spot for organizations regarding exceptions, which leads to management not knowing about actions that are taking place on tasks and projects.

Also, e-mail seldom provides the full and proper context for a process. Previous conversations that may have taken place outside of the e-mail thread, the most up-to-date version of attachments, the real-time status of a project – these are often lost when e-mail is used. The various problems associated with e-mail lead to wasted time spent re-creating the missing contextual materials, which often ends in frustration and missing or incorrect information being used as the process moves forward.

Social Software Tools in the Enterprise

The emergence of enterprise-strength social software has created a separate communications channel that enables users to keep tabs on colleagues, projects, and topics via activity streams that catalog events in near real time. In the consumer world, Facebook and Twitter reign supreme, and their success has inspired countless enterprise-friendly versions to pop up.

Ironically, increased consumer use of these tools has contributed to the increase in text messages, as services such as Facebook and Twitter can be configured to alert users to new updates via text message. AT&T reports that, in October 2009, 400 million social media updates in the form of text messages were sent over its wireless network; almost a year later, in September 2010, that number had jumped to 1 billion.

Because some social software applications also send out notifications about activity and new communication via e-mail (unless you turn off the notifications), they actually have the potential to drastically increase the amount of information that is pushed to users. For example, one posting left on a user's Facebook page could prompt a text message, an e-mail, and a new post notification on the Facebook page.

Business-focused social software contains less clutter and is, in theory, linked into the rest of a user's communications toolbox, so it should generate less extraneous information. Social software that links together communications with relevant background material and provides collaboration spaces that retain the context of communications has the potential to make up for some of e-mail's shortcomings if it is used properly.

What Should I Use When?

Most work-related communications issues are managed today via telephone, e-mail, IM, and, to a small extent, social software.

For the moment, we'll confine ourselves to those tools and figure out what method works better when in terms of effectiveness and less Information Overload.

The first and all-important step when initiating communication is to consider the nature of the issue(s) one wishes to communicate. Human beings are self-absorbed creatures; we have a tendency to assume that every issue we have is both urgent and important (see Chapter 9 for more on that) not only to ourselves but to those around us. The vast majority of the time, this is simply not the case.

So before picking up the phone, sending an e-mail, starting an IM conversation, or posting on your colleague's social networking page, take a minute to think about the relative importance and urgency of what you have to say.

The importance and urgency of any task (and thus the appropriate communication channel) has to be measured against these criteria:

- Personal importance, or how important is this issue to me?
- Group importance, or how important is this issue to others involved in the process?

- Institutional importance, or how important is this specific issue to the organization when measured against other problems the organization is dealing with?
- Urgency, or how urgent is this issue (which is not the same as important)?

The relative urgency and importance of an issue must be determined first before the correct communications tool can be selected and employed. For example, an issue may be of the upmost importance but of low urgency. Therefore, a phone call that would interrupt a colleague would not be the most appropriate method of raising the issue; instead, an e-mail message that can be dealt with at a moment when the recipient has time is more suitable.

When an immediate response is required, phone calls and instant messages are the obvious choices. There are, however, five reasons why a phone call might not be the best means of communication, as compared to an IM:

1. The telephone rings (sometimes loudly), and others may be made aware of the call. With IM, one can discreetly answer someone's inquiry (and avoid a third party overhearing).
2. One can carry on multiple IM conversations simultaneously. This is not possible on the phone, movies showing Hollywood moguls with three phones in hand notwithstanding.
3. IM is discreet. If someone is already on a phone conversation and needs additional information, that person can query someone else via IM without putting the call on hold.
4. IM is synchronous but decidedly less synchronous than a telephone conversation. Pauses of more than a moment on the phone are considered rude; this is generally not the case in IM, as only much longer pauses are noticeable.
5. Using IM, several people can "talk" (type) at the same time without being disruptive.

These reasons beget the question: Under which circumstances is IM "better" than old-fashioned telephony? And, while we're at it, under which circumstances might IM be more appropriate than e-mail?

There are some discussion topics that truly do not have to be memorialized in e-mail, which may, as Oliver North found out, be archived for future generations. In addition, when considering the appropriateness of IM, the user must be aware of others' presence awareness states, such as "available," "do not disturb," and "away from my office momentarily," presuming that these have been set.

The introduction of IM brought with it a new set of issues, challenges, and problems for the worker and the workplace. Included are:

- A need for an IM-specific etiquette.
- The need to set availability (i.e., one's presence state).
- New avenues for interruptions.

Without a doubt, the advent of IM has allowed us to increase the number of interruptions we cause to others, and it allows us to attempt to multitask more as well.

As discussed in Chapter 16, attempts to multitask basically slow us down rather than speed us up. That doesn't stop us from trying, however.

One phenomenon I have observed more and more, to the point where it is quite common today is a type of meeting that we might call a "background meeting." We can define a background meeting as one where participants do not have to pay 100 percent attention and can do other work simultaneously. These discussions are informal and can go on in the background for long periods of time.

For better or worse, this kind of communication is supported quite nicely by IM, since, unlike leaving a telephone conversation for 30 seconds, one can see everything that was "said" in the IM client. Additionally, participants in a background meeting can jump in and out as necessary. In fact, participants can be in more than one background meeting concurrently.

There are IM-like systems that support persistent communications, but an in-depth look at these is beyond the scope of this book.

From my own experience with colleagues, I have found these background meetings to be far more effective than teleconferences. Why? In many teleconferences, one or two people predominate, and others follow along silently. But the vast majority of participants must stay glued to the phone regardless, in case a tiny tidbit of information requires their attention or someone directs a specific question to them. With background meetings, the lesser-involved participants are able to pay the necessary amount of attention to the dialogue but not devote their exclusive attention to it.

So what works better when? Here is what I have observed:

IM is better than telephone when . . .
- There are many people participating and all need to talk/be active.
- At least one participant is in an environment where people could listen in, and privacy or confidentiality is an issue.
- There are a number of many-to-many conversations taking place.

Telephone is better than IM when . . .
- There are many people participating passively and one person is speaking (such as when the CEO announces a merger or acquisition).
- A more personal touch is required and the nuances of voice matter (e.g., breaking bad news).

E-mail is better than IM when . . .
- The text needs to be memorialized (archived for future reference, although more and more companies are archiving IM sessions).
- It contains an announcement to be sent to many people.

IM is better than e-mail when . . .
- An issue demands a faster response than an e-mail would allow, but is not so important or urgent so as to necessitate a phone call.
- The issue is relatively trivial, such as lunch plans.

Although still not standard formal communication tools for enterprise use, social tools can be helpful to:
- Aid search – to search for other users or experts or content.
- To join together users or content or areas of interest.
- To tag content.
- To allow knowledge workers to "subscribe" to the work of other workers or to specific types of content.

- To recommend (in terms of expertise) specific users or content.
- To support informal authoring (wikis, blogs).

10 Tips to Help Lower Information Overload

While there are literally tens of thousands of things that knowledge workers can do to lessen the impact of Information Overload, I recognize that the times we live in demand things short and sweet. Accordingly, I have developed (with apologies to David Letterman) a top 10 list that, when observed, will lighten the burden for everyone.

E-mail

1. I will not e-mail someone and then two seconds later follow up with an IM or phone call.
2. I will refrain from combining multiple themes and requests in a single e-mail.
3. I will make sure that the subject of my e-mail clearly reflects both the topic and urgency of the missive.
4. I will read my own e-mail before sending to make sure it is comprehensible to others.
5. I will not overburden colleagues with unnecessary e-mail, especially one-word replies such as "Thanks!" or "Great!" and will use "reply to all" only when absolutely necessary.

Instant Messaging and Presence Awareness

6. I will not get impatient when there's no immediate response to my message.
7. I will keep my presence awareness state up-to-date and visible to others so they know whether I'm busy or away.

All Forms of Communication

8. I will recognize that the intended recipient of my communications is not a mind reader, and therefore I will supply the necessary details in my messages so nothing is left to the imagination.

9. I will recognize that typed words can be misleading in terms of both tone and intent, and I will strive for clarity and simplicity in my messages. (The use of an occasional, well-placed emoticon can do wonders here.)

10. Finally, because I understand the complexity and severity of the problem of Information Overload, I will do whatever I can to facilitate the transfer and sharing of knowledge.

EPILOGUE

2084: OUR FUTURE?

Storytelling reveals meaning without committing the error of defining it.

—Hannah Arendt

Hank Jensen wakes up in the morning in his hotel room in London at 6:30 A.M. and an information beam silently reminds him of his important meetings that day. As he washes, an information beam transmits important news, customized for his interests, without his having to lift a finger. As he slept, a sleep beam, a relatively recent innovation also found in some of the better hotels, gave him a brush-up course on business Spanish in preparation for an upcoming meeting in Madrid.

While most executives don't travel for business meetings anymore, Hank, at age 50, still likes the more personal touch of face-to-face meetings, and he remembers a time when it wasn't technologically feasible to send your avatar halfway around the world to represent yourself in a meeting.

Hank's home, in a Manhattan tower near Central Park, is typical of a Generation Ier. Smart sensors abound and walls can display color or images upon command. With the introduction of the food replicator in 2060, the need for a separate kitchen space diminished greatly. Once Knowledge Acquisition Corp. ("We own it all so you don't have to") had completed digitizing all of the world's knowledge (a project begun by Google, a search engine company founded in the 20th century that became obsolete with the advent of information beams), bookshelves were no longer required because Generation Iers didn't own books.

There are those who maintain that the Generation I moniker came out of a self-centered reputation, but, in reality, those born in the years 2025 through 2050 were among the first to live in an information society that was all-inclusive and emblematic of the new world order without information borders.

The information beam, first announced in 2020 and perfected in the 2030s, heralded the dawn of this new information society. As i-beams (as they came to be called) came down in price, practically every person on earth gained access to the total sum of human knowledge. The sleep beam was a later innovation, introduced in 2055. It allowed humans to assimilate information during certain sleep stages.

The i-beam was revolutionary; it banished computers from walls and desks, making them as relevant as the home motor (a popular household appliance that was banished to irrelevancy once individual appliances included their own motors) of 1901. It eliminated interaction with such machines as well. Old-timers recall when obtaining information meant actually going to a computer and using a device known as a keyboard, a mechanical device consisting of a set of buttons with letters of the alphabet, which the user pressed to input individual characters. Most young adults today would not even recognize a keyboard, although they may have seen them in the movies from more primitive days. Such movies are quite popular now, and several companies are capitalizing on the nostalgia by offering holographic replicas of twentieth-century desktop and laptop computers.

With the i-beam, an individual could keep current on news from CNDR (news-gathering service CNDR was formed in 2012 from the remnants of the giants of the television and information ages of the twentieth century), locate friends (i-friendster was the most popular of these services), take a course (i-school had replaced high school, and advanced coursework at universities had become obsolete since the government had mandated continuing i-education via i-beam in 2044), and maintain a virtual presence at the workplace and at meetings (the world's dominant IT and communications provider, I-bea-M, had released immersive presence tools that would allow a lifelike virtual avatar to attend work and meetings; the popularity of avatars, however, had resulted in a new traffic problem when millions of avatars go to work in the morning and return during the rush hour via the i-way).

In part thanks to the new technology, Generation Iers are a fairly sedate group, and physician groups constantly warn parents (via i-beam public service announcements, of course) that allowing their children to sit idly while information is beamed into their heads – without any physical exercise – will result in health problems down the road.

The i-beam brought with it a few problems, the greatest one being a new wave of Information Overload due to the fact that everyone had continuous and direct access to all human knowledge as well as continuous feeds of new knowledge with only rudimentary filtering. Some early testers of the first i-beam units had used the systems without any filtering; what happened to them was never made public, but it was rumored that they lost their minds.

Indeed, an island in the tropics near New Guinea is rumored to house a sanitarium for those early i-beam testers, who reportedly pass their days screaming facts, figures, and statistics out loud.

As a result of these problems, the government began requiring further testing and eventually mandated rudimentary filters in an attempt to keep Information Overload in check. Unfortunately, the filtering system has not been working too well, given the exponential rate at which new information and knowledge are being created.

The World Psychiatric Association officially recognized Information Overload Syndrome (IOS) in 2066 and, thanks to mid-century cures of most forms of cancer and heart disease, IOS became the number one cause of hospitalization by 2080.

Hank's supervisor, Laura Adler, had just returned from a six-week cure at an information detox spa. (Forced commitments to such institutions are on the rise, and over 10 percent of the world's population is estimated to have spent at least one week in such a facility – although an additional 40 percent of the population has reportedly sought outpatient treatment from new IOS detox clinics that have recently sprung up).

Although Laura was completely cut off from all information beams during her stay, she was able to assimilate all the information she needed for work through a special i-beam post-cure update process that was monitored by her doctors. When Hank's and

Laura's avatars gathered in the virtual workplace for a meeting, they were able to move forward with projects as if Laura had been present all along.

Hank and Laura work for I-bea-M in the content distribution division. Their job is to develop new i-beam services. (There are thousands of suppliers right now, ranging from one-person/one-avatar companies to giants such as I-bea-M and its arch nemesis, AT&Beam). The current project is i-filters, a new technology that has been made necessary by the sheer volume of information being generated each day, not to mention the total sum of human knowledge available via i-beams, which continues to be overwhelming.

I-filters started in the 2070s as a cottage industry. Entrepreneurial types offered, for a fee, to sort through information and beam information to individuals based on specific wants, tastes, likes, and past experience. Some i-filter services opted not to charge a fee and built up large customer bases, making money selling beam-time for commercial messages customized to the individual i-beam user's interests.

The popular i-filter services competed with one another for the ability to provide news and information to subscribers before the competition (a pattern somewhat reminiscent of the blogger wars of 2020, which culminated in violence as rival blogging gangs attacked one another). At the same time, the ability of more advanced i-filters to selectively transmit information via i-beams based on subscriber preferences made them valuable to customers, and the information they amassed about their customers became valuable to advertisers, who started to purchase subliminal product placements within the i-beam streams.

A World Parliament committee has been holding hearings about such advertising, given the potential to inflict even greater overload on the population, but no legislation has made it out of the committee despite a decade of research.

By 2084, i-filters had become very popular, and their increased use seemingly did much to restore a balance and equilibrium in the world. Researchers observed a small but measurable decline in forced commitments at information detox spas and predicted that IOS would quickly become a thing of the past.

Plus ça change, plus c'est la même chose.

Meanwhile, Hank gets dressed and leaves for his meeting in London, after which he will continue on to his meeting in Madrid via the new high-speed, 600 km/h i-trains. He has reserved a seat in the quiet section, the one with no i-beaming allowed.

REFERENCES

Autonomy. *Software answer to information overload.* 2 March, 1999.

Baumeister, Roy F., Ellen Bratslavsky, Mark Muraven, and Dianne M. Tice. "Ego Depletion: Is the Active Self a Limited Resource?" *Journal of Personality and Social Psychology* 74.5 (1998): 1252–65.

"Beloit College Mindset List." *Beloit College.* 2010.

Berners-Lee, Tim, and Mark Fischetti. *Weaving the Web: The Original Design and Ultimate Destiny of the World Wide Web by Its Inventor.* San Francisco: Harper San Francisco, 1999.

Block, Jerald J., M.D. "Issues for DSM-V: Internet Addiction." *American Journal of Psychiatry.* 165 (March 2008): 306–07.

Bohn, Roger E., and James E. Short. *How Much Information? 2009 Report on American Consumers.* Global Information Industry Center, University of California, San Diego. Dec. 2009.

Burke, Cody. "Information Overload to Swamp The National Archives." *Basex Research Brief.* 2 Jan. 2009.

Bustillo, Miguel, and Ann Zimmerman. "Paid to Pitch: Product Reviews By Bloggers Draw Scrutiny." *Wall Street Journal.* 23 April 2009.

Bryan-Low, Cassel, and Aaron Lucchetti. "George Carlin Never Would've Cut It at the New Goldman Sachs." *Wall Street Journal.* 29 July 2010.

Cawood, Andrew. "'Reply to All' Function to Be Disabled." Memo: To All Nielsen People – Worldwide. 27 Jan. 2009.

Cairncross, Frances. *The Death of Distance: How the Communications Revolution Will Change Our Lives.* Boston, MA: Harvard Business School, 1997.

Christoff, Kalina, Alan M. Gordon, Jonathan Smallwood, Rachelle Smith, and Jonathan W. Schooler. "Experience Sampling during FMRI Reveals Default Network and Executive System Contributions to Mind Wandering." *Proceedings of the National Academy of Sciences of the United States* 106.21 (2009).

Coviello, Decio, Andrea Ichino, and Nicola Persico. *Don't Spread Yourself Too Thin: The Impact of Task Juggling on Workers' Speed of Job Completion.* Working paper. 2010.

Cutts, Matt. "Google Search and Search Engine Spam." *Official Google Blog.* 21 Jan. 2011.

D'Aurio, Jarina. "In Defense of Gen Y Workers." www.cio.com. 20 Nov. 2007.

Desk Set. Dir. Walter Lang. Perf. Spencer Tracy and Katharine Hepburn. 1957.

Dullea, Georgia. "Is It a Boon for Secretaries or Just an Automated Ghetto?" *New York Times.* 4 Feb. 1974.

Dworak, M., T. Schierl, T. Bruns, and H. K. Struder. "Impact of Singular Excessive Computer Game and Television Exposure on Sleep Patterns and Memory Performance of School-aged Children." *Pediatrics* 120.5 (2007): 978–85.

"For Those Who Think Young." *Mad Men.* Season 2, Episode 1. 19 July 2007.

Gross, Bob. "Happy Information Overload Day." CNN. 20 Oct. 2010.

Gross, B. M. "Operation Basic: The Retrieval of Wasted Knowledge." *Journal of Communication*, Volume 12, Issue 2: 67–83, June 1962.

Hardin, Garrett. "Tragedy of the Commons." *Science.* 162:1243–1248, 13 Dec. 1960.

Hamilton, Jon. "Multitasking In The Car: Just Like Drunken Driving." National Public Radio. 16 Oct. 2008.

Huff, Charlotte. "Brain Freeze." *American Way.* 1 Nov. 2007.

"Information." *Oxford English Dictionary.* 2010.

Information Overload: The Movie. Dir. Jonathan B. Spira. Basex, 21 May 2009.

Jackson, Maggie. *Distracted: The Erosion of Attention and the Coming Dark Age.* Amherst, NY: Prometheus, 2008.

Johnson Jr., John. "NASA's Early Lunar Images, in a New Light." *Los Angeles Times.* 22 March 2009.

Johnson, Steven. *Everything Bad Is Good for You: How Today's Popular Culture Is Actually Making Us Smarter.* New York: Riverhead, 2005.

Kedrosky, Paul. "Dishwashers, and How Google Eats Its Own Tail." *Paul Kedrosky's Infectious Greed.* 13 Dec. 2009.

Lenhart, Amanda, Rich Ling, and Kristen Purcell. *Teens and Mobile Phones.* Pew Internet & American Life Project. 2010.

Levine, James A. "Health-chair reform: your chair: comfortable but deadly." *Diabetes*, 59.11: 2715–6, 2010.

MacLuhan, Marshall, and Quentin Fiore. *The Medium is the Message: An Inventory of Effects.* 1st Ed.: Random House; reissued by Gingko Press, 2001.

Martin, A.H. "The Demand for the Illustrated Information Article." *The Editor: The Journal of Information for Literary Workers*, Volume 42, 1915.

Mehl, Matthias, R., Simine Vazire, Nairán Ramirez-Esparza, Richard B. Slatcher, and James W. Pennebaker. "Are Women Really More Talkative Than Men?" *Science* 317.5834 (2007): 82.

Messenger, James R. *The Death of the American Telephone & Telegraph Company: How MA Bell Died Giving Birth to the Information Age – an Eyewitness Account.* Marietta, GA: Alexander LLC, 2008.

Moskowitz, Clara. "Airport Security Unlikely to Spot Hard-to-Find Weapons." *LiveScience*, 14 Jan. 2010.

National Highway Traffic Safety Administration. "NHTSA, Virginia Tech Transportation Institute Release Findings of Breakthrough Research on Real-World Driver Behavior, Distraction and Crash Factors." 20 April 2006.

Nielsen: Internet & Social Media Consumer Insights. Nielsen, 2010.

Occupational Employment Statistics Survey. Bureau of Labor Statistics, Department of Labor, 2007.

Paul, Waddington. *Dying for Information?* Reuters, 1998.

Pisant, Bob. "Time Management." CNBC, 2 March 1993.

Priest, Dana, and William Arkin. "Top Secret America: A Hidden World, Growing beyond Control." *Washington Post.* 19 July 2010.

Reuters, "Glued to the Screen: an investigation into information addiction worldwide." *Reuters Business Information Report.* 1997.

Richtel, Matt. "Growing Up Digital, Wired for Distraction." *New York Times.* 22 Nov. 2010.

Richtel, Matt. "Lost in E-Mail, Tech Firms Face Self-Made Beast." *New York Times* 14 June 2008.

Rideout, Victoria J., MA, Ulla G. Foehr, PhD, and Donald F. Roberts, PhD. *Generation M2: Media in the Lives of 8- to 18-Year Olds.* Kaiser Family Foundation, 2010.

Rosman, Katherine. "Y U Luv Texts, H8 Calls." *Wall Street Journal.* 14 Oct. 2010.

Schmidt, Eric. "How Google Can Help Newspapers." *Wall Street Journal.* 1 Dec. 2009.

Spira, Jonathan B. "Addressing Information Overload – A Steering Committee Forms." *Basex Research Brief.* 19 Jan. 2007.

Spira, Jonathan B. "Carpe Data: The ROI of Data Mining." *Collaborative Business Knowledge In-Depth Insight.* June 2002.

Spira, Jonathan B. "Information Overload Now $997 Billion: What Has Changed?" *Basex Research Brief.* 16 Dec. 2010.

Spira, Jonathan B. "Information Overload – The Answer for 2008 May Be As Simple As Hot Chocolate." *Basex Research Brief.* 4 Jan. 2008.

Spira, Jonathan B. *Interview with Dan Bricklin.* 18 Nov. 2010.

Spira, Jonathan B. *Interview with Colonel Peter Marksteiner.* 5 Nov. 2010.

Spira, Jonathan B. *Interview with Paul Atchley.* 22 Sept. 2010.

Spira, Jonathan B. "The Document Jungle." *Basex Research Brief.* 16 Feb. 2010.

Spira, Jonathan B. "The Knowledge Worker's Day: Our Findings." *Basex Research Brief.* 4 Nov. 2010.

Spira, Jonathan B. "The LazerBook Story." *Basex Online Journal of Industry and Commerce.* April 1996.

Spira, Jonathan B. *Managing the Knowledge Workforce.* New York: Mercury Business Press, 2005.

Spira, Jonathan B, and Cody Burke. *Intel's War on Information Overload.* Basex. August 2009.

Spira, Jonathan B., and Cody Burke. *Three Variations on a Theme: An In-Depth Analysis of Office Suites from Google, Microsoft, and OpenOffice.org.* Basex. May 2010.

Spira, Jonathan B., and Cody Burke. *What's New in Microsoft Office 2010.* Basex. May 2010.

Spira, Jonathan B., and David M. Goldes. *"Calculating Information Overload."* Basex *Research Brief.* 26 Dec. 2008.

Spira, Jonathan B., and Joshua B.Feintuch. *The Cost of Not Paying Attention: How Interruptions Impact Knowledge Worker Productivity.* Basex. 2005.

Stephenson, Neal. *Snow Crash.* New York: Bantam, 1992.

Stone, Linda. "Continuous Partial Attention." *Lindastone.net.* 2008.

Stone, Linda. "Time Management Continuous Partial Attention – Not the Same as Multi-Tasking." *Business Week.* 24 July 2008.

Suarez, Luis. "I Freed Myself from E-mail's Grip." *New York Times*. 29 June 2008.

Taycher, Leonid. "Books of the World, Stand up and Be Counted! All 129,864,880 of You." *Inside Google Books*. 5 Aug. 2010.

Taylor, Frederick Winslow. *The Principles of Scientific Management*. New York: Norton, 1967.

Television Audience 2009. Nielsen, 2010.

The Global Online Media Landscape. Nielsen, 2009.

The Guinness Book of Records. London: Guinness World Records Limited, 2009.

Toffler, Alvin. *Future Shock*. New York: Random House, 1970.

U.S. Department of Transportation. *U.S. Transportation Secretary Ray LaHood Announces 2009 Distracted Driving Fatality and Injury Numbers Prior to National Distracted Driving Summit*. 20 Sept. 2010.

"U.S. Wireless Quick Facts." *CTIA – The Wireless Association*. 21 Dec. 2010.

Vascellaro, Jessica E. "Why Email No Longer Rules . . . And What That Means for the Way We Communicate." *Wall Street Journal*. 12 Oct. 2009.

Wallis, Claudia, and Sonja Steptoe. "Help! I've Lost My Focus." *Time*. 8 Jan. 2006.

Watson, Jason M., and David L. Strayer. "Supertaskers: Profiles in Extraordinary Multitasking Ability." *Psychonomic Bulletin & Review* 17.4; 2010: 479–85.

Watters, Audrey. "U.S. National Archives Asks Whether Politicians' Tweets and Blogs Are 'Official Government Records'" *ReadWriteWeb*. 4 Nov. 2010.

Wurman, Richard Saul. *Information Anxiety*. New York: Doubleday, 1989.

Xerox. *For Government Workers: Easing Information Overload Will Save*. 19 Feb. 2009.

ABOUT THE AUTHOR

Jonathan B. Spira is CEO and chief analyst of Basex, a research firm focusing on issues companies face as they navigate the knowledge economy.

Mr. Spira is recognized as one of the technology industry's leading thinkers and pundits, having pioneered the study of knowledge workers and how information technology impacts them. He began studying the problem of Information Overload more than two decades ago and his findings, which include data on the lost productivity of knowledge workers, have been cited by thousands of papers and articles on the topic.

Mr. Spira, who directs all research and analytic activities at Basex, is a founding board member of the Information Overload Research Group, a consortium of large companies created to help stem the tide of Information Overload.

He is author of *Managing the Knowledge Workforce: Understanding the Information Revolution That's Changing the Business World* (Mercury Business Press) and co-author of *The History of Photography* (Aperture), which was named a best book of the year by the *New York Times*.

Mr. Spira speaks regularly to industry and business groups on Information Overload-related subjects. He is a frequently cited news source and commentator for a broad range of business, trade, and broadcast media in the U.S. and abroad (including *Time* magazine, the *New York Times, Business Week*, and the *Wall Street Journal*).

OVERLOAD STORIES: THE WEB SITE

This may be the last physical page of the book, but the story of *Overload!* does not end here. Overload Stories, the online companion to this book, continues its mission and provides a place where you can share your own experiences and stories about Information Overload.

Information Overload is an ongoing problem and, consequently, new challenges and solutions are cropping up every day, so join us at www.OverloadStories.com

Overload Stories continues the research and discussions begun in this book. In addition to being able to post your own stories about how Information Overload has impacted you, your organization, and your life, you will be able to read and comment on stories written by other knowledge workers from a wide variety of organizations and cultures.

In addition to providing feedback, I will present new case studies and research, host discussions, and expand the ideas that have been developed in this book.

Think of Overload Stories as a twenty-first century version of the nineteenth century literary salon, where people gathered to exchange ideas and learn from one another. By participating in Overload Stories, you will be part of a community that is not only concerned about the problem of Information Overload but is taking steps to lessen its impact.

Point your browser to www.OverloadStories.com and join the fight.

INDEX